P9-DFO-956

WOMEN OF A CERTAIN AGE

Also by Lillian B. Rubin

Busing & Backlash: White Against White in an Urban School District

Worlds of Pain: Life in the Working-Class Family

Women
of a
Certain Age

The Midlife Search for Self

by Lillian B. Rubin

PERENNIAL LIBRARY

HARPER & ROW PUBLISHERS, New York
Grand Rapids, Philadelphia, St. Louis, San Francisco
London, Singapore, Sydney, Tokyo, Toronto

A hardcover edition of this book is published by Harper & Row, Publishers.

WOMEN OF A CERTAIN AGE: *The Midlife Search for Self.* Copyright © 1979 by Lillian B. Rubin. All rights reserved. Printed in the United States of America. No part of this book may be used or reproduced in any manner whatsoever without written permission except in the case of brief quotations embodied in critical articles and reviews. For information address Harper & Row, Publishers, Inc., 10 East 53rd Street, New York, N.Y. 10022.

First HARPER COLOPHON edition published 1981. Reissued in PERENNIAL LIBRARY 1990.

LIBRARY OF CONGRESS CATALOG CARD NUMBER 79-1681

ISBN 0-06-090833-5

90 91 92 93 94   MPC   20 19 18 17 16 15 14 13 12 11 10

Contents

Acknowledgments

Appearances notwithstanding, no one person and no one research project is ever responsible for a book. Writing, it is true, is a private task, a lonely process. But the creation of a book begins long before the writing of it and is, ultimately, the sum of the author's life and experience. In some fundamental way, then, a book is a social product in the same way as is an individual—both infant and idea born into a culture that shapes growth and development. The infant experiences life through the filter of family and society. The idea for a book and its execution is the product of some combination of those experiences and their integration inside the individual who conceives and writes it. That means that others have a hand in it as surely as if they had held the pen or punched the typewriter keys. So it is with this book.

Many of those others, I don't know. They're just there—in my present as well as my past—part of the background of the world I live in, helping to shape and mold me and my work in a thousand small and large ways. The women's movement —the most recent wave in the long feminist struggle—is one such influence, a movement that has helped me to understand myself and my life in sometimes startlingly new ways. The debt I owe to that movement and to the brave women who first raised their voices is incalculable. It is easy to see that this would have been a different book if it had been written a dozen years ago, before the voices of the women's movement were heard. More difficult, however, is to understand that it probably never would have been born. For even if I had been able to think clearly about these issues and to write about them all those years ago, who would have published it? Who, at that time, was interested in the problems of women, let alone women at midlife?

There are also others to whom this work owes important debts—family, friends, colleagues who have participated in the ongoing process of thinking, writing, and revising.

The women who worked with me on the project are, of course, an indispensable and integral part of it and of the final product. Barbara Artson and Loni Hancock did a superb job in helping with the interviews. Elaine Draper handled difficult library assignments with exceptional intelligence and creativity. And Kristin Meuser oversaw it all with dispatch, while she also typed everything from the transcripts of the interviews to the final manuscript. We all worked closely, talked together often. In such a situation, ideas fly back and forth so quickly, are accepted and discarded so often that, in the end, claiming or attributing ownership makes no sense. In any case, ideas are, or ought to be, public property—part of the riches of the community. It is in this spirit that our work went on, and in this spirit that I thank them for their contribution, not only to this book, but to my intellectual growth and development.

To Barbara Artson, a special salute. We started the project as close friends and struggled throughout with the problems of integrating and separating the work and friendship roles. In the end, both work and friendship benefited from the experience—an accomplishment of pride and pleasure for us both.

The Faculty Women's Research Seminar in Berkeley, California, provided an open forum and wise minds with whom to discuss and test ideas.

Gloria Alford, Robert Alford, Robert Cantor, Nancy Chodorow, Troy Duster, Barbara Heyns, Arlie Hochschild, Carole Joffe, Dorothy Jones, Pepper Schwartz, Arlene Skolnick, Jerome Skolnick, and Lenore Weitzman read all or part of the manuscript in process and offered perceptive criticisms that surely made this a better, stronger book.

Kim Chernin was an exceptionally giving, provocative, and insightful critic whose thoughtful commentary stimulated some of the best ideas in this book. Michael Rogin, close to my work for many years, was, as always, an important source of intellectual and emotional support. Two women, extraordinary friends over the last twenty-five years, deserve thanks as well: Joyce Lipkis, who traveled from Los Angeles to Berkeley with the manuscript in hand just to give me her wise counsel; and Anne Marcus, who spent hours on the long-distance telephone sharing her responses to the work.

My patients—middle-aged and young, women and men—have a continuing share in the process. They remind me always of the many dimensions in human problems. They renew my faith that we can, if we will, solve even the most seemingly intransigent ones. Indeed, they contribute to my life and my work in more ways than they imagine. The members of the Tuesday night women's group, in particular, have been an invaluable source of learning and inspiration as we have shared their struggle with all the issues of which this book speaks.

My agent, Rhoda Weyr, deserves my appreciation, not just for representing my interests so well, but for being also a good friend.

At Harper & Row, Erwin Glikes has, for some years, given me the kind of support and encouragement that every writer dreams of getting from a publisher. Editor, publisher, friend —he was close to this project from first to last. Both this book and I owe him much. Barbara Grossman turned the often difficult relationship between author and editor into a warm friendship as she edited the final version of the manuscript with tact and sensitivity. And Margery Tippie copyedited it all so deftly that hardly a hackle was raised in the process.

The Behavioral Sciences Research Branch of the National Institute of Mental Health supported the research on which this book is based with a three-year grant (#MH 28167). To Joyce Lazar, chief of that branch, a special note of thanks. She is a midlife woman who could be a model for us all.

Then there is my family for whom no words of thanks will ever be enough. My daughter, Marci Rubin, gave me her ear and her heart whenever I needed it, while also reading every word of every draft and responding with unfailing intelligence, sensitivity, and honesty. Her support, both emotional and intellectual, is a mainstay of my life. My husband, Hank Rubin, did all those things for which I have thanked others, and so much more that there is no way to recount his contribution, no words to give adequate expression to either my love or my gratitude. He, above all others, nourishes my life in all of its facets.

Finally, there are the women who opened their hearts and their homes to us, giving more generously of themselves than anyone had a right to expect. This is their story. And it is also their book, for without them it would not exist. They are a wonderful lot—intelligent, competent, sensitive, thoughtful observers of their own lives and of those around them; the finest teachers I could have had. It is to them that I dedicate this book.

1
Of Beginnings and Endings

I am a midlife woman. Like most women of my generation, I gave over much of my adult life to marriage and motherhood. Like so many others, I awoke one day from the childhood dream that I would be forever cared for—that being some man's wife and some child's mother would occupy my mind and my hands for the rest of my life. And I lay on my couch, listened to music, and wept with despair.

I was thirty-eight years old, already divorced and remarried to a man with whom I expected to spend the rest of my life, the mother of a beautiful fourteen-year-old daughter whom I loved dearly. But it wasn't enough. My daughter was busy with her teenage activities, my husband with his career. And I? I awoke each day wondering how to fill the time, wondering how I'd ever gotten into this fix, wondering how I'd ever get out.

But it was only 1962. The women's movement hadn't yet arrived to reassure me that others suffered a similar anguish. Betty Friedan had not yet given my feelings a voice, had not yet given my problem a name. So I suffered silently and, I thought, alone.

I had until then spent my life in and out of the labor force, sometimes doing small jobs, sometimes bigger ones. When restlessness overcame guilt, I went to work. When guilt won out, I quit. In between working for wages, I worked without wages, often putting in longer days and nights in volunteer labors than I would ever have permitted myself to do at paid work. But no complaints. It was better than staying at home wondering how to keep useful and busy. And more importantly, those volunteer jobs—for me, done mostly in the political arena where I have a lifelong interest—kept me connected to the world and taught me skills that I was able to turn into reasonably well-paid work in the period of my divorce.

But here I was, married again and living in another city— four hundred miles from the political community I knew so well, four hundred miles from old friends. Four hundred or four thousand—in such moments in life, they are effectively the same. I felt isolated, lonely, and furious with myself. I had a man I loved and a child I loved. What was the matter with me? Why wasn't I happy? What did I expect of life anyway?

In 1962, I had no answers. But shout at myself as loud as I could, rage at myself as much as I would, none of it helped; nothing abated the restless yearning inside me—a yearning that called for something more, something different, in this life of mine.

I tried to go back to the world of volunteers. But it didn't work. Once having been paid to do the same kind of work, it felt odd, awkward, almost disrespectful to myself to work without pay.

But returning to the paid work force had its own problems. Without a college degree, the only way I could get a job that would interest me was through personal contacts—through people who knew me, people who were willing to put aside bureaucratic regulations because they believed in me. And I had left all of them behind when I married and moved those four hundred miles away.

As I recall that time, I'm met with an inner sense of shock —shock, not because I gave up the life I had built for marriage, but because it never occurred to me not to. I remind myself: It was only 1962, five years before most women even thought such thoughts. And I ask myself: Would I do it differently today? And I ask you: Would you?

I had two choices. One, to pack up and go back to the life I had left. The other, to go to school. Both filled me with dread. Although I had always mourned the fact that I had been too poor to go to college in my youth, at thirty-eight I was scared—scared of competing with talented, well-educated eighteen-year-olds, scared that I'd find I wasn't as bright as I wanted to think I was, as I wanted others to believe. Still, on balance, I suppose the other option looked the worse one. A year later, I went to school—a college freshman at thirty-nine. Eight hard but exciting years later, I left the campus with a doctorate in sociology and postdoctoral training in psychology.

Eight years—years when I was literally buried in my books, years when most family responsibilities took second place to my studies. Even as I write that sentence, I experience again the guilt. And I wonder: Do I really want to let it stand bald and naked that way? Can I really be comfortable telling the world that my family took second place to a term paper? I'm not comfortable, but I'll let it stand because I must if I'm to tell the truth about the price a woman with a family pays when she embarks on such a road.

Eight years of guilt and excitement playing counterpoint to each other—years of finding out who I am, what I can do; years of struggle and years of growth. None of it would have been possible without the support and cooperation of my husband and daughter; none of it possible without their protection, not only from their own needs, but from the criticisms and intrusions of friends and family who warned about the dangers to my marriage, the costs to my child. They were warnings well founded in observation and experience, it's true. When a woman embarks on such a course, her marriage often *is* under threat. But there was something else underlying these expressions of concern from people whose lives touched mine—something related to their own needs and their own resentments because I was no longer able to give them the time and attention they wanted. How often my brother's voice came across the miles of telephone line, anger masking his hurt: "Can I come to visit, or is my forty-year-old sister too busy doing her homework?" How often a friend responded to my inability to make a lunch date with: "Oh come on, surely you don't have to take it all *that* seriously." How often my mother sighed: "Some people are so lucky; their daughters come every Wednesday." And I suffered, even while I understood. On the one hand, she wanted another kind of life for me, a different kind of old age. On the other, her own need, her own emptiness, was intensely felt. And her fantasy still was that I could fill the void in her.

It's true, as Marya Mannes says: "No one believes [a woman's] time to be sacred. A man at his desk in a room with a closed door is a man at work. A woman at a desk in any room is available."[1] It's true, not only in a room in the family home, but on a college campus as well. Ask any woman who has served on a faculty how often a student will pass a male colleague's office to come into hers with a request. If she asks that student why he or she didn't go to the male professor next door—a man who serves on the same committee, can answer the same question, grant the same request—she's very likely to hear something like: "I didn't want to bother him; he always seems so busy." A man, at work or at home, is the symbolic father, not to be disturbed—too busy, too preoccupied with the large tasks of life. A woman is the symbolic mother—always nurturant, always available—even when she is at work.

It was in 1963 that I started back to school—the only person over twenty-five in any of my undergraduate classes. It was in 1963 that Marya Mannes wrote of the "long burden of guilt" creative women would bear for their desire to do their work. It was in 1963 that she said: "No woman with any heart can compose a paragraph when her child is in trouble or her husband ill; forever they take precedence over the companions of her mind."

Fifteen years have passed since then—fifteen years of political and social turmoil; fifteen years during which, one by one, different segments of the American society have stood and roared their grievances; fifteen years during which women, too, translated their personal injuries into a social movement. At first this new feminism—the last great shout of the 1960s —was treated as a bad joke, or passed off as the cry of a few malcontents. Now, as the 1970s draw to a close, it is taken seriously enough to merit an articulate, highly organized, and well-financed opposition.[2]

By the time the 1970s were well under way, however, the great force of radical social protest that had powered the decade before had turned inward—at least for that historical moment. That didn't mean, as some commentators have suggested, that the grievances went away, that people forgot their anger and their pain. It meant that, exhausted from the struggle with powerful institutions that resist change so ferociously, they turned inward for R & R. Only, instead of *rest and recreation,* for the activists of the sixties R & R meant *respite and reanalysis*—a reanalysis that sought to understand more firmly how individual consciousness and social institutions interact to maintain the existing structure of social arrangements.

Whatever the initial intent, that turning inward has been capitalized on in the popular commercial culture. The decade of the seventies has become the *Me* decade. Gone, or at least muted, not audible under all the noise, is the old ethos of duty and responsibility to others—exchanged for detailed instructions on how to look out for "number one." Dozens of books now appear regularly, all aimed at reminding millions of readers that their primary duty is to self.

Enter the midlife woman of the late 1970s. In its early years, the women's movement was by, for, and about the young. But these are times in which diffusion—whether in ideas or fashion —works both ways. The styles of the student and the peasant are taken up by the rich; the ideas of the young, embraced by the old. Today's midlife woman had lived by the old rules— rules that promised kudos, congratulations, and fulfillment of self for giving up her own life to meet her responsibilities to others. Now, in the face of a movement that raises serious questions about her life, she wonders: What was it all about? Now, in the face of a culture that exhorts us all to a concern only for self, she asks: Is that really the kind of life I want for me? For my children? Now, in the face of a departing family and a lifetime of empty days, she worries: What am I going to do with the rest of my life?

It's a strange time, midlife, perhaps especially for women— a time of endings, and also a time of beginnings. As with all endings, there's pain, and the sadness of loss. But *this* ending brings with it also relief—relief because a task undertaken is finished, one phase of life done; relief because it presages a beginning.

Beginnings, too, carry with them a complex set of feelings. There's fear of the unknown, and anxiety about the capacity to meet whatever life's new challenges may be. And there's excitement— the excitement of a heightened sense of adventure. Life takes on a new charge, an increased energy; there are new possibilities, perhaps to develop potentialities only dreamed of before. Maybe there's even a second chance.

The feelings, contradictory as they are, war with each other, buffeting us about, pushing us first to one side, then to the other—the sadness of the ending, and the relief; the joy of the beginning, and the fear.

Until recently, midlife seemed little more than a way station between youth and old age, not worthy of much thought or discussion. Then, suddenly, it became a crisis—a moment of high drama when we supposedly struggle with the recognition of our own impending mortality, when life's unfinished tasks loom large and painfully in our consciousness. In fact, it's neither way station nor crisis, but a stage in the life cycle like any other—a time of life with its own dilemmas, its own tasks, its own pleasures, its own pains.

How is it, then, that we seem to swing so readily from not acknowledging its existence to a loud and insistent concern with midlife as a crisis? How is it that the very *idea* of a midlife transition comes upon us as a sudden discovery? The answer lies in the fact that middlehood as a stage in the family life cycle—a period when the tasks and responsibilities of earlier phases of adulthood are done—is a relatively recent part of human experience, the product of the closely intertwined biological and cultural changes of our century.[3]

Appearances notwithstanding, for women, at least, midlife is not a stage tied to chronological age. Rather, it belongs to that point in the life cycle of the family when the children are grown and gone, or nearly so—when, perhaps for the first time in her adult life, a woman can attend to her own needs, her own desires, her own development as a separate and autonomous being. Thus, the mid-thirties career woman, married two years and about to bear her first child is not concerned with midlife issues. She's worried about diapers and feedings, about hard days and sleepless nights, about how she'll continue her career, about whether she can manage motherhood and wifehood without sacrificing one to the other, or her own life to both. Compare her with a woman of the same age, married eighteen years, whose youngest child is fifteen. For good or ill, she has answered the questions that face the recently married new mother. For good or ill, that part of life is done. Now, she must find a way to give meaning to the rest of her life—something to do, some way of being, that makes each day worth living.

It's true that most people go through the various stages of life at roughly the same chronological age. But, in these modern times, that's a cultural fact, not a biological or psychological one.[4] That's because—within the biological limits, of course—every culture has a preferred age for marriage, a favored time for childbearing, and, in any given era, some general expectations about the ideal number of children per family.[5]

But why talk about this now? Aren't these customs and expectations changing? Haven't we all heard that young women are refusing marriage and motherhood in ever-larger numbers? Given the increases in our population, the *numbers* may, in fact, be larger than before. But numbers tell only part of the story—perhaps the *least* relevant part at that. For the other part, we must look at trend statistics that present quite another picture. There, we see that the proportion of women who never marry has *decreased* over most of the last eighty years—from almost 9 percent in the first decade of the century to 7 percent in the seventh.[6] There, also, we see a remarkable decrease in childlessness as well—from almost 14 percent of all married women in the 1900s to a shade under 4.5 percent in the present.[7]

And what about the wholesale delaying of marriage among the young that we keep hearing about? In fact, the average age at which men enter a first marriage shows a substantial drop —from 25.4 years eighty years ago to 23.6 now.[8] And for women? The age at entry into marriage remains relatively unchanged—21.4 years in the 1900s, 21.2 years in 1975.[9] But, contrary to expectations, women who marry now are expected to be slightly *younger* when they bear their first child than they were eighty years ago.[10]

There are, then, important similarities across the years— similarities that often are overlooked in all the noise of modern life, in all the shouting about changing customs. But there are also differences—differences in life expectancy, differences in the number of children we bear, which make for profound alterations in how and how long we live. With more of us living longer, healthier lives than ever before, more of us live through a period of middlehood, and more of us must deal with the choices, tasks, and changes that time of life requires.[11] Since we now have fewer children in this eighth decade of our century—2.3 per family compared to 3.3 in the 1900s—women today bear their *last* child younger than before, which means they reach the end of their child*rearing* period earlier as well.[12]

Those two facts alone account for a dramatic change in family life—a change that has important implications for both the marriage relationship and for the way the individuals within it will live their lives. At the turn of the century, the average couple could expect to survive together for just over a year and a half after their last child married. Now, they can expect to live together without children under their roof for just under thirteen years before death takes one of them (most likely the husband) off.[13]

But why talk about marriage when everyone knows that the divorce rate is spiraling crazily? Why worry about who lives together and for how long when everywhere we turn we hear that the nuclear family is dying, that marriage will soon be a relic of an archaic past? The answer: Because some respected population analysts already are predicting that the divorce rate is, at the very least, stabilizing, and possibly heading for a decline.[14] Because right now, well over three-fourths of the population between the ages of twenty and sixty-four are married.[15] Because in almost 85 percent of *all* families, a husband and wife live together.[16] Because in seven of every eight of those husband-wife families, the husband is still in his first marriage.[17] Because even if the rising divorce rate eventually means that one-third of all first marriages are dissolved, two out of three couples will remain married "until death do them part."[18] And finally, because three-fourths of the women and five-sixths of the men who divorce eventually remarry, usually within a three-year period.[19]

And among midlife people—those between thirty-five and fifty-four? Despite the rising divorce rate, 82 percent of the women in that age bracket and 87 percent of the men are married, by far the vast majority of them in stable, long-term first marriages.[20] For the women who live in those marriages, the increasing life span and the decreasing number of years spent in bearing and rearing children have come together to present them with a set of problems and opportunities unknown to earlier generations.

There are today nearly 25 million women in America between the ages of thirty-five and fifty-four—about one-fourth of the total female population of the country, compared to less than 20 percent eighty years ago.[21] If the projections of government demographers are accurate, these figures will increase to almost 40 million and 30 percent respectively by the end of the century.[22] The future aside, today's statistics alone make a powerful argument for attending to the problems of women at midlife. For they are the largest segment of the adult female population.[23]

Twenty-five million women—at least half of them awakening

daily to wonder how to fill the time. *Twenty-five million women* —the other half managing to keep busy, often at paid jobs, sometimes not, but, in any case, rarely ever anywhere near to tapping their talents and potential.

But enough of the big picture; enough of the large, sometimes startling, facts. Important as they are, they often obscure the human lives of which they are made. And it is those lives that are my central concern in this book, the reason why I chose to write it.

To do so, I talked with 160 women between the ages of thirty-five and fifty-four—long conversations lasting no less than three hours, sometimes as many as ten, during which they shared with me their lives, their hopes, their dreams, and their pains.

They are ordinary women, the women I met—women who come from all walks of life and represent a cross-section of "women of a certain age" in America today. Some are rich, some poor; generally they fall in neither extreme. Most are high school graduates, many have college degrees. A few never finished high school, many more have advanced or professional degrees. About 80 percent live in long-term marriages, the rest are divorced.[24] (See Notes and Appendix for detail on the representative nature of the group.)

Now, at an average age of just over forty-six, they all have children in varying stages of leaving the family home. For some, the children have all been gone for a few years; for others, a few months. A few still have one or more children living at home, but most can anticipate their departure within the next year or two.

Almost half now work in paid jobs outside their homes.[25] Most are clerks, receptionists, secretaries, salespersons; a few are factory workers, a few professionals. Of the rest, a small group are heavily committed volunteers, a few have returned to school to prepare for a career, and most—well over half—call themselves *homemakers* and say they intend to stay that way.

Large differences, these—enough to raise some large questions. How common, after all, are the problems of the rich and the poor? How common are the issues of the high school dropout and the woman with a graduate degree? Of the clerk, the factory worker, the homemaker, the teacher, the lawyer?

That's what this book is about. For all this diversity is overshadowed by one compelling fact of their lives. They all gave up whatever jobs or careers they may have had in their youth to devote themselves to full-time mothering and housewifery for some significant number of years—usually *at least* ten—after their first child was born. That fact alone puts them at the midlife transition with a common core of experience and a common set of problems—indeed, with a bond that is common to all women of that generation who lived their lives in compliance with the cultural mandates of their time. This is the story of that shared experience—an experience, it should be clear, that is not given to midlife women alone, but to all women at any age who take marriage and motherhood as their primary life tasks.

2

The Empty Nest: Beginning or Ending?

Lonesome? God, no! From the day the kids are born, if it's not one thing, it's another. After all those years of being responsible for them, you finally get to the point where you want to scream: "Fall out of the nest already, you guys, will you? It's time."[1]

It's time—an urgent cry that wells up from deep inside, an impassioned plea that rises from the knowledge that too soon there will be no more time.

Time for what? Almost universally, the answer is:

Time, finally, for me. Time to find out who I am and what I want. Time to live for me instead of them. All my life I've been doing for others. Now, before it's too late, it's time for me.[2]

Until quite recently, this stage of women's lives was the province of clinicians. If a woman became depressed after her children left home, the relationship was assumed to be one of cause and effect. Children's leave-taking, they said, causes depression, a particular kind of depression that even warranted its own name. The empty-nest syndrome, they called it. Nothing to worry about, they assured us. It's a loss like any other. And as with any loss, the normal processes of grief and mourning would produce their healing effect. Although the healing didn't always come, few questioned the theory.[3] Instead, such women were characterized as neurotic—pathological in their inability to separate from their children, in their incapacity to manage internal conflict without breakdown.

As consciousness heightened about the nature of the life problems women face, as more women moved into the social sciences where such theories are born, ideas about the empty-nest syndrome underwent a reinterpretation. Now, the pathology was located *not* in the woman, but in the system of social roles and arrangements that makes it always difficult, sometimes impossible, for a mother to develop an identity that rests on alternative roles.[4]

An important shift in understanding, this. But not yet enough. For, in fact, these new explanations still rest on the same unspoken assumptions as the old ones—assumptions that depression in midlife women is linked to the departure of their children, that it is the loss of the mothering role that *produces* the sadness and despair. Like the old ideas, these new ones too often still take as given the belief that a woman is little more than the builder of the nest and the nurturer of the young, that her reason for being is in that nesting and nurturing function.[5]

Think about the language we unquestioningly use to characterize this period of life: *the empty nest.* Not *the awakening,* not *the emergence,* not words that might suggest that inside that house all those years there lived someone besides a mother; no, we say *the empty nest.* And think, too, about the associations to those words. Do we picture a father filled with sadness because his children have left the home? Of course not, because the nest is so intimately associated with mother that it is difficult to separate the two. Indeed, the very words *empty nest* conjure up a vision of a lonely, depressed woman clinging pathetically and inappropriately to a lost past—a woman who has lived for and through her children, a woman incapable of either conceiving or desiring a "room of her own."

That's the stereotype which permeates the culture, dominates our image of women at midlife. It's so consonant with our view of Woman-as-Mother—a view so widely shared and, until recently, so unconsciously held—that the phrase *empty-nest syndrome* has slipped into the language as if it speaks to an eternal and unvarying truth.[6] Since we have failed to take heed of the assumptions that underlie the words, however, we also have not noticed that most of the ideas we have about depression in midlife women comes from research done on hospitalized patients.[7]

Does this sad creature of the stereotype exist in the larger world where women live their lives and dream their dreams? Not among the women I met.

It's true that some are sad, some lonely, some are even depressed. It's true also that some are hesitant, some unconfident, and most are frightened as they face an uncertain future. But except for one, none suffers the classical symptoms of the empty-nest syndrome.[8]

Certainly, there are differences among them—differences related to how long the children are gone or whether they are gone yet at all;[9] differences related to how successfully a woman feels she has handled the tasks of mothering, how she feels about her adult children;[10] differences related to how a woman has lived her life until this period, how she has prepared for the transition, how she feels about her marriage—or her divorce—as the case may be.[11] Important differences, these, which merit attention and examination. But underlying all those differences is a more important similarity. *Almost all the women I spoke with respond to the departure of their children, whether actual or impending, with a decided sense of relief.*

Among those whose children already are gone, almost every one is unequivocal in those feelings.

> I can't tell you what a relief it was to find myself with an empty nest. Oh sure, when the last child went away to school, for the first day or so there was a kind of a throb, but believe me, it was only a day or two.[12]

Even those most committed to the traditional homemaker role—women who have never worked outside the home in the past and say they don't intend to in the future—speak in the same vein.

> When the youngest one was ready to move out of the house, I was right there helping him pack. We love having the children live in the area, and we love seeing them and the grandchildren, but I don't need for any of them to live in this house ever again. *I've had as much as I ever need or want of being tied down with children.* [13]

A few—generally those who are a little closer to the time of the transition—are more ambivalent.

> It's complicated; it doesn't just feel one way or the other. I guess it's rather a bittersweet thing. It's not that it's either good or bad, it's just that it's an era that's coming to an end and, in many ways, it was a nice era. So there's some sadness in it, and I guess I feel a little lost sometimes. But it's no big thing; it comes and goes. [Suddenly straightening in her chair and laughing] Mostly, it goes. [14]

Women who have seen one child leave usually are ready for the next one to go.

> I think when my son left—he was the first to go—we suddenly realized that this family unit wasn't going to go on forever, and that things were going to be different from then on; you know, I mean that eventually everybody would go off and lead their own lives. So the first month or so after he left was hard, but no big problems since then. And there won't be big problems when the girls' turns come. I'm ready now—maybe more than ready. [15]

Even women who have not yet watched a child leave home speak passionately of their readiness to turn their attention to their own lives.

I'm ready to feel some freedom; I'm just itching for it. I'm looking forward, finally, to having a life of my own again. It's been such a long time.[16]

But what about women who are divorced? Wouldn't women who have no husbands around to claim their attention — perhaps no prospect of marriage in sight—find the departure of the children more troubling? Surprisingly, the answer is *no.* Like their married sisters, they're relieved to be freed of the responsibilities of mothering, glad to be able to call their lives their own.

A little more than one-fifth of the women I met are divorced —some for almost a decade, some for only a few weeks or months. Those for whom divorce is relatively new are still in the process of adjustment—a few suffering acutely because the rupture in the marriage came as an unexpected blow; most grappling with the fear, the loneliness, the sense of loss that are almost always part of the immediate aftermath of divorce.[17] But whatever the issues a divorced woman suffers, the departure of the children is not high among them.

It's true that some of those who are recently divorced are frightened at the prospect of a lifetime alone. But having the children at home does nothing to still those fears.

It's hard to face that I might have to live alone forever.

Is it harder now that the last of your children has just married?

No. I thought it would be, but it's not. I was talking to a friend about it just yesterday, and she said, "Why should it make a difference if the kids are home or not? They don't warm up the bed."[18]

Women who have lived longer with divorce are simply and plainly relieved to be freed from the daily burdens of single parenting.

It was hard not to be in a marriage when the children were smaller. During those years, I felt it was incumbent upon me to provide a full family life for them—I mean, to provide them with a two-parent home where there was at least a substitute father. I guess I blew that one because I didn't remarry, and felt pretty guilty and uncomfortable about it for years. But now that the children are grown, there's no compelling reason to be married. [Interrupting the flow of her words for a thoughtful moment] What I'm saying is that it's great not to have to worry about them any more. Now if I decide to get married, it'll be for me, not for them, which, of course, is the only way it ought to be anyway.[19]

Whether married or not, it seems as if there's a kind of revolution of rising expectations among midlife women. With children in the teenage years, they have more freedom than ever before, but it's not enough to satisfy. Instead, a taste of freedom opens up the hunger for more—not just for more time to themselves, but for the opportunity, finally, to claim themselves.

You know, when the kids get a little older, you can actually go away for a weekend by yourselves, and that's great. But somehow, your head is still at home worrying about what's going on there. I'm ready to be able to go away and have all of me away. I'm *ready*. [Groping for words to express the depth of her feeling] Oh hell, it's not just going away that I care about. I want all of me. It's as if I want to take myself back after all these years—to give me back to me, if you know what I mean. Of course, that's providing there's any "me" left.[20]

Are there no women, then, who experience feelings of loss at their children's departure, none who feel the grief and sadness that inevitably accompanies such loss? Of course there are. Most women do. But there's wide variation in the duration of those feelings—some speaking of days, some weeks, much more seldom, months. And whatever their intensity, such feelings rarely devastate women, rarely leave them depressed and barely functional.

Sometimes the leave-taking is more problematic for working-class than for middle-class mothers.[21] But notice first the word *sometimes.* And notice also that this says nothing about depression. In fact, in those instances where such problems exist for working-class women, they are almost always short term and of limited intensity. Still, there is a difference—a difference related to the *process* by which the children of each class generally leave home.

Almost from birth, most middle-class parents know when the big break will come—at eighteen, when the child leaves for college. There's plenty of warning, plenty of time to get ready. But in working-class families, college attendance is not taken for granted—often these days not even desired—and children are expected to live at home until they marry.[22] Even among those working-class girls and boys who are college bound, most know they will live at home during those years —both because it's part of the family expectations, and because generally they cannot afford to do otherwise.[23] Since the age of marriage is not clearly fixed, that means the time of departure is also indefinite—for both parents and children, somewhat like living with an indeterminate sentence rather than a firm release date that's agreed upon and understood by all. That difference alone—the unpredictability of the departure date—makes preparation for separation more difficult in working-class families.

Indeed, often middle-class mothers speak of the child's senior year in high school as the year in which much of the separation work is done—what sociologists call "anticipatory socialization."

> By the time my daughter left for college, I had really dealt with the issues. From time to time in her senior year in high school, I'd get a pang thinking about what was coming. I must admit, though, that by the time it actually happened, even I was surprised at how easy it was. I guess I had just grown accustomed to the idea by then.[24]

But for the working-class woman, there is no such clear marker, no date known years in advance when she can expect a child's departure. For her, therefore, preparation is different, separation perhaps more difficult for some brief period of time. But almost always the difficulty certainly is brief, and it surely does not approach anything that rightfully could be called a depression.

In fact, regardless of class, those who suffer most are women who are disappointed in their children, whose relationships with them are unsatisfactory, whose disapproval of their life-style makes their interaction difficult and tenuous, at least for the moment.[25] The most difficult times for a mother are those when she looks at a child and says, "I'm disappointed," when she looks inside herself and thinks, "It didn't work out the way I planned." Partly that's because it's almost impossible for a mother to experience that disappointment in her children without blaming herself. After all, if her main task in life is to raise the children and it doesn't come out right according to her standards, who else can she blame? Indeed, who else will be blamed?[26]

> I lie awake many a night wondering what I did wrong that my daughter lives the way she does—the dope and the living together, and all that kind of thing. I don't know; I couldn't stop her. God knows, I tried. I try to tell myself it's a different world and it's not my fault. But it's hard to believe that. It just feels like I failed at my job.[27]

It may not be reasonable that women take that burden all unto themselves. There are, after all, fathers who, by their absence if not by their presence, must take some responsibility for how their children grow and develop, for what kinds of adults they become. And there's a society outside the family with which children interact from very early childhood—schools, classmates, peer groups, each with a culture that helps to shape and mold its participants. Yet, from all sides the finger of blame is pointed at mothers—blame that, until now, they have accepted and internalized unquestioningly.

> I try to tell myself differently, but I still feel the things they do reflect badly on me—you know, like it tarnishes my image and makes me look like a failure. [Shaking herself as if to push away unwanted and turbulent feelings] I guess you could say it's not only that I've needed them to prove themselves, but to prove me too.[28]

But there's more than pressure from external sources, more than blame and its companion, guilt, involved. For most mid-life women, becoming a mother meant that they aborted their own hopes and dreams and invested them instead in their children—an investment whose costs lie heavily on both mother and child since it asks nothing less than that the child validate the mother's life.

> My only career has been my children. If I can't find success in raising them, then what? Where am I going to look for any sense of pride or fulfillment? There's nothing else I've done that I can judge myself by. My husband has his career, and he finds success and fulfillment in that. He's proven himself someplace, so he doesn't feel the disappointment the way I do. For me, it's the only thing I tried to do, and I failed. You know, when you look at your children and see that they're not going to be what

you dreamed, when those fantasies and illusions go out the window, it's hell.[29]

"My only career has been my children"—words that suggest that if a woman has another career, she can more easily tolerate the disappointment of her dreams for her children, that it won't be such hell. And if it's possible to measure hell, that's probably true. Women who have work from which they get substantial independent gratifications *can* more easily avoid the pain by burying themselves in their work. They have other things to think about, other ways of relating to the world and to themselves. They have at least the beginning of another identity, an emerging sense of their own separateness. Like a newborn colt, that developing identity may not yet stand firmly, but its existence alone is enough to make a difference. It is demonstrable proof that a self lives apart from the children, clear evidence that a future exists.[30]

Important though it may be, however, who suffers more from such disappointments and who less is not the central issue here. The question is: How do women handle the departure of their children under these circumstances? The answer: With pain, but also with relief.

> It hurts that he's gone because things are terrible between us now, and he doesn't come around much any more. But, I don't know, I think it's better since he's gone. It's a relief not to have to see him every day. Oh, I don't know. What can I say? It hurts not to see him, but it hurts more to see him and be reminded.[31]

Yes, she's relieved that he's gone—glad not to be burdened by his presence, not to be reminded daily of her pain. But it hurts, too—hurts because, even though he's not there, she can't help remembering, can't help believing she failed, can't help reflecting on the past with regret, can't help wondering how it could have been otherwise.

And there's something else as well. For those memories, those questions, mean also that the separation from the child is more difficult than usual because she's stuck with feelings of incompletion—with the sense that one of life's tasks is not finished, yet is now outside her control. It's somewhat akin to having to deal with the death of a parent with whom conflicts remain unresolved. The departing child is not dead, of course. But the psychological *experience* of the loss can be the same. Psychologically, it feels like it's the last chance to heal the divisions, the last chance to make peace. Thus, just as in a death, the departure of a child with whom there is conflict means that the loss is experienced more keenly, the grief more difficult to manage and work through.

With all this—whatever the disappointments, the sense of failure, the loss; whatever the time span of the suffering or the intensity of the pain—one thing is certain: The women I met are not debilitated by it. Indeed, they cope quite well with whatever feelings of failure, disappointment, and loss they may suffer, for alongside these feelings there exists another powerful set of needs and emotions that helps to neutralize the pain—the longing for freedom, the wish to find and claim a well-defined and differentiated self, and the relief that, finally, this may be possible. It is these feelings that dominate the transition period and beyond, this struggle that engages women, perhaps for the rest of their lives.

> If it's hard now, it's because I don't know what I'll be doing, not because the children are gone. Their going is a blessing; it's time. But I'm scared.[32]

How then can we account for the persistence of the myth that inside the empty nest lives a shattered and depressed shell of a woman—a woman in constant pain because her children no longer live under her roof? Is it possible that a notion so pervasive is, in fact, just a myth? No simple questions, these; and no easy answers. For they touch the deepest layers of social structure and personality, and the interconnections between the two.

To start, let's grant that, as with all stereotypes, there's a kernel of truth in this one. The midlife transition is, in fact, a difficult one for most women—a time often filled with turmoil and self-doubt, a time when old roles are being shed and the shape of new ones not yet apparent; a time of reordering long-held priorities, of restructuring daily life. From that small truth, however, has grown a large lie—a fabrication based on the one-sided and distorted view of women and womanhood; a view that insists that womanhood and motherhood are synonymous, that motherhood is a woman's ineluctable destiny, her sacred calling, her singular area of fulfillment. Until quite recently, this view has remained largely unchallenged—one of the accepted verities on which our social and economic system was built.[33] Man worked outside the home, woman inside. Her biological destiny was to nurture, his to provide the safety within which she could do it.

Never mind that it never really worked that way, that the ideology and the structure of the economy are at odds. Never mind that many men in this society can't provide that safety, not because they don't want to or are lacking in skills, but because there aren't enough jobs. Never mind that, even where jobs exist, most don't pay enough to ensure much safety for the family. Never mind that poor women have always had to work, or that among married women with children under six years old, well over one-third now work outside the home —most out of economic necessity.[34] Never mind that this represents more than a threefold increase over the last two and a half decades, and continues to rise as inflation pushes the cost of living ever higher. The myth lives—a kind of cultural conspiracy that blinds us all to such realities.[35]

That myth—that image of the madonna-mother—has disabled us from knowing that, just as men are more than fathers, women are more than mothers. It has kept us from hearing their voices when they try to tell us of other aspirations, other needs; kept us from believing that they share with men the desire for achievement, mastery, competence—the desire to do something *for themselves.*[36] Worse yet, it has aided and abetted the distortion of feminine consciousness—a distortion that makes it difficult indeed for women to accept and acknowledge their inner experience, whether in relation to their own aspirations or to their feelings about the end of their active mothering years.

> I felt terrible when I didn't feel bad enough when the last of my children left. I'd walk around wondering, "What kind of a mother are you?"[37]

Even when a woman can say clearly that she's glad it's done, rarely can she let the statement stand without qualification or equivocation. Instead, she covers it at once with some evidence that she really is a good and loving mother.

> I mean, I really love them. You know, I gave them my life for all those years. And I miss them, too, I really do.[38]

Why the hasty retreat? Partly it's because she's concerned about the impact of her words on her listener. But more importantly, it's because the acknowledgment of those sentiments—the act of speaking them aloud—activates her own guilt and discomfort, violates her own expectations about how a good mother should feel. Still, the relief is so powerfully felt that she can't help adding, with a self-conscious smile and a self-deprecating air—a manner that suggests *these* words about to be spoken are not to be taken too seriously:

> It's just that it's nice to have the house to ourselves.

It's in such comments that we can come to understand a woman's yearning, to comprehend the totality of the experience of motherhood and the profound ways in which it colors daily life. It's in such comments that we come to know something of the things she holds dear. Yet, because they are so incongruent with the set of expectations we bring to the situation, these are the very lines we too often fail to hear; these are the words whose real meaning eludes us.

But often enough as well, we are not told. It's difficult to speak of such feelings in the face of the myth. Often they're repressed and denied long before they ever surface into consciousness. When that doesn't work, the guilt that attends them can be excruciating, and the fear of being found deficient —labeled *unnatural*— is felt keenly enough to still the tongue. A fifty-one-year-old mother whose last child left home a year ago speaks compellingly about just those fears:

> I sometimes worried that I was unnatural, so I didn't really like to talk about it. You know, when you hear all around you that women are pining for their children, you feel as if there's something wrong with you—that you're not a natural mother—if you don't.[39]

What do women mean when they speak the words *natural mother?* Why is it that about one-fourth of the women I met admitted guiltily, shamefacedly, that they don't consider themselves natural mothers, don't feel they were "made for motherhood"? Perhaps because the ideal we all hold is anything but natural.

In our minds lives the madonna image—the all-embracing,

all-giving tranquil mother of a Raphael painting, one child at her breast, another at her feet; a woman fulfilled, one who asks nothing more than to nurture and nourish. This creature of fantasy, this myth, is the model—the unattainable ideal against which women measure, not only their performance, but their feelings about being mothers.[40]

Who, under those circumstances, is "made for motherhood"? Who can acknowledge, let alone speak easily, their real feelings? It's a setup for failure, an invitation to heartbreak, as Doris Lessing understood so well when she wrote about Martha Quest:

> She sat down and consciously tried to pull herself together; she felt herself to be a hopeless failure; she was good for nothing, not even the simple natural function that every female should achieve like breathing: being a mother.[41]

Still, everyone knows there's more talk now about such issues, more public discussion, more critical examination of long-cherished ways of thinking about women and femininity. If the new feminist movement has done nothing else, it has raised these issues and forced us into a national dialogue about them. And, indeed, often enough women now say that they know others who feel relief at the departure of the children. But whether speaking of self or friends, rarely is it said without some sign of distress. Always there's the sense that maybe it's true that other women share these feelings, but no one can be quite certain that it's all right. Thus, when discussing the subject, women often look about uncertainly, lower their voices, and generally give signals of discomfort—as if they fear being overheard. Typical is this forty-five-year-old who leaned forward in her chair as if to bestow an important confidence, dropped her voice to just above a whisper, and said:

To tell you the truth, most of the time it's a big relief to be free of them, finally. I suppose that's awful to say. But you know what, most of the women I know feel the same way. It's just that they're uncomfortable saying it because there's all this talk about how sad mothers are supposed to be when the kids leave home.[42]

"Most of the women I know feel the same way." How is it, then, that this woman, like so many others, doesn't really know what she knows? Why the discomfort with her own feelings? Why the guilt? Some women respond to those questions by labeling themselves and their friends as deviant or aberrant, assuming that the rest of the world is different.

I don't think my friends are typical or representative, or anything like that. I think most women still are in very traditional places, and most women really do miss their children terribly when they go. It's as if their lives just end. I'm different and so are my friends. That's because I picked them, I suppose.

Others simply deny the reality of what they hear.

Well, people say that now because, you know, women aren't supposed to be such gung-ho mothers any more. We're supposed to be liberated and all that stuff.[43]

All this, then, suggests the enormous complexity in the interaction between cultural expectations, their internalization, and personal experience. For what I have been saying here is that, at one level, it's no big news to women who live it that the empty-nest syndrome doesn't exist for most of them. At another level, however, they are so mystified by the ideology of motherhood that they deny their own inner experience as well as the evidence their eyes and ears bring to them from the outer world.

In fact, it should come as no surprise to anyone that the end of the active mothering function is greeted with relief. Only someone who has never been a mother would fail to understand how awesome are the responsibilities of motherhood as they are presently defined in our culture.

> You know, you love them, but there's times you wish they didn't exist, too. It's frightening to feel like whatever they're going to do or whatever they're going to become is up to you.[44]

Over and over women speak with great emotion about that responsibility, the exhaustion and anxiety it generates.

> I wanted to be a perfect mother. I was terrified of making mistakes, and I was always worried that I might damage them. It was so hard. I was always trying to contain my anger and to be there and say the right thing when they needed me. I felt exhausted all the time. I used to think it was because I worked so hard around the house with three kids and all. But now I know it's because I was too anxious.[45]

Even where the responsibility is carried without so much consciously experienced anxiety, for most women the obligations of motherhood are rooted deeply enough so as to color, not only their living in peace, but also their prospects for dying in peace.

> Maybe you'll think I'm crazy, but when they were younger, I used to worry about what would happen if I died. Don't misunderstand me, I'm not ready to die. But if I have to die now, at least I can go knowing my kids could tolerate it, and that they don't really need me any more. *What a relief to know that!* It would be a tragedy, wouldn't it, to be a mother and to die before you thought your kids were ready?[46]

A tragedy? Perhaps. But at least equally tragic is the burden she carries. For every mother who reads these words understands them deep inside herself; every one believes that, indeed, her premature death would be a tragedy from which her children might never quite recover. She may never have spoken such words or thought such thoughts consciously, but when she hears them, she knows their truth.

Some women say that one reason they feel relieved to see their children grown and independent is because they don't have to worry any more about how the kids would fare if they were to die. Have you ever thought about that?

> My God, no, I haven't. But it's true, isn't it? I just never thought about it like that. I mean, I never *knew* I thought about it, but as soon as you said it, it hit me right here [pointing to her midsection] in the solar plexus.[47]

Others know more directly and at a more conscious level, as reports of the disappearance of flying phobias show.

> It's astonishing, I never had any fear of flying until my kids were born. Then I lived with that terror in an airplane for twenty-five years. As soon as they became independent, I lost my fear of flying.[48]

So what? one might ask: Don't fathers also feel keenly their parental responsibilities? We all know men who are burdened with the need to plan for death as well as for life—men who struggle, not only to make a living today, but to provide for tomorrow as well. Insurance companies grow fat and rich as they offer to protect against those fears—fears that are the price men pay for their unquestioning acceptance of the present division of labor in the family. With a wife and children wholly, or even largely, dependent upon him, a man works all his life partly, at least, to ensure their support in the event of his death. A few women spoke compassionately about this issue.

My husband is seven years older than I am. And that means he's probably going to die before I do. Then what'll happen to me if he hasn't been able to provide for me? I simply couldn't make it on my own. So he has to carry a terrible burden. All these years, he not only has to worry about supporting all of us now, but he has to worry about my future. It's no wonder he's so snappish.[49]

Of course fathers worry. But there's a crucial difference. A mother fears leaving her children before they're emotionally ready, a father before they're financially ready.

This is not to suggest that mothers feel more deeply about their children than fathers, nor that the differences in their responses—in the nature of their concerns—belong to natural differences between women and men. There's nothing natural about mothers being the care givers and fathers being the money givers. Rather, those are social arrangements—both women and men responding to long-established, socially defined roles and functions within the family. As a consequence of that family structure, however, a father can feel he has fulfilled his responsibility if he leaves enough dollars behind him. But what replaces mother? What can she plan to leave behind to help her children until they become emotionally independent adults?

They carry with them heavy costs, these social arrangements—burdening both women and men in painful, if different, ways. Mothers suffer when they bear the burdens of childrearing alone, it's true. But the reward is an intimate connection with their children. And fathers? Contrary to all we hear about women and their empty-nest problems, it may be fathers more often than mothers who are pained by the children's imminent or actual departure—fathers who want to hold back the clock, to keep the children in the home for just a little longer.[50] Repeatedly women compare their own relief to their husbands' distress.

For me, it's enough! They've been here long enough—maybe
too long. It's a funny thing, though. All these years Fred was
too busy to have much time for the kids, now he's the one who's
depressed because they're leaving. He's really having trouble
letting go. He wants to gather them around and keep them right
here in this house.[51]

Repeatedly they tell stories of their husbands' sorrow.

My son's marriage was very hard on my husband—very hard on
him. He was terribly upset. I was so shocked, I could hardly
believe it. She's a beautiful girl and we both love her, so it
wasn't that. I couldn't figure it out for a long time, but after a
couple of months, we finally talked it out. It turned out he was
suffering because he felt like it was the end of our little family.
He felt terrible because it would never be the same again. He
doesn't say much about it any more, but I can just tell it's still
hard for him. My daughter is going with a very nice young man
now, and it's quite possible that they'll get married. But Alex
ignores it; I mean, it's like he pretends it isn't happening—you
know, like if he doesn't look it'll go away.[52]

Interesting observations. And surprising at first—until I
began to reflect on the different experiences men and women
have in the family in general and in parenting in particular.
Then it seemed reasonable that fathers would suffer the loss
of children, sometimes even more than mothers. Foremost
among those differences, perhaps, is the fact that, for mothers,
the departure of their children comes as the culmination of a
developmental sequence, the result of a natural process in
which they have participated rather than a sudden break—a
fact that empty-nest theorists generally ignore. As one woman
laughingly put it:

Mother nature had it all figured out. By the time they're ready
to go, you're ready to see them go.[53]

Indeed, she figured it out well from first separation to last. By the time the ninth month of pregnancy arrives, a woman doesn't object to birthing the child. She doesn't suffer from an empty womb; she rejoices in a full crib. This is not to deny the existence of postpartum depression in some women. It simply asserts that, no matter how much a woman may enjoy and appreciate the experience of pregnancy, no matter what feelings the separation of the birth may eventually evoke, by the time she has carried a child to term, she's ready to give it up. So it is through all the stages of a child's development. One young mother with whom I spoke recently described her feelings as she watched her seven-year-old son ride off on his first "big boy's" bicycle. With a tender and loving smile, she said:

> I stood out there and watched him riding off down the street on that bike. It was scary; he could get hurt. But there was pride, too. I guess the way to say it is that there was a sad joyfulness.

A sad joyfulness, did you say? What a lovely phrase.

> Yes. I started to say it the other way—a joyful sadness—but I turned it around because I realized that "a sad joyfulness" says it better. There's more joy than sadness.

Indeed, for all mothers, a child's growth brings both. Each stage brings with it some loss, some sadness. Each brings also some joy, some pride, some sense of accomplishment—another step taken, another phase negotiated successfully. And in each, there is preparation for the next—an ending, but also a beginning—not alone for the child, but for the mother as well. Children crawl before they walk, walk before they run—each generally a precondition for the other. And with each step they take toward more independence, more mastery of the environment, their mothers take a step away—each a small separation, a small distancing.

The child moves from its mother's arms, to the floor, to its own two feet. For mother and child, a shared miracle that is also a shared separation. By the time a mother sends a little one off to school for the first time, she's ready—a readiness born of the experience of hundreds of such small separations, of her intense involvement in each stage of the child's growth that already foretells the next. For her, then, the preparation for the child's eventual departure is continuous, even if not always experienced consciously, its inevitability long ago etched in her psyche.

> I've been thinking a lot about how I'll feel when they go because it seems as if it won't be hard for me. I've been wondering about that, and thinking about whether I'm just kidding myself. But you know, you grow toward it all the time you're raising your children. Where I wasn't ready to lose them a few years ago, I've grown now to where I look forward to it.[54]

It is this developmental process that too often is missed by those who write and speak of the pain of the empty-nest stage —this process that makes it possible for a mother to speak of relief while yet acknowledging the sadness, this process that makes this, too, a period of "sad joyfulness."

Over and over, women speak of that process, recounting the steps of separation—what the children did, what they themselves did. Some deal with the broad sweep of the process.

> I had heard so much about how hard it was supposed to be that, when they were little, I thought it would be horrible when they got married and left. But that's silly, you know. It would have been horrible when they were little. But by the time they grow up, they change and you change. Eventually, they're not the

same little kids and you're not the same mother. It's as if everything just falls into a pattern and you're ready.[55]

Others describe it much more graphically.

It came about in little bits and pieces. Take my son, for instance. First, he wasn't home so much in his late teenage years in high school. Then he went to college and, even though he still lived here, he was home even less. Then, he met this girl, and we hardly knew he still lived here for a while. So, by the time he got married, the space that had been his in the house was sort of filled up with other things, and I was used to it.[56]

Still others focus more on the ways in which they reclaim their own lives.

I was fortunate in that with four kids it took eleven years for them all to leave, so that I had lots of time to get used to it all. Each time one of them left, I took on another "me" thing. Each one of those "me" things filled up the space they left. For example, before my children were born I had started to weave, and I really enjoyed it. When the kids came, I stopped weaving. I concentrated on being a homemaker and mother, and I didn't weave for nineteen years. The loom stood in the living room and collected dust. No one ever used it. When my first child went to college, I went back to the loom, and I got into it and other things as well, more and more deeply as each child left.[57]

All this suggests that, generally, there are no shocks, no surprises, no sudden jolts. Of course, there are moments of heightened realization: *My children are leaving.* Of course, there are moments when that knowledge is hammered home —a child goes to camp for the first time, an older one to college, another marries. But even those moments of high drama take place in the context of a long and subtle process —a process that usually happens outside the immediate awareness of the people who live it, one they may understand only in retrospect.

Compare this with father's experience in the family. While mother has been feeding, tending, nurturing, teaching, watching, and sharing inside the home, father has been working outside. Sometimes he spends so much time at work because it is, in fact, the major emotional commitment in his life; sometimes, simply because it's his job to ensure the family's economic stability. More often, it's probably some mix of the two—his work being both a source of satisfaction and oppression.

But whatever his feelings about his work, he generally spends most of his life at it—most of his emotional and physical energy being spent in the pursuit of economic security for the family. Consequently, he's not there when his children take that first step, when they come home from school on that first day. He's not there to watch their development, to share their triumphs and pains. Then, suddenly, one day it's too late. One day they're gone—gone before he ever had a chance really to know them.

For him, indeed, it must seem sudden—one day infants, the next, they're grown and gone. There's nothing natural about the process. He hasn't watched it, hasn't shared in it. One can almost see him passing his hand over his eyes wearily, wondering, "How did it all happen so fast?"

Long ago, he had some dim sense of being cheated, some wish to relate more and differently to his children. Long ago, he promised himself he would—some day, when he wasn't so busy, wasn't so tired. But there was never the time, never the energy. And besides, he never quite knew how to relate to them, what to say—how to play with them when they were little, how to talk with them as they grew.

Over and over, women—ironically, even those married to

child psychiatrists and psychologists—tell of being the interpreter between father and children, the buffer, the mediator, the one whose task it is to explain each to the other.

> I always felt as if I had a foot in two different worlds, as if I was the one who walked across that no man's land that always seemed to exist between them. Oh, it was better at some times than others; I mean, they were able to talk to each other some of the time. But even at its best, I was always there as mediator and explainer, the one who knew what the other wanted and tried to explain it.

It's true that women complain a good deal about this.

> I hated always to have to explain the kids to him. They're his kids, too. Why couldn't he take the trouble to get to know them?[58]

And it's true also that, with all their complaints, it's a role they often hold onto because it gives them a sense of power, of control, of mastery in a world where, in fact, they have little.

Was it only that you resented being in that position, or were there elements of it that you also liked?

> Well, when I could make it work, I have to admit it could be very satisfying. It's like in a job you set out to do—when it works, it's just fine. You feel challenged and useful and important, as if there's at least one thing you can do that nobody else can. I guess in order to give up that role, you have to know there's something else waiting for you; I mean, you have to know there's something you can do as well.[59]

On the surface, it looks like a functional division of labor —both parents get what they want or need at the moment. She gets to feel important; he gets left alone to do his work. But the cost, especially for father, is high. Just when he has more

time, just when they're old enough to be talked to like real
people, just when he's beginning to notice what he's missed
—his children are gone. No wonder he wants to shout, "No,
don't go, not yet!"

Since mothers usually don't miss any part of the process,
the end of active mothering doesn't come with any sudden
wrench. Indeed, for women who can look at their children
and think: "There's a job well done," the sense of accomplishment transcends any feelings of loss; the relief is unequivocal. For those who suffer disappointment, the relief is
mixed with painful feelings of failure. And yet, not one of
those women yearned for another chance. For good or ill,
they were glad the job was done, ready to move on to the
next stage of life.

That doesn't mean there are no problems at this life transition, only that they lie in the contemplation and confrontation
with the next stage of life, only that they have to do with
anxieties about the future, not with nostalgia for the past.

Some women talk of fears for the marriage. It's been so long
since there were just the two of them. Will they know how to
relate to each other without the children mediating?

> I'm fond of saying, "You start with the husband. Then, the kids
> are around for a few years. Then, you pick up with the husband
> again." So, intellectually, I feel my first role should be as a wife,
> but when you think of how much time being a mother takes, I
> know it hasn't been that way. Now, when the last of my kids
> go, I'm going to have to learn to be a wife again—just a wife.
> I don't know how graceful I'll be at it; I'm not very practiced.[60]

Will they be able to talk?

> It isn't that I want to hold the children here, it's just that I worry
> about what our life will be like. I don't know what we'll talk
> about, just the two of us, after all these years.[61]

But alongside those fears, there's also excitement—the feelings vying with each other as women contemplate an unknown future. For many families, especially those in the working class, there's some financial freedom for the first time in their years together; for some, for the first time in life.

> It's a whole different ball game, really, to live without having the boys as our first responsibility. We always lived on a very tight budget worrying about them, you know, always trying to do for them. Now we have money to spend on ourselves for the first time in our lives. Even if I just want to blow a few dollars on myself, I can do it now. That's like a whole new life for us —just to go on and do things for yourself.[62]

It means there are possibilities that, until now, existed only in fantasy, if at all—the possibility for adventure, for freedom, for travel; the possibility for the flowering of the marriage relationship in new, even undreamed-of, ways; the possibility for the development of a self only hinted at in earlier life stages. Recall the woman who said: "I want to take myself back after all these years—to give me back to me." And recall, also, her fearful caveat, that inner voice that warned her against expecting too much: "That's providing there's any 'me' left."

All these possibilities—exciting, yet frightening. How will it be? What kind of changes will it require—in him, in her, in their marriage? For her, the greatest unknown—and her central problem in this period—is what the next thirty or forty years of her life will look like. What will be its shape and texture? What will be its daily flavor?

> The children's leaving hasn't been traumatic at all. What has been and still is traumatic is trying to find the thing I want to do, and being able to pursue it to a successful conclusion. I'm an artist—a good one, I think. But it's hard to make the kind

of commitment that real success requires. I'm afraid of what it'll do to my marriage, and also to the rest of my life. And I suppose I'm afraid to really try and fail. But that's the stuff that's so hard and painful right now; it's not knowing what I'll be doing, or even what I *can* do. And from forty-five to seventy-five is a lot of years if I don't have something useful to do.[63]

The ending, then, is difficult, not because the children are gone, but because it brings with it a beginning. The beginning has the potential for adventure and excitement, but it brings with it also the possibility of failure. Some will negotiate it successfully, some will not. Sometimes the failure will be theirs; more often it will lie in the social constraints by which women's lives have been, and continue to be, hemmed in. But for all women whose central life task has been bearing and raising children, one question is heard like an urgent demand: "What am I going to do with the next thirty years of my life?"

3
Who Am I? The Elusive Self

> When your body has to deal all day with shit and string beans, your mind does too.[1]

Clever words, compelling in their simplicity—too clever, too simple. We read them, and they strike a chord. We think about them, and we know they speak to a particle of truth. But only a particle.

They carry with them a sense of compassion, a cry of outrage. But they also distort. For they present us with an image of single-dimensional cardboard characters—women who virtually have *become* "shit and string beans."

Where are such women? Who are they? Surely not those millions who, whether defining themselves as feminist or not, have responded so spiritedly to the issues the movement has raised. Surely not those millions who, long before the movement, felt stirrings of discontent—whose bodies were busy for years with "shit and string beans" while their minds, in fact, made doing those tasks possible by lifting them up and out of that drudgery even while they were engaged in it. Surely not even those women who, we now understand, were driven crazy by those grimy details of their daily lives. For it was that very insanity that was their rebellion—their statement that their minds would not, could not, be taken over by shit and string beans.[2]

Most women—flesh and blood women—do not have minds

that turn to mush. Instead, they struggle with a daily life of unending trivia—struggle with it, and generally conquer it. Most women find ways to give sense and meaning to daily life —ways to be useful in the community, to keep mind active and soul growing even while they change diapers and cook vegetables.

> The secret is that when you're doing all those mindless tasks, you're thinking about something else—maybe a book you're reading, or some dreams you're having. Maybe you're involved in some group, or the kids' school, or something like that. It all gives you something else to think about when you're doing the dishes or making the beds, or whatever.[3]

Still, the issue of identity—a troubling one for women at any age—is brought to center stage at midlife. Who am I? A lifetime of doing what they're supposed to do, of putting the needs and wishes of others before self, gives a particular urgency and poignancy to the question. Who am I? No easy question precisely because for so long women have mystified themselves and others as they sought to comply with socially prescribed roles, sought to obey external mandates about who they are, how they should act, what they should feel.[4]

As with any powerless group, women have learned well how to please, how to ingratiate, how to present themselves in accordance with the definitions and expectations of the powerful. Thus, they have learned to look helpless even when they may not be, learned to suppress elements of self the world doesn't want to see, doesn't want to know about.[5] Unfortunately for them, behavior and consciousness are not so easily separable. And too soon, the act becomes a reality—or at least a woman no longer can tell one from the other. Too soon, she no longer knows whether her smile stems from her own genuine pleasure or her need to appease another, whether she's really dumb about numbers or she's responding to social expectations. Too soon, she no longer knows herself.[6]

No wonder man complains of woman as mystery, as enigma. Others have explained that in connection with ancient male fantasies around the miracle of conception and birth—part of the collective unconscious carried forward from the era when that indeed seemed a miracle and a mystery.[7] But the fact that those fantasies persist so long after the miracle is no longer a mystery suggests other explanations as well.

First, let's agree that there *is* a mystery about woman's nature. There is an elusiveness about her, a mercurial quality born of her uncertain identity that, at least in part, rests on socialization practices that practically guarantee a highly ambivalent adult.[8] Indeed, it is that ambiguity and ambivalence which often is so puzzling in women—the quality of shifting from child to woman, the seeming helplessness one moment and the utter self-reliance the next that baffle us, that seem so difficult to understand. These are the qualities that make her a mystery, the qualities that provoked Freud to complain, "What does a woman want?"

But those shifts, that elusiveness, are not just a display for a man. It's true that the very power of a man's position makes him the least likely confidante, the least likely person to whom a woman would reveal much of what she does understand about herself.[9] But it's also true that oftentimes she's almost as much a mystery to herself as she is to him. That is the meaning of the *elusive self.* It's fraught with ambivalence and ambiguity—not because of anything that inheres in the nature of women, but because they have been forced to suppress and repress so much of that nature. Recall the nursery rhyme:

> What are little boys made of?
> Rats, and snails, and puppy dog tails.

What are little girls made of?
Sugar, and spice, and all things nice.

Not just a child's harmless ditty, but a reflection of a culture's expectations—a mandate that girls repress the mischievous, the curious, the intellectually seeking parts of self; a statement that girls are expected to hover quietly and sweetly in the background of life being "all things nice."[10] No surprise, then, that when I asked the women I met, "When you were growing up, what did you have to do to please your parents?" the answers came as with a single voice.

> Be a good girl and don't talk back. The "be a good girl" says it all. I was never supposed to say or do anything that might be even faintly rebellious.[11]

Or from another:

> Just be good. I always knew you were supposed to do whatever you could to please the other person—practically any other person. Whether you wanted to or not, it didn't matter; that's what a woman was supposed to do.[12]

But such repression never works completely. Eventually, the repressed parts of self demand expression—generally not directly because that would violate the expectations, would seem to risk threat to self and other. Instead, they leak out, sneak out, finding their way into behavior if not consciousness —seen often only as a sudden change of mood, a flash of anger, an unpredictable emotional display, a seemingly unreasonable demand, none understood clearly either by actor or onlooker.

Still, the problem of woman's nature—and, therefore, a woman's identity—would be relatively simple and straightforward if women were expected *only* to repress parts of self. Instead, it is immeasurably complicated by the fact that from

girlhood to womanhood the mandates are contradictory—
each containing two messages, each urging her on while at the
same time holding her back.

Achieve, but not beyond what is appropriate for a girl!
In my earlier school years, they were very proud of me because
I did so well. But when I got to college, my mother nagged at
me, always telling me I shouldn't work so hard. She'd keep
saying, "You don't need to get A's; B's are good enough. It's
more important for you to get out more, have a good time, and
learn how to get along with boys better." When I would argue
with her, she'd say, "At least don't let them know you're so
smart. Boys don't like such smart girls."

Strive, but be careful never to damage your marriage chances!
I always liked clothes and I was always interested in business.
So I dreamed I could be president of Saks Fifth Avenue. My
parents always supported me in whatever I wanted to do; they
really encouraged me. But then, when this man came along with
the right chemistry and the right education, my mother reminded me that I'd have to make a decision about whether I was
going to be my own person and be lonely all my life or be a
wife.

Be smart, but not smarter than your brother!
They loved it that I was smart in school until my brother began
to get B's and C's when I was getting A's. Then my parents
always said that he was really smarter—I mean, naturally
smarter. They said I did better only because I worked harder.

*Be knowledgeable enough to impress, but never so much as to
overshadow a man, any man!*
It was okay to be smart, but there were limits. My father would
shout at me, "Okay, so you're smart, but who wants to sleep
with an encyclopedia!"

Ambiguous messages, these, each contravening the other, leaving girls puzzled and women ambivalent. What is smart enough; what too much? What dare they show? What must they keep hidden? Questions without clear answers, mandates that create an impossible bind for both the child and the adult who grows from her.

> I have two selves—one at home and in the social world I live in, and one at work. My husband doesn't like aggressive women, and if people in my home world had to deal with me the way people in my work world do, it wouldn't work at all.[13]

"I have two selves"—an astonishing statement, spoken with force and clarity but without the slightest hint that there is anything unusual in it. For all women sense, even if they don't always know clearly and consciously, that, in important ways, they have two selves.

Two selves—always in skirmish if not full-scale war, the source of a lifetime of painful conflict. No wonder women often seem erratic and unstable, given to sudden changes of mood, unpredictable emotional displays. The effort to juggle those two selves, to walk that fine line, to keep parts of self neatly in check—to be interesting but never center stage, to be intelligent but never more than her man—is always difficult, often impossible.

Two selves—one advances, the other retreats; one achieves, the other fails; one is intelligent, the other defeats that intelligence. *Two selves*—born of contradiction and confusion, of different expectations at different life stages. Almost all the women I met recall that they were encouraged to achieve when they were small and that limits were imposed upon that achievement as they grew older.

When I was little, I was expected to be smart and to get good grades in school. But by the time I was halfway through high school, my parents got nervous about it. Then, they would be more interested in whether I was going to the junior prom than what my grades were.[14]

Over and over, that's the story—the tale women tell about the ways in which achievement and the use of their intelligence outside the area of human relations were discouraged once they hit their mid-teens. Sometimes it was subtle . . .

All my life I remember talk about what my brother was going to be when he grew up, but nobody ever asked me. They liked it that I was smart in grade school, but later it didn't matter any more.[15]

. . . sometimes not so subtle.

When things began to get harder for me in high school, my parents just kind of shrugged it off. I remember my father saying to me all the time, "You don't need to worry your pretty little head about school." The idea was always that in a couple more years I'd get married and have babies so none of it made any difference anyway.[16]

In some families, where education was highly valued even for a girl, the brakes came later—in the college years, usually at the first sign that she might have serious career plans in mind.

I was a very good student, and in college I began to think about going for a doctorate. But my parents really opposed that. They were afraid I'd have too much education. Either they argued with me that no man wants a woman with a Ph.D., or else they would worry that if I went on and got a professional degree, I'd never be satisfied to settle down and get married.

Class background, the educational achievement of parents —these made a difference only insofar as the timing of the active discouragement and limit setting. Girls from working-class families who somehow might have forgotten their place —who threatened to display competence beyond what was seemly—were likely to feel it soon after they entered high school; those from college-educated middle-class families, not until college.

Such differences were not related primarily to differing parental expectations for daughters, nor did they generally stem from some middle-class value in developing children's potential regardless of sex. Rather, college was a business proposition, an investment that was expected to pay dividends.

What were your reasons for going to college?

> To find an appropriate husband. What else? Isn't that what all girls of my generation went to college for?

Thus, even when a girl grew up knowing that she was expected to go to college, it was almost never an expectation in the service of a future that included anything but marriage. Middle-class girls generally went to college plainly and simply because the duties of a middle-class wife are broader than those of her working-class counterpart—more often requiring her presence outside the home, her involvement in her husband's work world, her appearance in public in the role of a literate, charming hostess and companion.[17] A college education is a prerequisite for the job.[18]

What were your reasons for going to college?

> I always knew I was going to marry a professional man; that's what I was brought up to do, and that's why my parents made sure I went to college. Well, you just knew that if you were

going to hold onto a man like that, you'd better be educated and interesting. It helped, too, that I could help him advance his career, you know, by doing all the things women do—entertaining nicely, belonging to the right groups, all of it.

By the time they get to high school, however, most girls of any class need no reminders of how to behave in appropriately feminine ways. Long ago, when they were still small children, they had heard the latent as well as the manifest content of the mixed message.[19] Long ago they understood that they must mute, if not outright hide, important parts of self—understood what boys like and how to give it to them, what they dared risk in terms of displaying their intellectual capabilities. Whether college bound or not, long ago most girls learned to still their dreams lest they be stolen away—and in so doing, made it unnecessary for any external agent to do the stealing. Thus, when I asked whether in childhood or teenage years they had any aspirations to be or do something when they grew up, the answers came with monotonous regularity:

> I just assumed I'd grow up, marry, and raise a family. Oh, I suppose vaguely, somewhere inside me, I knew that I *could* do something else, but it wasn't ever real. I mean, it wasn't anything that was *really* in the cards. The cards said you're going to be a housewife and mother, and, you know, it's hard to argue with the cards.[20]

Perhaps one does not—cannot—"argue with the cards." Still, such parental and social ambivalence leaves its mark, producing women who are cleft in two—torn between the intellectual and intuitive parts of self, between the need to achieve in the larger world and the need for human relatedness, a choice only women are forced to make.

But, one might argue, isn't it true that social role expectations also require men to make such choices? Not quite. For men, the more successful they are, the more likely it is that they will marry and live inside a family. For women, it's the other way around. The more successful they are in the world outside, the less likely they are to have the comforts of home and family. For women, the choice is more immediate, the cost more clear. A life of achievement threatens to be paid for in the heavy coin of isolation and loneliness.[21]

Still, the argument might continue, don't social role expectations also result in a similar division in men? Isn't the difference only that men must move along the opposite path—the one that emphasizes achievement at the expense of human relatedness? Yes, men also suffer a divided self—a division that leaves their emotional, intuitive side less well developed than their intellectual, achieving one. And while that's no small loss, there are important differences both in what is lost and how the loss is experienced.

For one thing, men generally don't suffer the division so deeply because the messages of childhood were clearer, less contradictory. The mandates to achieve, be strong, take control were relatively clean and direct; the constraints on their feeling side—"Big boys don't cry!" "Only sissies play with dolls!"—not muddied by ambivalence and ambiguity. Consequently, in adulthood, they often are only vaguely, dimly aware that something is missing—made conscious of it largely through the prodding of women who keep reminding them of their repressed part by demands for more intimacy in the relationship.[22]

But even when men are conscious of the division within themselves, they live relatively more comfortably with the repression of their emotional side than women do with their suppressed achievement needs. No natural phenomenon, this; not a product of male nature, but a result of the fact that the culture places a higher value on the side of achievement.

There are, after all, no Nobel Prizes for housewifery or motherhood, no prizes of any kind for expertise in love, loyalty, devotion, and self-sacrifice. For women, then, the repression is more painful, more difficult to maintain, precisely because their repressed part is the one most highly valued in society.

Call it what you will—the active, the passive; the doing, the being; the rational, the nonrational—it's all the same. That's the division women are consigned to for most of their lives— two halves, one less developed than the other to be sure, but alive. Alive, even if not so well. For it is not possible both to encourage and discourage a child's intellectual development —not reasonable to glow with pride at A's when she's seven and frown with concern when she's seventeen—and expect a clear, developmental outcome. Such contradictory and confusing expectations in childhood set women up for a lifetime of vacillation and ambivalence about their identity in adulthood —characteristics that can be seen more or less clearly in every interview, but are most striking around the issue of their competence.

Thus, when I asked the question:

I wonder if you could briefly describe yourself in some way that would give me a good sense of who and what you are?

I got a melange of answers that were puzzling and disturbing —not susceptible to easy analysis, not presenting a clear and readily discernible picture.

It isn't an easy question, of course, so it's no great surprise that many women had trouble answering it. Yet, there was no rush, plenty of time to think. And they had answered other difficult questions. Why should this one present such problems that almost one-quarter could not answer the question no matter how much I pushed, prodded, probed, or tried to help?

No amount of sympathetic waiting, no offering what in other contexts had been construed as "permission giving" worked. In embarrassment, they finally said one version or another of:

I'm blank. Maybe there just isn't much of a self there.

In embarrassment, I generally let the subject drop.

But it puzzled me. Many of the women who described themselves as a blank were, in fact, in struggle about their identity; were, in fact, anything but a cipher. It's true that the very fact that they were in the process of change could have accounted partially for their inability to deal with the question. But that could not be all of the answer. It seemed too simple, didn't take account of the fact that, on the average, these women had lived for over forty-six years. Surely, after so long, something of an identity—something of a grounded and bounded image of self—remains even when undergoing the most profound situational and personal changes.

I kept talking, kept wondering, kept asking questions. Eventually, understanding dawned. It's the inner turmoil wrought by this time of life, the struggle with the emerging other self, that such women are trying to avoid.

"I'm a blank." Almost always these words come from women whose earlier years show signs of a mighty struggle to make peace with their inner restlessness, with their sense that deep inside them there's something, perhaps even someone, else. These are the women who, until now, have been most successful in denying those other parts of self, who long ago accepted social definitions of womanhood and femininity with seemingly few reservations, few questions—the women who have been "good girls" most of their lives.

Almost forgotten is the child who got A's. Almost effaced is the adolescent who once dreamed of doing something important in the world outside the home. Almost, but not quite.

For by midlife, even for such women, the old definitions no longer work so well. Something else is emerging—a restlessness long denied, avoided, pushed away; a yearning for something different, something more; a view of the past that's touched with more than a little irony, more than a little regret.

> I was the one with that good Girl Scout image. Trustworthy, loyal, kind, true blue—that was me. Ask anyone, they'll tell you. I guess I'm just beginning to know now that if you're so busy being good all the time, it gets pretty hard to tell who you really are after awhile. God, what a waste.[23]

But along with the emergence of these new stirrings, there's fear—fear of change to be sure, but, before that, fear of the feelings themselves. They're new and strange. Who can know what they mean, where they will lead? It's frightening even to acknowledge such inner struggle, more terrifying still to feel one may stand on the brink of some transformation of self. Just the contemplation of such change can feel threatening—threatening to the existing order of a life, threatening because its course and consequence may be outside personal control. Some people are carried past those fears because their lives already are too painful, too limiting, too confined; some because the adventure of discovery and change has its own rewards. But for some, such a moment in life is so unsettling that it virtually dictates getting a tight grip on the past and holding on as if for life itself. Those are the women who draw a blank.

> I'm Dennis and Derek Clark's mother, and Mike Clark's wife. That's who I am, right there. After that, I'm just a blank. I don't know if I'm anything else; it's been so many years.[24]

What of the rest of the women—the 75 percent who answered the question, who offered some definition of self?

I wonder if you could briefly describe yourself in some way that would give me a good sense of who and what you are?

Almost invariably the question was met with a surprised, uncomfortable silence; almost invariably the first response was some version of, "Do you mean physically or what?" Always I replied, "You choose."

Most start with some description of their physical attributes: I'm short, tall, blond, fat, pretty, not so pretty any more, average—testifying to the primacy of their appearance in their image of self. No surprise in a culture where a woman's looks are her most highly valued commodity. No surprise either that few are satisfied with their looks, least of all those who are quite beautiful. Indeed, it is the beauties who now have the most trouble with aging—who peer worriedly at every wrinkle, speak anxiously of every bulge. In fact, the subject of bulges must surely amount to a national obsession. Well over half the women I met speak about being fat, say that's the thing they'd most like to change about themselves. Yet, few are anywhere near fat, most not even discernibly overweight. A heavy toll we pay for our national mania for thinness—millions of women whose distorted perceptions of their own bodies give them little peace and rest.[25]

Eventually, most women manage to say more—to speak about themselves as something more than a physical entity. Almost always the words they use are those that stereotypically define feminine personality: *warm, sensitive, kind, outgoing, considerate, caring, concerned, responsible.* And almost always the words *mother* and *wife* are included in the list.

So far, no surprises. That, after all, is how women generally are defined, therefore how they define themselves. Moreover, those are qualities that merit pride, so why not display them? No reason. But these were long, open-ended discussions—

plenty of time, plenty of encouragement for a woman to give a more rounded picture of herself. Yet, few did. *Most striking was the fact that, although half the women I talked to hold paid jobs outside the home, not one—including those who work at high-level professional jobs—described herself in relation to her work.* [26] It made no difference how the question was worded or sequenced— whether it came before our discussion of their work lives or after, at the beginning of the interview or the end, whether the conversation took place in office or home. [27] Not one said, "I'm a teacher," "I'm a secretary," "I'm a psychologist," "I'm a seamstress," "I'm a personnel manager," "I'm a lawyer." Few included the words *competent* or *capable* in their definition of self.

Noticing the omission time after time, I asked to meet professional women in their offices, assuming that if they were speaking to me in their workplace, they would be more likely to think of themselves in terms of a work identity. Not so. The words they used remained the same: *loving, kind, concerned about people, committed to relationships, accepting, nonjudgmental, a good listener.* Finally, I began to ask about it, posing questions that brought a wrinkled brow, a sense of puzzlement; questions that brought them face-to-face with a reality they had not thought about before.

I'm interested in the fact that we're sitting here in your office, that you're clearly committed to your work, yet your description does not include one word about yourself in relationship to your work.

Some gasped in disbelief.

My God, that's true, isn't it? If you hadn't noticed it, I never would have even thought about it.

Some sat silent, thoughtful, for long moments.

> I'm stunned. I'm quiet because I can't think of what to say. I'm running the conversation over in my mind trying to see if it's really true. I'm sad to say, it is.

One of those meetings was particularly revealing. I walked into the small, cluttered office of a woman who is an executive in a large social service agency and was struck at once with the power and immediacy of her presence. Here was a dynamo, a woman filled with energy and excitement. She waved me to a chair, apologizing for the mess, and asked me to be patient while she completed an expected telephone call that required her immediate attention. I sat down and waited. The phone rang, she identified the caller and began to speak rapidly, forcefully. "No, George, that won't do," she insisted. "It simply has to be *this* way." The man at the other end of the line demurred. They argued; she remained adamant. She won. I sat, admiring her performance, her forthrightness, when it suddenly occurred to me that George wasn't just some ordinary associate; he was the mayor of the city. I was delighted —no, joyous, gleeful. Finally, I thought, a setting and a circumstance in which a woman can't possibly fail to acknowledge her work identity. As she replaced the telephone in its cradle, she turned to me, smiling. "Okay, let's get started. I've told my secretary to hold all other calls for the next few hours." Given what I had just witnessed, I decided to start the interview with the question of identity.

Before we get into the rest of the interview, could you briefly describe yourself in some way that would give me a good sense of who and what you are?

She leaned back in her chair, looked thoughtfully out the window for a moment, then said:

Okay, I guess that's not too hard. I'm a very considerate, generally agreeable person. I'm a good wife, good mother, and a very
good daughter. In general, I think it's accurate to say that I'm
kind, loving, warm, and very nurturant.

It was my turn to gasp in disbelief. What about the performance I had just witnessed? Why had she not said anything
about her work, her capabilities, her power—those parts of
her that moments earlier had been on display? I asked the
questions. The answers were unclear, out of focus. Finally I
said:

What if I were to change that question to ask how you would
describe yourself if you were trying to impress someone?

Discomfited and puzzled, she replied:

I don't know. Actually, I thought I'd done that—answered to
impress you, I mean.

I, too, was puzzled. I continued to meet women in their
offices where possible, continued to probe the issue.

I'm interested in the fact that we're sitting here in your office,
that you're clearly committed to your work, yet your description does not include one word about yourself in relationship
to your work.

All the women struggled for understanding, both for themselves and for me. In the process, all spoke to a fundamental
theme in women's identity—the distinction they experience
between *being* and *doing*. [28] *Being* is internal, *doing* external;
doing is work, *being* identity.

I don't really know why I didn't say anything about my work.
It's certainly very important to me; I love what I do. I think

maybe it has something to do with how I see myself as a whole person. [With a bright smile of sudden understanding] Yes, that's it. Being a lawyer is what I *do;* you asked me what I *am.*

However it was said—with more or less subtlety, more or less clarity, more or less complexity—the idea was the same. "My work is what I do, not what I am."

But is this uniquely a woman's response? I thought so, but I couldn't be sure. Is it perhaps a sign of the changing times—indicating a shift away from a work-related identity and toward a fuller, more rounded picture of self? I doubted it, but again, I couldn't be sure. Of one thing I was certain, however. The picture each woman gave was not more rounded but a flat caricature—a description of a stereotype, not of the alive, complex person who was sitting before me.

To still my doubts, I talked with thirty-five men, asking them the same questions I had asked of the women. Some were the husbands of the women I was meeting; more were not.[29] They were men in blue-collar jobs as well as white—lathe operators and doctors, carpenters and salesmen, mechanics and engineers, factory workers and professors. Not one failed to define himself in relation to his work. "I'm a writer," "I'm a laborer," "I'm a carpenter," "I'm a doctor"—these are the first things they said about themselves. Even where men do work they hate or work at jobs that have no widely acknowledged social identity (some of the less well-known work on an assembly line, in a refinery, or a factory), work was still the reference point for identity—not just the work they do by day, but the do-it-yourself tasks they do by night.[30] No man included the word *husband* in his definition of self; very few said *father.*

Only one man responded in the same way as the women had —looking startled, troubled, fumbling. He was unemployed. Struggling to find words, he spoke painfully, haltingly.

> It's hard. Let's see. I'm a forty-five-year-old man. Most of my life I've been in heavy construction—an operating engineer. You see, right now I can't really describe myself because I'm in a very big transition period. I'm unemployed. The bottom fell out of construction and I haven't worked regularly for two years —only occasionally, and lately not even that. So, you see, I can't say who I am right now.

I find it interesting that, since you can't say what kind of work you do right now, you feel you can't say who you are.

> Yeah, well, isn't everyone that way? [Getting up to pace back and forth] It does seem funny, doesn't it? I guess a man's something else besides his work, isn't he? But what? I just don't know. I don't know if I am or not. I mean, you know, I'm a father of four kids, but that's not who I am.

It's not who he is because from infancy he's been trained to *do*—to achieve, to master, to conquer the environment. For him, adulthood means to do something in the world out there. For him, there is no *being* without *doing*. For her, it works the other way. All her life, she's been expected to *be*—*be* good, *be* pretty, *be* patient, *be* kind, *be* loving. *To be*—the quintessence of woman.

Banished from the world of doing, prohibited from seeking to conquer the outer world, she has become master of the inner world—the world of emotions . . .

> Living with Greg is like having a very complicated and delicate mechanism around which I've been trained all my life to service. That's what my life in the family is about, that's my func-

tion—to serve, to soothe, to heal. I'm the one who always knows what everybody is feeling, and the one who explains and interprets all of them to teach other. It's my job to test the emotional climate all the time, and to make sure it's just right.[31]

. . . and the world of relationships.

Until very recently, I never thought much about me as an individual. I never thought about who I (I mean, *I* as an individual) was, or what I could do. I thought about myself always in relationship to others; I mean, like how I relate to other people and how they relate to me. I guess you could say that's always been the center of my life.[32]

Whether she works or not, that's still the way she most likely defines herself, still what she returns to when asked for a presentation of self, as these words from a woman who is now a successful executive show.

I was raised to make other people feel good—there's no question about it. And when you ask me to describe myself, it's in those terms that I immediately think about myself.

Such definitions of self—the disconnection of being from doing, the focus on relationships and relatedness—are not simply a response to external demands. Identity is formed through the process of internalizing the external. A self exists in a social context; it grows and develops as part of an ongoing process of interaction with the social world. *External becomes internal.* [33]

If that's true, then how is it that so many women who clearly are in the process of changing their lives are not able to speak of a new and different sense of self?

I have trouble telling people I'm the director of this institution. Somehow, it still doesn't feel like that's *really* me. You know, my husband doesn't have any trouble saying he's a professor; it's part of his identity—maybe even most of it. I'd like this to be part of mine, too. But it isn't yet.

Partly that's because it takes time, perhaps years, to incorporate a new definition of self—to internalize a new self-image, to claim it as one's own.

It's really very interesting what happened to me over the years. When I first went back to school, I felt guilty if I was studying and not doing the housework. Then, by the time the six years were over, I felt guilty if I was doing housework and not studying. It's a matter of your identity changing. My sense of self— of who I really am—has finally begun to change.

But time alone is not enough. For if the formation of identity takes place in the context of social interaction, then we must look to the social world in which women live to understand why the integration of a new or expanded definition of self is so difficult. There, we hear women say:

I have to park my professional self outside the door when I come home. That woman—the aggressive one, I mean—just couldn't live with my husband.

There, we hear men say:

A smart woman doesn't come home all wrapped up in herself night after night. She knows it makes her man uncomfortable and insecure when she's that high about something that doesn't include him. So she keeps the lid on.

There, also, women complain:

When we go someplace together, nobody ever asks me what I do. They just assume I'm nothing more than David's wife and somebody's mother.

A common experience, that one—one I know well. It happens not only when my husband and I go together into *his* world, but in mine as well. More than once, he has joined me at meetings of *my* professional association, there to have people who know neither of us ignore me and ask him: "Where do you teach?" More than once, a colleague has introduced us as Mr. and Dr. Rubin, only to have the stranger turn to my husband and say: "It's a pleasure to meet you, doctor." More than once, he has accompanied me to a TV or radio station where I was invited to do a guest appearance, only to have to explain that it was not he who was to appear on the show.[34]

All these and more are familiar experiences for a midlife woman who is trying to incorporate a new identity along with the old. All are reminders that the achieving woman violates social expectations; all render her invisible. A woman may not be surprised by such responses. She knows, after all, that people in the world respond to her in these ways out of stereotypic social definitions that insist, irrespective of the evidence or the reality, that a mid-forties woman is somebody's wife and mother, nothing more. Still, each such experience brings with it a subtle message of degradation; each serves to invalidate the nascent sense of self; all make her both angry and fearful. She's angry because it's so hard to struggle always against this kind of invalidation, against the depersonalization that comes from feeling invisible. She's fearful because the implicit message, whether in the family or outside it, is that there's danger for her if she insists upon being seen and acknowledged in her new role—danger to her marriage, danger also of being ignored or treated with condescension, of feeling trivialized and humiliated. Consequently, she remains ambivalently connected to both the old self and the new, vacillating between wanting to assert herself in the new role and wanting to remind the world that she remains all those things a good woman is supposed to be.

Interestingly enough, the women who most often describe themselves as competent and capable are those who spend much of their time in volunteer activities in the community—women who call themselves homemakers but who, in fact, spend many hours each week as unpaid administrators in community and civic organizations.

Another puzzling finding—one I pondered over for a long while. What sense did it make? Why would women doing unpaid work feel more comfortable about expressing confidence in their abilities than those who work for pay? Perhaps, I thought, it was self-evident to the working women. After all, no one continues to pay a salary to someone who is incompetent. Perhaps. But it was not enough to explain what I was seeing and hearing. The men I spoke with also were paid, and they had no trouble either in defining themselves with reference to their work or in talking about their competence. It felt like an unsolved mystery—as if I had my hands on a piece of the puzzle but couldn't quite make it fit. Then, a few weeks later, a personal experience gave me the crucial clue.

I was giving a presentation at a local university, talking to colleagues who were almost exclusively middle-aged men. As I began to raise these issues about women's identity, my listeners became restless—the signs clearly evident in the rustle of shifting bodies and papers, the sounds of throats being cleared, of feet shuffling across the floor. Soon, they began to challenge what I was saying. Before long, discussion turned to argument—both they and I quickly becoming fixed in positions from which we were incapable of hearing each other. As words flew around the room, my discomfort rose. An inner voice warned against expressing my anger, fearing that I would appear too strident, too aggressive, too (Dare I think it, let alone say it?) too unfeminine.

Finally, one of the men, an old friend, intervened, hoping to cool the heat so we might see some light. He spoke in my behalf, arguing that there was perhaps something that I, as a woman, was trying to communicate that they were not ready to hear and understand. I was relieved to have someone speak for me, relieved to anticipate the breaking of the tension—so relieved that I lost track of the discussion. Then, over the din of my own inner turmoil, I heard him say: "And Lillian here is one hell of a good cook!"

Out there in the room, the clatter of words and voices continued; inside me, everything stopped in a stunned silence —not so much at what had been said, but at my own inner reactions. For my head reminded me that I should be angry, even outraged. My head shouted, "What does your ability in the kitchen have to do with your competence in this room?" But my woman's soul retorted, "Oh, shut up! You know you're glad that your 'feminine' credentials have been established—that they now know the other side exists; that you're not just an aggressive, angry, 'castrating' woman."

There it was—that instant of recognition, that moment of knowing what previously had been unknown. Once turned the right way, the piece of the puzzle fell easily into place. The women who are volunteers can speak comfortably of themselves as competent because the work they do is congruent with social role definitions—with definitions of womanhood and femininity we have all long since internalized and that, most of the time, lie outside the context of awareness. For them, there are no conflicts around this issue of work and competence, no need to deny those parts of self in fear that an observer might miss the other, the "feminine," side. By working long hours without pay, by working, not for personal gain but for the good of others, they are demonstrating how caring, concerned, selfless they are—the epitome of all a good woman ought to be. No need to display the womanly side, it's built into the system—validated both inside the house and out. Family, friends, community all applaud her energy, her devotion, yes, even her competence. A husband who consistently refuses to agree to his wife working for pay encourages, even takes pride in, her volunteer work. Why not? Since she doesn't earn a salary, she remains in a subordinate and dependent position. His authority in the family isn't threatened; the traditional balance of power remains undisturbed. While her work fulfills important community needs, it competes with no one—at least no one of consequence. It is, in a word, appropriate.[35]

It's true, he complains sometimes that she's too busy, that the house is not clean enough, meals not given the attention he'd prefer. But precisely because of the nature of the work she does—because it's volunteer and not paid—his complaints don't come with great force. Because she's engaged in activities that benefit the community, because she's lauded as altruistic and selfless, he isn't comfortable demanding that she stop. It feels too clearly selfish, too markedly self-centered. For the same reasons, she can hear his complaints, make some small efforts to palliate his discontent, and continue on her way without much dislocation to her activities outside the home.

This is the social context that permits volunteer women who work long days and many nights to insist that, unlike women who are employed for pay, they are not bound to the job. Children, home, husband all come first, they claim. It's irrelevant that this is a fantasy—that, in fact, the woman who is regional president of the PTA or director of her school district's volunteer program is no more likely to miss a meeting she is expected to chair than is her employed sister to miss a day's work because a child is home with a cold. It's irrelevant because the fantasy is shared in the family, in the community

—a collusion that denies and transforms reality. That transformed definition of the situation determines the volunteer woman's experience, and it is her experience that counts. The simple fact that women in high-level volunteer jobs universally experience themselves as free to choose home over job is enough to liberate them from the painful conflicts that dominate the lives of so many women who work for pay. The volunteers can claim their competence, acknowledge their abilities, say it out loud for the world to hear. Not for them the fears that come to women who move toward a world where they'll compete with men. Not for them the pain of struggle with either the internal conflicts or the external ones.

Once the context is clear, other things fall into place. For example, women who are secretaries more often speak of their competence than do the lawyers and executives. On reflection, it makes sense. One is doing woman's work; the other, man's. The secretary could say with pride:

I'm good at my job. My boss really appreciates me.

On the job, she's validated for tasks not much different from those for which she's appreciated at home—service to others. Little threat there to her own sense of self, no threat to his. But the lawyer could only look startled at her own success, speak in wide-eyed wonder about it, behave as if it somehow had happened to her outside her own volition.

I'm amazed I've gotten through law school. I'm amazed I've graduated. I'm amazed I passed the bar the first time.

To claim this new identity is to claim the right to compete in the world of men. To openly acknowledge her own capabilities is to confront the prohibitions of a lifetime—powerful prohibitions that forbid women to come into serious contact with their ability to achieve, to be powerful, to be masterful. No wonder competent, strong, capable, powerful women refuse that definition of self even when it is offered.[36] Listen to this dialogue with one such forty-eight-year-old who holds down an important job.

It's exciting to listen to you describe your work because you do it with such energy and power.

[She flinches, as if struck] Ummmm!

You flinched, as if I said something you didn't want to hear. I don't understand.

Yes, well, if you had just said *energy* that would be okay. But *power*—that's different. I would certainly choose a more flattering word than powerful.

I meant it to be flattering.

Thanks, but that's kind of hard to believe. I don't like to be described as powerful; I don't want to be. People don't really like it—not in a woman. It can get you in trouble, being powerful.

How so?

People just don't like it, that's all; they don't like it. My husband doesn't like it, either. He says I'm too forceful and too aggressive. God, how I hate that damned word. *I hate it!* When you're a woman and someone says words like that about you, you know it's no compliment.

So, what words would you use to describe yourself?

I'm a good cook, although a lousy housekeeper. I'd like to have everybody think I'm charming, and sometimes I am. I'm a good mother and a good wife. And I'm a caring, concerned person.

[Then, as an afterthought] Oh, yes, and I suppose I've got enough brains to get by okay.

Power—a word that belongs to men, not to women. *Power* —men seek it, kill for it; women fear it, resist even knowing they have it. "I don't like to be described as powerful; I don't want to be." Why? "People just don't like it," she says. "My husband doesn't like it either." But that only describes the facts, it doesn't explain them. Then why?

Power—in men, described as cool, dispassionate, rational, contained. And in women? From the mythic Medea to the Jungian archetype, power in women is seen as dangerous, destructive, devouring—too fiery, too impassioned, too uncontrolled and uncontrollable to be permitted expression.

But male power, too, has some terrifying representations in the culture. Look at the imagery of the wrathful God who comes down from the heavens to smite his sinful children. Still, there's a difference between such imagery and the ones that relate to women. For the male God in all his anger remains reasonable and potentially within control. He's the keeper of the rules, the avenger of transgressions, it's true. But at least there are rules—rational ones, some say—that provide guides for behavior, that, if followed, offer the promise of safety from his anger and security in his love. The message is clear: Obey the rules and there's nothing to fear from this God, this father.

It makes little difference that, without cause, without reason, men with power always have killed, maimed, damaged, destroyed beyond repair. The images of the cultural archetypes that live inside us resist such mundane realities, defy such reasoned and reasonable responses. Instead, it is women who are designated as capricious, women with power who seem to pose a danger beyond all control. Such myths, and the fearful fantasies they generate, live in all cultures where oppression exists. In our own land, they have a long history. The target changes with the historical moment and the geographical setting: the Irish in nineteenth-century Boston, the black slaves in the South, the Chinese when the West was settled. But the content remains the same; always the despised group is described as defective, ignorant, immoral, amoral, and above all, dangerous—a threat to be contained.

They serve a purpose, these myths. They are necessary both to justify the oppression of one group by another, and to maintain it. They justify by attributing all these deficiencies and more to members of the target group, thus making them seem to be of a lower order of the human species. And they instill fear in large segments of the population who, believing it to be a matter of self-preservation and/or the preservation of a valued social order, become complicit in maintaining the oppression.

So it is also with the subordination of women. But between men and women something else goes on as well—something that lies in the structure of family relations as we know them. For in fact, as helpless infants, mother did have life and death power over us—not for reasons necessarily given in nature, but because the modern nuclear family is arranged so that mother is the first and primary care giver, the agent of survival. From the moment of birth, the child needs another to sustain life—to feed, tend, nurture it. But that other, that mother, seems to appear and disappear in unpredictable and capricious ways. Sometimes a cry brings her comforting arms, her nurturing breast; sometimes it does not. No way for the infant to know why it happens, why it doesn't. In those circumstances, mother is, in fact, the repository of all pain, all pleasure, the embodiment of all power. Her presence means safety, her absence danger, even death—terrifying power that is experienced as arbitrary, outside control, because she, not the child, can choose which it will be.

Still, there's plenty of evidence that father's power also is experienced as profoundly frightening. But in the nature of family life as we know it, the incorporation of father as a powerful figure comes later. Indeed, because fathers are not the primary and earliest care givers, not the survival figures of infancy, their presence most often is not very deeply felt in those first weeks and months of life. By the time father becomes more than a shadow in the consciousness of the child, the primary experience with the all-powerful mother already has been internalized, already has laid the foundation in the unconscious for the fear of women.[37] By that time, also, the child has learned to manipulate the environment, learned how to get at least some of the most basic needs met in stable and predictable ways. The world, therefore, seems more reasonable, more controllable. And father, precisely because he is incorporated at this later developmental stage, is invested with those attributes of our inner experience that give evidence of the world's order and rationality.

For all of us who have been brought up in a traditional nuclear family, then, mother's power was once experienced as awesome and arbitrary, once feared as potentially deadly. Small wonder that the idea that woman's power is dangerous is so firmly rooted in the culture myths. Yet, there's an apparent contradiction here. Everyone knows, after all, that in real life women are not the powerful ones. But I speak here of life at another level—that inner unconscious life, that life which exists outside awareness and on which so much myth and fantasy is based. At that level, those myths, those fears, reflect our deepest and most primal experience, the experience of our first days on earth.

Still, the world of everyday experience plays a part in the

drama as well. For girls who grow up to be women, those fears are dissipated as they experience another reality both within themselves and within their assigned roles in the family and society. They come to understand their own relative power-lessness in the social world—an understanding that modifies their interpretation of their earlier experiences and that, at the very least, attenuates their connection with the myth of the dangerous mother. And they come to know some-thing of the complexity of the motherhood experience, something of the bond that ties mother to infant in ways that are anything but arbitrary and capricious.

For boys, however, it's another story. Without such correc-tive inner experiences, most men spend their lives trying to palliate those unconscious, archaic fears by rendering women powerless in the world of daily experience. Only then can they feel some safety from the terrifying, all-powerful mother. Un-fortunately for all of us, efforts to control our inner fears by externalizing them onto the world outside rarely work for more than brief moments. Therefore, men must engage in a constant ritual repetition of the subjugation of women—a rit-ual, however often repeated, that leaves their deepest fears untouched.

It would seem, then, that so long as the present structure of the family exists—so long as the infant must depend only on mother for life itself—the myth that woman is dangerously powerful will flourish, the fears will persist, and most women will be fearful enough of reprisals that they will be reluctant to hear the word *powerful* applied to themselves.

But even when women stand ready to claim their power, competence, and mastery, the world withholds acknowledg-ing them in such roles—as every woman who has ever wan-dered into the man's work world knows all too painfully. Ask any lawyer who, in job interviews, repeatedly is asked whether she can type. Ask any doctor who must continually explain she's not really a nurse. Ask any college professor who is looked upon suspiciously—as if she has somehow illegitimately upgraded herself from a high school teacher. Ask any professional woman who must make her way in the world ready always to defend her professional identity, so consistently is it denied and invalidated.

My own life is littered with such experiences—enough to fill the pages of this book. With a strong stomach and a sturdy ego, sometimes they can seem funny. On days less good, they can be hurtful. On any day, they're denying and invalidating of a self I have struggled to develop and now must fight to preserve. One example here will serve the point.

A year ago, my own dentist sent me to a specialist for consultation and some specialized work. Long ago, I learned that if I wanted service in a doctor's office, I had better be more than just a woman who, the feeling seems to be, has nothing better to do than to wait. Therefore, when I telephoned for the first time, I introduced myself as *Dr.* Rubin, stated the name of the referring dentist, and asked for an appointment.

I arrived for my visit at the appointed hour and announced myself to the receptionist who asked me to fill out a personal history form. I left blank the questions about my marital status and my husband's occupation, filling in only my own—"Professor of Sociology and Psychology"—and my employing institution. In the space that asked me to check whether *Mr.*, *Mrs.*, or *Miss*, I inserted *Dr.* Then I returned the form to the reception desk and sat down to wait.

Very soon, a dental assistant came on the scene, collected the form from the receptionist, and ushered me to a dental chair. The dentist, holding the form I had filled out, arrived moments later and greeted me heartily. "I'm Dr. Smith. I'm certainly glad to meet you, Mrs. Rubin. Is your husband the well-known restaurateur and wine connoisseur?" He talked *at* me through the entire visit—talked about himself, about my husband, but never acknowledged that I had any independent identity.

I was angry, but too embarrassed to comment. Long ago I learned the pain and heartache of fighting for validation, of demanding that my status be recognized. As a sociologist I know also that if I have to ask for acknowledgment of my status, I am already in a singularly disadvantaged position.

Nevertheless, as I drove to keep my next appointment, I determined to confront the situation if it should recur. Soon after my arrival, I was led into the office and seated in the dental chair. The doctor arrived. "Well, Mrs. Rubin, how are you today?" I replied, "I wonder why it's so hard for you to address me by my proper title, which is *Doctor?*" He was silent for a few minutes, then muttered, "It just seems odd." Then, with that false brightness with which adults speak to children, "But we'll try if it'll make you feel better."

I went to that office twice more. He addressed me as *Doctor* from then on—albeit with that studied politeness and ever-so-slight exaggeration that borders on mockery. As I was preparing to leave after my last visit, he leaned toward me and spoke. "Would you mind if I ask you something?" "Of course not," I replied. He smiled ingratiatingly, lowered his voice, and asked in a "friendly," confidential tone, "Aren't you proud of being married to your husband? Wouldn't you really rather be called *Mrs.?*"

4

"Sex? It's Gotten Better and Better"

> Sex? It's gotten better and better. For the first years of our marriage—maybe nine or ten—it was a very big problem. But it's changed and improved in lots of ways. Right now, I'm enjoying sex more than I ever did in my life before—maybe even more than I ever thought I could.[1]

"It's gotten better and better." That's what most women say. Better than what? Where did they start from, these midlife women? Where have they gone?

It's simple enough to cite statistics on the sexual behavior of the women I met. Over half of those who are married have sexual intercourse once or twice a week, another 20 percent do so three or four times a week.[2] Close to 90 percent presently are capable of achieving orgasm, well over half doing so more than half the time. About two-thirds engage in oral-genital sex, almost half of them often enough to consider it a standard part of their sexual repertoire.[3]

But having said those things, what do we really know about the *quality* of their sexual interaction, about its meaning in their lives, about its history? Ask midlife women about their sexual histories, and the stories come tumbling out—stories of their early sexual repression . . .

> During the dating years, I was constantly putting on the brakes, and I just couldn't reverse on command. It took years of feeling inadequate and of hating myself, which didn't help me *or* our sex life.[4]

. . . stories of their painful struggle to bring to life that repressed part of self.

> Sex was a constant source of difficulty for me as an individual
> and created nothing but conflict in my marriage. I was so closed
> off sexually, I really thought of myself as an asexual person.
> Getting through all that took lots of years and meant some
> terrible suffering for both of us—my husband *and* me.[5]

With only few exceptions, the memories of marital sex in
the early years bring with them an outpouring of deep feelings.

> What words can I use? They were *hard* times, *plain hard times.*
> It was the key issue in our marriage for years. It was the one
> that nearly wrecked us. [A combination of anger and bewilderment in her voice] And it wasn't anybody's fault. We were both
> incredibly ignorant. Both of us were only doing whatever was
> expected, you know, what we learned God knows when—
> maybe with our mother's milk. All I know is that for me, sex
> was all one big NO.[6]

Over and over those memories call up their anger at the
bind they found themselves in—a bind born of the mandate
of virginity and the expectation that they would turn into
sexual sirens at the pronouncement of the marriage vows.[7]

> He wanted me to be a virgin—that was very important to him
> before we were married—and he also wanted me to be skilled
> in bed right from the start. Imagine! It wasn't just awful, it was
> *impossible.* When I think of it now, I feel outraged because it
> wasn't even our fault. We were both just playing our parts, like
> puppets on a string.[8]

What parts were they playing? Who was pulling the string?
The parts were those assigned by the culture—the stereotypic
versions of sexuality with which girls and boys of that generation grew. These are women and men who came to adulthood

in the 1940s and 1950s when the wave of sexual liberation that brought the Victorian era to a screaming end was past. By the time they reached sexual maturity, it was clear that the Victorian heritage was not entirely gone, the double standard of sexual behavior not wiped out by the revolution of the 1920s. It had simply changed its form. By the 1940s, it was granted that women were capable, even desirous, of sexual pleasure. But the time, place, and manner were carefully circumscribed—limited only to one man, only in marriage.

Thus, almost without exception, the women who came to the marriage bed were naïve, repressed, inexperienced. Even among those who had had premarital intercourse, it was the rare woman who found the experience enjoyable, rarer still the woman who had orgasms in that period of her life. Indeed, most described those experiments in illicit sex as unsatisfactory and guilt ridden, acts usually so hasty and rudimentary that they barely qualify as full-fledged sexual intercourse.[9] As one woman said, "It all happened so quick each time, it was over before I really knew what was happening." And another, "Technically, it was having sex, but actually it wasn't. There was a coupling, but not a real experience."

Yet, about that, there were no complaints. They were, after all, engaged in forbidden behavior. Most women didn't expect to enjoy it.

After marriage, though, after sex became licit, then it was a different story. Then all of them—technical virgins or not—expected something more, something special, something magical to happen. They were filled with romantic fantasies that their own special prince would unlock the secrets of their bodies, their souls. They dreamed that "the earth would move," that "waves would be crashing on the shore" as they were swept away by his magical touch. And, of course, they were bitterly disappointed.

The first time I had intercourse, I thought: Is this what I've been saving myself for? [Her face registering the surprise she felt so long ago] *I couldn't believe it; it was such a big nothing.* I had read all those romantic novels about violins playing and bells ringing, and I absolutely believed some fantastic thing would happen. My God, what a disappointment it was![10]

This was the gift of the liberated sexuality of that era—incredible fantasies and magical expectations that were bound to fail.

I had tremendous hopes that I would flower as a sexual being after we were married. I looked to my husband to give me all the sexual pleasure I was afraid of before marriage. And when he couldn't, I was bitterly disappointed and resentful.[11]

But the disappointment and resentment were not the women's alone. For the men shared this package of impossible expectations.[12] Both wife and husband believed it was his responsibility to open up the mysteries of sexual pleasure for her; both believed he held the secret key.[13] For both, it was a distressing surprise to find that a lifetime of sexual repression exacted a price—that a woman couldn't spring into sexual responsiveness on cue. When the fantasies didn't come true, both husband and wife were caught in a bind where each oscillated between angry blaming of the other and a deeply felt sense of personal inadequacy—often creating a vicious circle where the more the inadequacy was experienced, the more it was externalized as anger against the other.

We came to the marriage with such high hopes. But our sexual maladjustment turned it into a nightmare of self-consciousness and resentment. It seemed like there was no peace. I was either angry at myself or angry at him. And I think he felt pretty much the same way.

But, one might ask, were there no women who were sexually responsive right from the beginning of marriage? The answer: Very few. It's true that some speak of sexual pleasure in the early years. But very rarely did that pleasure include orgasms.

Some valued the sexual experience because it was the major means of communication in the new marriage—not exactly the life they had dreamed of, but better than nothing.

> I never even knew what an orgasm was then. I enjoyed sex because it was a coming together in an intimate-type way. It was the most intimate thing we ever did in those days because we didn't do much talking.[14]

For others, there was something else as well—the satisfaction that comes mostly from giving pleasure, a quality of caring and nurturing for which women are well schooled.

> Long before I ever had an orgasm myself, I used to have a feeling of joy out of giving him joy. It didn't make a big difference if it wasn't such a great thing for me. Having someone in my arms who I loved and to whom I was giving satisfaction was very important and gave me real pleasure.[15]

An interesting and provocative issue, this—women who take such satisfaction in giving pleasure that their own unfulfilled sexual longings become relatively unimportant. In this age, when the emphasis is so much on *taking* pleasure, we might be tempted to label such women with pejoratives —to speak of their socialization to passivity, to bemoan their tendencies to masochism and self-denial. But that's too easy. And it leads too often to a call to arms, to a shrill and insistent demand for change, that leaves many women feeling confused and angry, inadequate or misunderstood. Worst of all, it leaves them feeling as if some prized part of themselves were being denied and invalidated—the part that's tender, giving, nurturing; the part that gets "joy out of giving him joy."

But what does this say? What of the often tragic consequences of traditional socialization practices that encourage passivity, masochism, and self-denial in women? No denying that; no denying either that the behavior I speak of here may be related to those tendencies. But let's not deny the reality and complexity of their experience when women speak of the importance of being able to give pleasure to a loved one. Let's not wipe out such giving with words of disparagement. Indeed, to do so invalidates any possibility of an authentic altruism—that kind of behavior which was glorified in the pre-Freudian age, which once was lauded as the height of virtue. It's true that the post-Freudian view that directs us to the potential pathology in such altruistic behavior is an important corrective to earlier romantic notions about saintliness and self-abnegation. But it has been carried too far if, in this era of human history, we can no longer distinguish at all between the authentic desire to give and its pathological distortion—masochism.

When it comes to sex, it is this very quality of giving that is necessary to turn the sex act into a relationship. Only when two people wish to give at least as much as they wish to take does sex become a nourishing and enriching experience. Only then is the uniquely human separated from the animal.

Of course, it takes two. And until now, there too often has been only one—the woman—to do this kind of giving. The task now is *not* to exhort women to change or to thwart that capacity in themselves, but to encourage men to develop it more fully. No easy task, to be sure, but a necessary one if sexual relations between women and men are to fulfill their promise.

Unfortunately, in this culture, facile answers too often take the place of real struggle. Thus, we now have a whole new vocabulary of assertiveness for women and a lucrative industry to match that supposedly teaches them to assert themselves and their needs. But the programs are problematic: first, because their focus on individual change rests on implicit assumptions that the problem lies in the personal inadequacies of individual women; second, because much of their rhetoric mistakes "assertiveness" for selfishness and seeks to teach women to abandon those giving parts of self.[16] In fact, *real* assertiveness would mean that women would respect those gentle, tender, giving qualities enough to assert their value. *Real* assertiveness would mean that they would continue to give such care and concern in their relationships *and* would insist on getting it from their men as well. Difficult demands for women to make, difficult for men to understand and respond to—especially so because, for so long, such values have been ruled out of men's lives; especially so because, for so long, those ways of being have been devalued with the label *feminine.*

These reflections aside, there was pain in the early years of these marriages. And there was conflict. But most women eventually won a victory in the struggle with their repressed sexuality—a victory of nature over culture, the triumph of female sexuality over the forces that for so long have conspired to obliterate it.

As long ago as 1953, Kinsey showed that the proportion of women experiencing orgasm in marriage rises steadily through the years.[17] So it is with the women I met. "I'm enjoying sex more than I ever did in my life before—maybe even more than I ever thought I could"—common sentiments, spoken repeatedly. But it took time. For some, it was a year or two before they experienced their first orgasm; for those less fortunate, it didn't happen for a decade or more. Others commented on the dramatic change after the birth of the first child, telling, not only of having their first orgasm, but of experiencing spontaneous sexual feelings for the first time in their lives.[18]

> All of a sudden I knew what it was like to feel sexual. I mean, I would get sexual feelings before that when I was stimulated, but they didn't just come by themselves. I used to wonder what people meant when they talked about being horny, but I never knew until after Lisa was born.[19]

Unfortunately, for women who are new mothers and who must bear the burden of child care alone, increasing sexual responsiveness is not an unmitigated blessing. For it is one of life's hapless paradoxes that the physiological development of this stage of the life cycle is so poorly matched with its demands. Certainly there's joy in those early months of motherhood, but there's also exhaustion. Of course there's the wonder of a new life and a new love, but there's also anxiety. Am I a good enough mother? Will I spoil my baby by holding her now? Or will I damage him forever if I don't? Is there something wrong with me that I sometimes feel restless and discontent? How could I have been so angry yesterday; she's only an innocent child? Question upon question, born of the myths and the mandates that attach to motherhood in our society—the myth of the all-loving, all-nurturing, madonna-mother; the mandates that remind her repeatedly that she alone is responsible for the healthy development of her child. Preoccupied with such fears, anxious about her adequacy in this new and demanding role, it's hard for the young mother to care much about sex. In fact, for most women—including those who by then were enjoying good sexual relationships—the arrival of the first child marked a significant drop in both sexual activity and pleasure.

Even among those who became orgasmic for the first time after giving birth, the experience usually wasn't met with pure pleasure. Rather, it was pleasure mixed with relief at finally having reached that long-sought goal.

> I suppose I was glad because it took the pressure off me. It was something my husband wanted very much, and I felt like such a failure not being able to do it for him.[21]

And there was frustration and anger as well.

> It was a damned irony. Just when I couldn't have cared less, it happened. And then for years, I was too tired and too preoccupied to want it much. God, what an aggravating time that was.[22]

In fact, from the time they're born until they leave home, the presence of children generally inhibits a woman's sexual responsiveness—a fact that is a constant source of conflict between many wives and husbands.[23] At first, the strain of a newborn infant leaves her tired and edgy much of the time. Later, other concerns about the care and welfare of children dominate her attention.

> He could be ready at any time of the day or night, no matter what was happening, and it made me very uncomfortable. You know, a child could be banging at the door, and he wouldn't be interrupted for anything. Or you could hear a kid screaming down the hall, and it wouldn't faze him at all. Well, I couldn't very well get into it under those circumstances.

These are trying times in a marriage. Whether at the breakfast table or dinner, in bed or out, young children are difficult, demanding, often irritating companions. Even when they're at their angelic best, spontaneous interaction and communication between adults is limited just by their presence.[24] That means there's often some distance between wife and husband —distance born of the fact that their daily lives are so separate while their evenings are too short, and altogether too full of distractions, to reestablish a connection quickly.[25] For most women, that spells difficulty in the sexual relationship—a consequence of the fact that, for women more than for men, sex is *part* of the total relationship not something that stands *a* part from it.[26] Over and over, they speak of not being able "to turn on the minute the kids go to bed," of needing "some time together before jumping into bed," of not feeling "very close or sexual after we've barely talked to each other for a few days." And over and over, they tell of the conflict these differences with their husbands create.

When children get older, they need less, demand less. Then the irritation at their seemingly unceasing demands, the constriction of their constant presence, and the worries about their physical and psychological well-being are replaced by embarrassed concern about what they might think their parents are doing behind the closed door, or what they might hear in the night.

> Just knowing that the bed could squeak or they could hear some noise makes it hard to get into sex sometimes. I feel nervous that they could walk in any time, too. We've thought about putting a lock on the door, but after twenty years of not having a lock on the bedroom door, I feel embarrassed to suddenly have one show up. What would I tell the kids? Even if they didn't ask questions, I know what they'd be thinking, and I feel like I'd have to explain. But what would I say?[27]

The fear of pregnancy is another important inhibitor of sexual desire and activity in women. Despite almost universal use of birth control measures, that concern remains alive for most women in their childbearing years. For some, usually those who have had the experience of an unwanted pregnancy —a child born of a birth control device that failed—concern turns to fear.

To deal with this fear, just over 15 percent of the men have had vasectomies.[28] Without exception, this has meant more relaxed and frequent sexual activity between wife and husband—the woman sometimes becoming orgasmic for the first time. When this happens, a woman credits her newfound sexual responsiveness to the freedom from fears of pregnancy.

> It made all the difference in the world not to lie there scared to death that I'd pay for this for the rest of my life. The last thing I wanted was another baby, and I never felt secure with either condoms or a diaphragm. After he had the vasectomy, I could begin enjoying sex for the first time in my whole life.[29]

"The last thing I wanted was another baby." No reason to doubt her words. But there's still another issue, perhaps equally important, in this complex drama between wives and husbands. Very often, a woman sees her husband's willingness to undergo vasectomy as a statement of his caring and concern for her, a statement of his commitment to something besides his own gratification and pleasure. Both together—the release from pregnancy fears *and* the reassurance about his love and commitment that the vasectomy seems to her to imply—become powerful forces in freeing a woman to more sexual responsiveness.

In several families, there was conflict about whether or not a man would take this step. And always, for the wife, that conflict centered on both these issues, as these comments from a woman in a deteriorating marriage show.

> I can honestly say to you that from the second year of our marriage to the fifteenth, I enjoyed sex as much as he did. But no more. Not one of my children was planned. No matter what kind of birth control we used, something always happened. Five years ago, I got pregnant again for the fifth time. Fortunately, I had a miscarriage, so I didn't have to have the baby. But it turned me off sex, and ever since we have big rows over it for the first time in our lives. [Tears streaming down her face] But dammit, he can

do something about it instead of just bitching at me. He could have a vasectomy and take care of me in that way—finally. Until now, it's always been my job. Well, since it didn't work for me, it's his turn. If he cares enough about something besides himself, he'll do it. But I just don't think he does.[30]

It should be clear by now that both life cycle and culture influence women's sexual responsiveness. At the beginning, it's youth, inexperience, and the prohibitions against female sexuality that have to be overcome. Later, it's children—small ones or teenagers—and the fear of another pregnancy that impose constraints. Through all this, however, most women move steadily toward a more expansive and open sexuality—partly because some life-cycle issues are resolved, and partly in response to the changing cultural context.

Between the time these midlife women grew to sexual maturity and the time they were raising their own daughters to womanhood, profound changes in the boundaries of acceptable sexual behavior had taken place. Whether in marriage or outside of it, what for the mothers had been inconceivable, for their daughters has become commonplace.[31] While a few of the most daring of the mothers had premarital sexual relations furtively, now most of their daughters are doing so openly—many living in arrangements their mothers once would have considered sinful. While most of the mothers speak with pride —albeit tinged with some sadness—about their premarital sexual naïveté, their daughters would be embarrassed to make such an admission.

I have written elsewhere about the costs to young people of this revolution in sexual behavior, of the difficulties they suffer as they struggle to cast off their parents' teachings and to change their old consciousness to match the new behaviors.[32] Imagine the impact on the parental generation. Suddenly, they find themselves living in a culture that not only gives license to formerly forbidden behaviors, but exalts them. Suddenly, their unmarried children become sexually active, shocking their mothers, but reminding them also of their own repressed girlhood and young womanhood, of the moments now when they dared to wonder—quietly and to themselves, to be sure —whether those old ways were indeed the best ways.

> When my daughters got old enough to have sexual relations with boys, I had to ask myself some very hard questions. Was it better the way I was? Did I want them to spend the first ten or twelve years of their marriage getting through the sexual hang-ups my husband and I had? I guess I was somewhat jealous of the opportunities they had even though I was upset about what they were doing and afraid for them.[33]

Wherever they turn—on film, on stage, in print, or in life —midlife women are bombarded with what seems like a newly liberated sexual energy, reminded of what they may be missing, told these joys can also be theirs. Simultaneously, for the first time, relatively large numbers of women are speaking and writing about female sexuality, launching a concerted attack on established myths and stereotypes. For the first time, women are speaking to and for women, insisting on defining their own experience, challenging existing interpretations of female sexuality—from the general conception of sexual inertia in women to the more specific myth of the vaginal orgasm.[34]

Despite the changes wrought by the public discussion of female sexuality, however, many, if not most, women still tend to see their sexual behavior in highly individualistic and personalized terms, suffering from guilt, feelings of inadequacy, and sometimes desperation when they are not meeting whatever may be the current standards for sexual behavior. This is the paradox of the new sexual freedoms: They are not simply *freedoms* but very often new *coercions*—new mandates for behavior that evoke guilt and discomfort in much the same way as did the old restrictions. Indeed, in our highly conformist and goal-oriented society, these new directives for sexual behavior can be more oppressive than the old ones since, when oppression comes in the name of freedom, it's more mystifying, hence harder to grasp and overcome.

Thus, if some women are found to be capable of multiple orgasms, it's not just a matter of pleasure for those who can or wish to, it becomes a requirement of adequate sexual performance—the end toward which sexual activity is directed. The pleasure a couple may have experienced before the discovery too often gets lost in the determined, sometimes tortured, march toward the new goal. If she doesn't have multiple orgasms, *she* feels terrible; if he can't make her, *he* suffers as well. From blaming themselves, they shift to blaming each other, and back again. Wherever they come to rest at any given moment, their sexual relationship suffers—all in the service of the quest for something more, something better. Nothing wrong with the search, of course, only in the way it's conducted, only in the fact that it's alienated from internal needs and longings, dominated by the latest sexual fad. This year it's multiple orgasm, last year it was vaginal—a quest that brought needless anxiety to millions.

> We kept trying and trying to get me to have a vaginal orgasm. That was the big "A"—"A" for being female, "A" for validating your husband. It was the focus of all our sex. We were no longer human beings, but guinea pigs in our own experiment.[35]

But it wasn't, in fact, their own experiment. They were responding, not to some inner mandates, but to external, social ones. To some, it must seem like the ultimate paradox that, while using the language of pleasure, the recent sexual revolution has managed to do to sex what even the Puritans couldn't quite achieve—to turn it into hard work.[36] Our concern for performance and technique leaves little or no room for a playful, pleasurable, sensuous sexuality—the kind of sexual play that would lead quite naturally to a woman's orgasm. Instead, we speak with a kind of grim resolve about the techniques for "getting her ready," both women and men missing the pleasures and delights to be found in the process. The word we use to describe this part of the sexual interaction tells the story—*fore*play: the part that comes before the real thing. If we understand the social context in which language, culture, and behavior interact, it comes, not as a surprise, but as another demonstration of the many contradictions in the American culture—in this case, the tension between work and pleasure that dominates public policy as well as individual life, a tension built deep into the American consciousness, part of our Puritan heritage.[37]

In this context, let's look anew at the issue of faking orgasm and its meaning to women who do it. A very small proportion of the women I met fake orgasm all or most of the time. But most have done it at some time in their married lives, and almost half still do it at least once in awhile.

That's no big news. The issue claimed my attention only because most of the women who fake orgasm, even those who do it only occasionally, speak intensely about the guilt and discomfort they feel now that the phrase *faking orgasm* has become practically an epithet. They tell of reawakened fears about their sexual adequacy; they talk about feeling judged. Most of all, they plead to be understood, wanting the meaning of what they do in bed to be known before the judgments are rendered.

But who's judging? Surely not the feminist writers who have spoken out so passionately about contorted social definitions of female sexuality. Surely not those who have written with such compassion about the sexual conflicts women face as a consequence of those distortions. Ask them. And the women I spoke with say they don't know who, only that they feel they're being judged and found wanting, that they feel misunderstood because there's not enough talk about what it means to them to fake orgasm, why they do it.

> It's every place you turn these days. And it makes me uncomfortable because I don't think those women who shout about how terrible it is to fake it understand what it's like and why a woman would do it.

And why do you do it?

> It's just easier sometimes, that's all. I never tell a lie about it; it just happens. [Squirming uncomfortably in her chair] Joe doesn't ask me, right? He doesn't say, "Did you or didn't you," right? So what if I just let him think I did? He needs to believe it's that way. So what if I just give him that impression?

The "so what" is that she—and others like her for whom these comments are typical—is asking those questions of herself, not of me, suggesting that she's not so sure any more that it's really all right.

You sound as if you're asking yourself that question, not me.

> Yeah, I never did before, though. I never thought it was a problem. I've never talked about my sex life to anyone, *never.* But there's so much talk about things like that now, you can't help hearing and reading things. And lately, people are talking about women faking it, so I worry about it. I guess now I ask

myself if it's honest or not. [Hesitantly] And you know, I begin to think maybe there's something wrong with me that I don't have an orgasm every time.[38]

How does it happen that way? How does it happen that she's angry at "those women who shout about how terrible it is to fake it"? How does it happen that she worries that "there's something wrong with me that I don't have an orgasm every time"? Certainly the feminist discussion about faking orgasm has dealt with the *why;* certainly it has tried to place the behavior in the context of social expectations, not personal responsibility. Then, how does it happen that this woman, and so many like her, hasn't been able to hear that message?

Perhaps women fail to hear the reassurances because their own internal anxiety about what they do is so great that it must be disowned—projected outward onto anyone who calls attention to it. Perhaps they have trouble listening because the emphasis on the social sources of their sexual behavior indeed misses something in their own experience that makes those explanations seem alien. It is, after all, the triumph of the socialization process that we internalize the mandates of our culture so profoundly that we believe we are acting on inherent and individual choices. Perhaps women don't integrate the new messages so readily because there's so much noise in the social world about sexual issues that it's hard to know who's talking, hard to know what's being said. Perhaps also because they have had quite enough of the changing and often contradictory cultural expectations that influence and shape their sexuality.

I came to the issue of faking orgasm with my own biases, believing that the only reason a woman fakes it is to please her partner and that, no matter what, no woman ought to deny her own experience and sexual needs in this way. But the women I met taught me anew that human behavior is never so simple, and that changing it requires understanding, not injunctions —understanding, not just of individuals, but of the social system in which they live.

It's true, of course, that one reason women fake orgasm is to please their partner. But rather than viewing that in its negative sense, let's turn the prism a bit. Then we see that the behavior is born of their caring concern for him—a gift that's born of love and the ability to give of which I spoke earlier.

> It isn't as if he's not a good lover, because he is. He doesn't rush and he's not abrupt. I need a lot of attention and loving, and he gives it. So why should I make him feel like he's fallen short or he's a failure just because I don't have an orgasm every time?

But there's another reason why women fake orgasm—one that speaks more to their own needs than to their husband's. Women's orgasms are now big business—books, films, therapies, and the like, all part of a highly profitable industry devoted to telling us how to make it happen, all selling the notion that good sex must end in orgasm. Anything else is portrayed as not quite good enough, not quite the real thing. That means that women are now under the same performance pressures that men have experienced for so long—pressures that may feel incompatible with internal needs, since many women insist that it's not necessary for them to have an orgasm every time they have sexual intercourse; that sometimes they can be quite content with a loving, tender sexual experience that does not culminate in orgasm.

Whether in men or women, such pressures ultimately generate a response. Some men become impotent. But there's no such out for women, no physiological response that makes them absolutely unable to participate in sexual intercourse. For them, faking orgasm is one way to make *in*congruent demands feel more congruent—a reasonable response to an unreasonable situation, perhaps the only way to take some of the pressure off.

> I never thought it was a big thing until now. After all, I don't have to have an orgasm every time. Sometimes I just don't need or want one, but it's important to him, so I just let him think I have it.

For some women, then, faking orgasm may be the most effective protective device available—a way of dealing with sexual mandates from a culture and a husband that are experienced, even if not always consciously understood, as alien and alienating; perhaps the only way a woman has at any given moment of pleasing her man who may be trying so hard, yet unsuccessfully, to please her.

Still, the act of faking is alienating in itself, one might argue, and ought to be dealt with in that context. Indeed, that's an important and complex issue for both women and men—one major reason why they must learn to be more open with each other about this and other sexual issues. But that alienation doesn't start with faking orgasm. Faking it is only a symptom of alienated sexuality that begins early in childhood when girls begin the process of internalizing social definitions of female sexuality that distort their experience and alienate them from the messages of their own bodies. From the beginning, it's those external cultural definitions of sexuality that dominate our consciousness, circumscribe our behavior, and define our relationship to the sexual side of our personal identity. And it's those cultural definitions and the way they are responded to that deserve our closest attention. For to allow the discussion of faking orgasm to take place outside that deeper cultural context is to burden women and men with yet more reasons for guilt and more feelings of personal inadequacy.

With all the constraints, with all the problems, there's also a liberating side to the public discussion about sex and sexuality. Whether young, middle-aged, or old, many women have been listening intently, hearing the new words, daring finally to believe their own experience, to give legitimacy to the messages of their own bodies.

> God, it was like a heavy load lifted from me—from both of us —to find we were okay. But it didn't come easy. It took years of reading all this stuff that's been coming out about women's orgasms, as well as some therapy, before we began to be able to accept that whichever way I get it, it's okay.[39]

It's true that some few still speak sadly about being unable to take advantage of a cultural climate that offers permission for more sexual freedom than ever before dreamed of.

> I wish I could be free sexually like the kids, but I can't. It just doesn't work for me. Too many years of repression, I guess, and too many lessons that I learned too well.[40]

But for most midlife women, life-cycle and cultural changes have come together to make for more gratifying sexual relationships even in long-term marriages. The years of sharing the same bed means they know each other better, are more likely to know what will bring sexual pleasure, are more trusting and, therefore, more able to be interdependent. With the children grown, there's more privacy, more opportunity for relaxed time alone.

> We're a lot freer sexually now than we ever were before. And now that it's just the two of us in the house, you can do it when you feel like it, and you can take your time—you know, just lie there together for an hour or two, or even more. It makes all

the difference when you don't have to worry who's listening in one of the other bedrooms.[41]

Such changes in personal sexual behavior do not come easily, nor do they come all at once. For some, one small change has led to more; for others, one has been quite enough. And most of the time, they are changes that, by current standards of sexual practice, are small indeed. But that they have come at all is testimony to women's will to struggle toward change, testimony to their capacity for growth and development in the face of repressive early training that presents formidable obstacles.

This expanding sexuality in women is not without its paradoxical effects, not without its positive side and its negative. For just as there is a distinct and different pattern in the work careers of women and men, so there are differences in their sexual careers and development as well.[42]

We know that for men the passage of years means a diminution of the sexual imperative. That lessening of sexual capacity has been discussed at length, usually with expressions of regret and sadness for the lost virility of youth. But rarely do we hear about the positive impact of that fact upon midlife marriage.

> It's not as frequent as when we were younger (it just seemed like all the time then), but it's more meaningful and it's more enjoyable. I don't ever feel pushed into it any more, and that's good for both of us. We don't start out with all that stuff between us—you know, his wanting it and me resisting it. Now I want it as much as he does—sometimes even more. So sex now is really very good and much more varied than it ever was. [Laughing] I guess this is one time when less is more. I mean, there's less quantity but more quality—a lot more.[43]

Indeed, for many women, the waning of the intensity and frequency of their husband's sexual need brings an important new dimension to their own sexual experience. Until this happens, many women never have the chance to feel the full force of their own sexual rhythm, never get to experience the frequency or potency of their own sexual desires. Until this time, that rhythm, that force, was coopted by the urgency of their husband's sexual demands. For the first time, many women discover that their sexual responsiveness is cyclical, the waxing and waning of its intensity related to the menstrual cycle.

> I'd heard talk that women were supposed to be sexier around their period, but I have to tell you that I didn't know anything about it first hand until recently. I always just thought I wasn't very sexy and that I didn't have any peaks and valleys—[with a self-mocking laugh] just valleys, you know. It was kind of a wonder to me to find out about the peaks, which happened after my husband kind of slowed down.[44]

It's not that this woman, and others like her, didn't often enjoy the sexual encounter in the earlier years. The point is simply that the initiative then usually came from the men and was related to their wishes, needs, and sexual rhythm, not to the women's. When that changes, when the men's sexual need is no longer so clamorous, women often learn for the first time about their bodies' capacity for sexual response.

> I didn't even know it then, but I never knew what it was like to feel horny. He was always there waiting and ready, and most of the time I felt I had to say "yes" even if I didn't feel like it. Now I *love* feeling that I'm a sexual person for the first time in my life. It's sometimes hard to believe the change.[45]

And now the paradox. For this very shift in the urgency of male sexual response which makes life easier in so many ways also means that women again are stuck with having to quiet their own rising sexual needs. For men, there seems to be no anxiety worse than the fear that their sexual powers are waning. Thus, at the first sign of diminished sexual capacity, a woman is likely to act as if on automatic pilot to protect her man from having to confront that reality. That means she doesn't initiate a sexual encounter even at the cost of muting her own heightened sexual imperative.

> There's nothing worse than to push him and have him unable to perform. If he fails, it causes more problems than it's worth. It's a shame because I feel deprived now when I never would have before. But I worry more about him than I do about myself. So I just wait for him to ask me. That's easier all around.[46]

Perhaps she's angrier about it now than she might have been in another era and at another time in her life—angrier because now the repression is more difficult to achieve, the deprivation experienced more keenly, and the culture somewhat more permissive of her acknowledging and expressing those feelings.

> I know now that this is denying oneself, that it's an enormous part of life that I've denied for a long time. It's denying feelings of self-affirmation which you need more as you get older. I can't deny those feelings so easily any more, and sometimes I get mad that I still have to because now it's not so easy for him to have sex any more.

Generally, however, most women don't speak that anger very readily—and surely not to their men. In fact, a woman who experiences this sexual turnabout in a marriage is likely to tread very gingerly. She's frightened for her husband— frightened that his fear of losing his sexual potency will, in fact, become a self-fulfilling prophecy. And she's frightened for herself—frightened because she knows his sense of manhood rests on his sexual performance; frightened because she understands how dangerous to him, to her, and to their marriage is any threat to that sexual capacity.

> It's a shame men are so sensitive about their virility. But it's true. When impotence hits a man, it's a real trauma. I don't want to put him in a position of having a failure and feeling so terrible that he won't be able to make it next time. Sure, I like sex; I enjoy it. But I'm not going to die without it for a while. So I just wait.[47]

It's true, she won't "die without it." But she *will* temper her sexual desire because of her concern for her husband's sense of manhood, moderate her own yearning because of his need to believe in his sexual competency. And although almost always she'll speak words of understanding, she's usually ambivalent, if not downright angry, about the situation.

> [Bursting out spontaneously] It makes me furious that just when I become a real sexual being, he cops out. [Then immediately wanting to modify the anger] Oh, that's not fair, is it? It's not *his* fault. Sex has always been so important to him, and I know how hard it must be not to be able to do it all the time. I guess he was what you'd call a sexual athlete until a few years ago when that all changed. I feel very badly for him, I really do. But I guess I can't help feeling bad for myself, too. It just seems like one of life's rotten tricks.[48]

Half a lifetime of struggling with her repressed sexuality and a woman awakens to find her husband getting ready for sleep. Indeed, one of life's ironies, "one of life's rotten tricks" —especially galling because for so many years the situation was reversed, especially so because for so long her active sexual interest is what he pleaded for, argued for. Finally, she's the one who would more often initiate sexual activity. And she can't—restrained by the fear that he'll experience it as pressure, that he won't be able to complete the act.

How often does this happen? Often enough to engage the attention and concern of about half the women I spoke with. To whom does it happen? It's hard to discern a clear pattern. But age makes a difference. The women between forty-five and fifty-five—all married to men from two to ten years older than they are—speak about the waning of their husband's sexual capacity more often than those who are younger. But even among the forty-year-olds, it already is felt, already is a subject of concern.

It's tempting to speak only of physiological differences—of the divergent developmental paths that put the peak of male sexuality a decade or more before the female sexual peak—to explain the diminution of sexual interaction in midlife marriages. But there's more than biology here, more than a regrettable physiological process at work. Indeed, that's too easy an answer, too static a notion—one that fails to take into account the fact that sexual behavior takes place in the context of a relationship, that it is an interaction between two people, that much of the complexity of the total relationship is expressed in the sexual interaction. Ask yourself: If it were just biology, how could we explain the man whose impotence or waning sexual interest is replaced by a clamoring sexuality immediately after a divorce?

In fact, where serious incompatibility of sexual desire exists, it's often related at least as much to power struggles in the marriage as to distinctly physiological issues—power struggles that, as anyone who has lived in a marriage knows, tend to get played out in bed.[49] Certainly it's true in over one-fourth of the families I met where those power struggles are alive, dominating the sexual interaction, determining its content and frequency. In some families, they're very old; in others, they're much newer—the product of a wife's emergence as a force to be reckoned with in this era when so many women are beginning to make their presence felt in new ways.

Where the struggle has a long history, it's played out in the sexual interaction in one of two ways. Either the husband is relatively indifferent to his wife's needs, taking what he wants sexually while she simply submits. Or the wife withholds—sometimes physically, by refusing to participate, more often emotionally, by becoming nonorgasmic. Where the struggle is more recent, it's usually manifest by a husband's failing sexual interest at exactly the time when a wife's increasing independence outside the home begins to make itself felt inside as well—whether in the kitchen, in the living room, or in the bedroom. She may be trying her wings on a job or at school at the same time she's beginning to experience and assert her sexual needs and desires. After years of hearing his complaints because she doesn't initiate sexual activity, she finally does. And he turns off.

> He always wanted me to take the first step, but when I began to do it, he was always too tired or [mimicking his posture and voice] he just didn't feel like it.

How did you feel about that?

> I didn't like it, but what can you do? With a man, you can't make him, can you? You just have to wait it out.

What do you think was going on for him?

> I don't *think,* I know. I had just gotten my first job and was very excited with my life. Things were changing around here and he didn't like it.[50]

In all families, such changes in longstanding interaction patterns are difficult. In some, they are met with resistance that expresses itself in a number of overt and covert ways—not least of them in the sexual dynamic. Another woman speaks:

> When we do have sex, it's good, and I always experience orgasm now, although it's a new feeling for me to feel like it's not often enough. There's nothing much I can do about it right now because he doesn't want me to be the aggressor. [Her eyes bright, voice tinged with a mocking anger] Oh, he doesn't say that; he has said exactly the opposite for years, in fact. But he doesn't have to say it; there are other ways to get the message across.

What do you mean? What other ways?

> I went through a period of time a year or so ago when I took him at his word. I mean, I got fairly aggressive and let him know when I wanted sex. It didn't take long to see how uncomfortable that made him.

If he didn't say that, how did you know he was uncomfortable?

> It was easy; he just wouldn't be interested. After the first couple of times, he'd just be too tired or too something. Whatever he was, he wasn't interested. In fact, he hasn't been terribly aggressive himself for the last few years.

The last few years—precisely the period when she was appointed to a municipal commission in her city of residence and enrolled in a university to finish a bachelor's degree dropped twenty-five years ago in favor of marriage. When these activities come together with a new assertiveness at home, as eventually they must, the change can be overwhelming, seeming to both wife and husband to threaten the stability of the marriage.

One unconscious mechanism for coping with the anxieties stirred by such a threat is to seek to reestablish the former equilibrium—which means to try to restore the relationship to the way it was. Even when that old way is recognized by both partners as far from ideal, they generally collude in the struggle to return to the past, since it is, at least, known. And psychologically, the *un*known can be more terrifying than the known, however bad that may be.

The sexual sphere, laden as it is with so many repressed emotional and cultural burdens—guilt, shame, rigidly sex-stereotyped notions of appropriate behavior—is probably the most readily manipulable, the most easily restored to the old balance. Thus, she stops being aggressive, and he regains the sexual initiative; not a perfect solution but a tolerable one, one that allows both to retain something—she, her outside activities; he, the feeling that he remains in control.

The issue, then, is not just sex, but also power—the struggle for one affecting the other in a continuing dynamic interaction. It's true, however, that the fact that these struggles are acted out in this particular way in the sexual arena is likely to be age related. Male impotence or sexual withholding is a more probable weapon—one not so hard on the person wielding it—at fifty than at twenty-five.

There we have it: A complex picture of a delicate and complex part of life—sex and sexuality. For women, there seems to be a disturbing disjunction between sexual development and sexual behavior. At the developmental level, women's sexuality breaks the bonds of early repressions and gathers force and power as they move into midlife. But at the behavioral level, something else happens. There, we see that despite the development and recognition of their own internal needs and sexual rhythm, despite all the talk about the liberation of sexuality for both women and men, we still can't discuss the sexual behavior of women in marriage outside the context of their relationships with their husbands—at least not when looking at the present generation of midlife women.[51] No matter how we turn the prism, no matter what facet of the sexual interaction we examine, women still are largely reflectors of their men's needs and wishes—responding to male initiatives and imperatives, subduing their own.

It's true that, like all peoples in subordinate positions, women have ways of striking back—covert ways that even they don't fully understand. Thus, women who are constrained from acting directly and forcefully by a lifetime of training to stereotypically feminine behavior may become nonorgasmic or unresponsive in an unconscious attempt to assert self and claim autonomy. Or they may fake orgasm to protect themselves from unwelcome demands. But the price for such behavior is high indeed, since it hurts the woman who does it at least as much as it deprives the man who is the object of it.

Whether their daughters' generation will effect some fundamental change is as yet unknown. For that answer, we must wait another twenty years. Today's young women may, indeed, be successful finally in rising "up from the pedestal,"[52] in developing a surer sense of their own sexuality, in gaining the ability to assert it, and in helping their men to develop those capacities of caring, concern, and nurturance that until now have been the almost exclusive province of women. We can only hope so and wish them well. But for most midlife women today, the needs and desires, the frustrations and discontents, that men bring to the relationship still dictate their behavior, if not their desires.

Still, there's something left to be said. With all the complexity, with all the difficulties, most midlife women will say: "Sex? It's gotten better and better." A remarkable experience, this, given the level of sexual repression with which they have lived for so long. A remarkable experience, given the number and magnitude of issues that beset the sexual interaction in marriage. And a remarkable expression of the strength, the tenacity, the force, of female sexuality. Despite all attempts to sublimate it, repress it, deny its existence, it forces its way into life and consciousness—there to be given a warm welcome by women who have spent a lifetime struggling to claim their sexuality, to define themselves as sexual beings.

5

Of Women, Men, Work, and Family

Why is it so hard to write a book about women without reference to men? The question nags. Is it *my* idiosyncracy, some failing in the way my mind puts together the material?

I go back again to the interviews—searching. Eventually, I see. It's not just I who can't talk about women, especially married women, outside the context of their relationships with men. *I* can't because generally *they* don't. Most women don't speak about, often don't even *think* about, themselves and their lives without reference to their husbands.

Ask a midlife woman about *her* plans for *her* future, and she more than likely will speak of her husband's.[1] Some talk about his retirement:

> In another ten, fifteen years at most, my husband will be retiring. Then we'll be able to do all those things we've always wanted to do and never had the time.[2]

Never mind that most can't spell out what "all those things" are, that under questioning they usually say some vague things about traveling or having fun. Never mind that these same women at other points in our discussion speak of their fear of those retirement years—wondering what they will do, how they will feel when their husbands are home all day; worrying about how their husbands will manage. The point here is simply that when I ask them about *their* future, they speak about their husband's. Imagine, if you can, forty-,

forty-five-, or fifty-year-old men responding in kind.

Some speak of their husband's work plans—a potential transfer, a sabbatical. Not surprising in a world where family life and the needs of other family members are expected to be subordinated to a man's work. What did surprise me, however, is that this is true also among women who have themselves gone back into the work force, even among those who are seeking advanced degrees in order to carve out a career for themselves. Listen, for example, to this forty-five-year-old woman, halfway through a doctoral program, who had talked excitedly and at length about how important it is for her to be en route to a professional degree.

Now that you're coming close to the end of this program, what do you see in your future?

> Oh, there's all kinds of possibilities, I suppose. I don't expect to have too much trouble finding a part-time teaching job. I *will* have to be somewhat careful about what I take on though because my husband is due for a sabbatical in a couple of years. So, of course, we'll be doing that.

Nonchalantly, as if it were the most natural thing in the world—"So, of course, we'll be doing that." Could it really be that, with a doctoral degree close at hand, her life still is planned around part-time work, and her husband's sabbatical is looked toward as an option in *her* life? I asked; she replied.

> Yes, of course. He's been planning for some years to go to Kenya to do some research on this sabbatical. Naturally, he expects me to go with him.

And you just as naturally assume that you'll go?

> Sure! What else could I do? I can hardly let him go alone.

And, of course, it's equally unthinkable to either one that he might change his plans to suit her needs.

But, some will say, such things are changing. Look at all the stories around about dual-career families, about families where husbands and wives work in different cities, even different regions of the country. Yes, look at them. They're written by, for, and about a select few—the academic couple, the wife and husband who are business executives or professionals. How many such marriages are we talking about? A few hundred? A few thousand? And how much will even these small numbers dwindle once there are children? To point to these families as the wave of the future is to delude ourselves about the difficulties of effecting large-scale changes in the culture—difficulties that are the expected consequences of any threat to the existing structure of power and authority in the society. And the entry of masses of women into the labor market on equal terms with men is just such a threat. That is why it is resisted so tenaciously, fought against with every weapon at the society's command—from the differential socialization of girls and boys to the development and elaboration of ideologies of femininity that serve to keep women in their place.

But never mind the future. What about the reality of the present, even among this small and privileged elite? For at least one alternative version of that reality, look in the daily press—not in the new women's sections, where such two-career couples sometimes are presented as if they represent a significant shift in family life and values, or in what's probable in the relationship between women and men, but in the news section. There, we read that on December 30, 1977, the director of California's Department of Conservation, a former professor of geothermal energy at the University of California, resigned her job to join her geologist husband who was to be on an expedition in Australia for eight months. "I had

a really tough choice to make," she said. "I really love the job
but it just seemed too long to be apart."[3] Eight months—a
long separation—just as long in Australia as in Sacramento.
But she leaves her job, his expedition goes on.

There, in the same news columns, we read also that the
President has had difficulty in finding women to fill high-level
posts in the federal government because they are loath to
leave their husbands behind in their city of residence. We read
this, and we hear the muttering—muttering about how
women can't *really* be counted on in such jobs, about how they
don't take advantage of opportunity even when it comes looking for them, about how their concern for family and their
need for security transcend all other commitments, even service to their government.

But who reminds the mutterers that a man doesn't have to
make those choices, that his wife and children are expected to
move with him when such an opportunity comes his way?
There are few indeed to make those reminders, fewer still
who will be heard and responded to respectfully—who won't
be written off as "another one of those libbers."

And who is there to say that a husband ought to support a
wife's career just as she has supported his? Who is there to
suggest that he ought to move to Washington so she can accept
the appointment the President offers and still live inside a
family? Who is there to talk to him about the importance of
his family and his responsibility for keeping it intact, to give
him the kind of advice that women in such situations get?
Surely not the same people who criticize, sometimes even
vilify, a wife who refuses to give up whatever she's doing so
her husband can accept such a high honor.

An overstatement? Read the daily press. There, on a day in
November 1977, two women wrote to "Dear Abby"—that
arbiter of morals and values read daily by many millions in

every corner of the land. The first, a thirty-eight-year-old recently married professional woman, complained that her husband had given her an ultimatum. Either she stopped her
overnight business trips or the marriage was finished. Abby's
advice? Invite him along on the trips in the hope that he'll feel
less threatened. "If that doesn't work, you will have to choose
between your husband and your business trips."

The second woman wrote to complain that her husband was
about to be transferred to a job in a city five hundred miles
away from the place where she and her children had lived all
their lives, where they had all their friends and family, and
where they had just built a lovely home—the dream of her
lifetime. "Every time I think of moving," she wrote, "I burst
into tears . . . I know I sound selfish, but I can't help it. My
husband wants to move. If I need a good lecture, let me have
it." And Abby did. A man's "greatest asset is a wife who is
always in his corner," she scolded. "You and your children
will make new friends. Help your husband climb the ladder
of success by being supportive and you will have another
lovely home that his 'Jack' built."[4]

Who is there to challenge such advice? Not Abby's readers
—or at least not very many. Not a word of protest appeared
in the column over the next few months. That is, after all, the
way of the world. Two lives devoted to one job—that is, if the
job holder is a man.[5] If it's a woman, then the advice is: Try
to change him; if you can't, do his bidding or prepare to lose
the marriage. No word to her husband about his obligation to
be supportive, no comment about his unreasonable demands.

And just in case this wife and others continue to insist on
their right not to be moved about as if they were pawns on a
chessboard, the corporate world is preparing its response. In
a feature story in May 1978, the *Wall Street Journal* reported
that several of the nation's largest corporations now favor

divorced men because they have no wives and children to inhibit their geographic mobility. Indeed, some corporations now either implicitly or explicitly encourage divorce where family considerations stand in the way of a man's transfer.

No wonder it's so hard to write a book about women without also dealing with their men. While the lives of both are inextricably interwoven, for women, family is at the core of their lives; for men, it's at the periphery. Thus, there are plenty of books about men—about men and their work, for example—that never mention the women in their lives, never consider the fact that most men live in families where their lives are entwined with others, never concern themselves with the way men's work affects women's lives. One could argue, of course, that this is a failing of those books—that in wrenching men's work lives out of the context of the rest of their lives, such books present a distorted view of the world in which both men and women live. One could quarrel also with the implicit judgment they carry about what's important and deserving of attention in the lives of men.

While such criticisms are valid, it must also be said that those books reflect quite accurately what the world is like—reflect the fact that work and family are distinct and separate spheres of living for most men. For a man, marriage is what he *does* in addition to what he *is.* First, he's a "doctor, lawyer, merchant, chief." Then, he marries and some small part of him becomes husband and father as well. Work, not family, is a man's most important social task—the task for which he was reared. Work, not family, is the basis of his social identity—his success or failure gauged by what he does on the job, not by whether his house is clean or how his children grow. I asked an engineer who is also the father of four:

When you were small, what did you think you'd be doing when you were grown up?

> Well, I didn't know what it would be, but I knew I'd work. I always knew I had to be something.

What about getting married and being a father? Did you ever think about that?

> No. I never gave any thought to having a family or being a parent. I don't remember having any fantasies about who I'd marry or about having children. I don't know. I guess I just assumed a wife and kids would be in my life one day, but it wasn't anything to dream about.

A crucial, life-shaping difference between boys and girls. For a boy, marriage and parenthood isn't "anything to dream about." For a girl, if it's not the only dream in her life, it's surely the dominant one. In adulthood, it's marriage and motherhood that define a woman, locate her in the world, ground her in a social identity. Therefore, it's how she defines herself. First, she's wife and mother. Work is permitted only in the interest of the family and/or only after all the needs of its members are tended. No matter if she works outside the home as well as in it, no matter how important her work or how successful she may be at it, the tasks by which she is defined, judged, and validated are those of the family; therefore, those are the ones by which she measures herself—as novelist Lois Gould reminds us with these wry words:

> My real work, writing, has never been fraught with . . . guilt. Nobody ever checks on my real work. I know there are spiteful strangers all over the world whispering about the dust in my apartment, but no one gossips about the fact that I only wrote three pages today instead of fifteen. No one cares if I write no pages. When am I going to dust that apartment, though?[6]

Indeed, in the lives of women a distinction that seems simple—the distinction between *homemaker* and *worker*—turns out to be complex, impossible, in fact, to distinguish between the two and write about them separately. Homemakers work; workers make homes. Their lives obstinately resist neat labels and clean categories.

Ask a woman what her occupation is, and one who works for wages outside the house may say she's a homemaker, while one who does not may say she's a worker. Both speak the truth. The woman who works outside the home also puts in long hours inside. The choice she makes when asked to define herself depends on several things—not least of them her class background, how she feels about the work she does outside the house, how she feels about the label *homemaker,* how she relates to the women's movement and feminist ideology.

The woman who says she's a worker but earns no wages usually is caught in her own special binds. She may speak four languages fluently and travel the world over as her husband's interpreter in his export-import business, but no matter what she calls herself, the world sees her as "just a housewife" because she doesn't earn a paycheck. Worse yet, whatever she calls herself, *she* has her own doubts. Without a salary, does she have a right to the title *worker?*

> I hate questions about my occupation. Whatever I say, it's not real. I'm not just a housewife. But the fact is that I don't earn any money for what I do. I'm an interpreter. My husband couldn't run his business—at least he certainly couldn't travel —without me or someone to replace me. But when I say that, people act as if I'm trying to upgrade myself from a housewife. A couple of weeks ago we met some people, and when I told them what I did, they said, "Oh, you help your husband out in your spare time." I was furious. But you know, when you hear

it often enough, you begin to wonder if maybe you're not just kidding yourself.

So it is also with the woman who is a serious but unknown artist, an unpublished writer, a talented craftswoman—all activities that earn little or no wages, therefore not recognized as work.

> My painting is my life, but it's not really acceptable to say it's my work, is it, if I'm not earning any significant amount of money at it? I'd feel very much better about saying I work if I could earn a reasonable income from it.

As Virginia Woolf knew so well, in a culture where productivity in the world of work is so highly valued, "Money dignifies what is frivolous if unpaid for."[7] Thus, only earning what she calls a reasonable income would give this woman the right to be taken seriously, to take herself seriously, to call her art her work. For that income would be the visible, tangible symbol of the worth of her art—the statement that it is valued in the world and, with it, that the person who creates it is valuable also.

Homemakers and workers, workers and homemakers—impossible to disentangle the two cleanly. Homemakers work both inside and outside the house. Some get paid; those are the easy ones to classify. Others don't—the woman who spends two days a week without pay in her husband's office, the volunteer who spends forty hours a week at high-level administrative work, the artist who works twenty hours at her easel, the full-time student in a degree program—these are harder. And what about the woman who invested a small inheritance in real estate twenty-five years ago and now manages her properties which earn $50,000 a year—all done from her home, all in an hour or two each morning? Asked for her occupation, she gestures as if to wave the question away and says, "I'm only a housewife." "And what about the work you do managing your property?" I ask. "Oh hell," she snaps, "that's not work."

Homemakers and workers, workers and homemakers. Perhaps the most we can say is that the balance between them differs according to a woman's situation, and that it shifts at different times of life as family needs and her responsibilities for them ebb and flow. Today's homemaker may be tomorrow's worker; tomorrow's worker, the homemaker of the days ahead. But whichever the dominant orientation at a particular moment in the history of a life, one generally does not wholly exclude the other.

It's this very flexibility that sometimes is pointed to as the singular advantage of women's role in the family—the fact that, when it works in its ideal form, women do not have to go out to work every day of their lives, that many women, at least, are protected from the harsh and bitter realities that most men face daily in the world of work. Often, especially for women in working-class and poor families, real life is far removed from that ideal, as the soaring proportion of young mothers in the labor force attests.[8] For those women, there's little advantage in the traditional role since it means only that they're stuck with two jobs—one inside the house, the other outside. Among the others—those who can afford to live out the ideal—some do, indeed, use that flexibility in their daily lives well, developing a broad range of interests that enhances growth and enriches life. But the world doesn't give much credit for such activities, doesn't validate them as important, worthy, socially productive. Consequently, women don't either.

Thus, while they tick off an impressive list of activities and accomplishments, the women I met often seem at sea—unsure of who they are, what they want, what interests them. "I've never had any *real* interests"—a theme heard surprisingly often, one that was difficult at first to understand.

What does it mean to speak of real interests? These women have plenty of interests—community service, politics, sports, church activities, weaving, ceramics, decorating, sewing, painting, all kinds of cultural and intellectual pursuits. Many have been taking classes at the local college or university for years—classes in literature, art history, music, psychology, child development, and the like. And although they have no credentials to show for these efforts because the work was not undertaken for credit in a degree program, many have become quite expert in one or another of these fields. Yet, this expertise usually is diffidently and ambivalently acknowledged, if at all.

Interesting, isn't it? Years spent in studying—in deepening interest and knowledge—years of activities that expand intellect and consciousness, tossed off as if they count for nothing. Why? The women agree that they have many things with which they keep busy, many things they enjoy doing, enjoy learning. But, most insist, these are not the kinds of activities that give meaning and direction to life. But what does that mean?

For some, it means that they don't bring in a paycheck, don't provide the resources to permit feeling like an independent adult.

> If you don't earn any money, it's hard to take yourself seriously or to feel like what you're doing is important or worth anything. I try to tell myself that's a very materialistic viewpoint and that I don't really believe it. But what's the difference what I believe? It's what the world believes that counts.[9]

For others, it means that the activities don't have any particular use in the world, that they're not productive of anything but personal satisfaction, that no one cares whether they do them or not.

> It doesn't make a damn bit of difference to the world what I do with my life or whether I do anything. It's as if I don't count; you know, like outside of my family the world wouldn't notice if I just stopped existing.[10]

Whatever they say, however they say it, one thing is clear: These activities are labeled as not real interests in part, at least, because they're not recognized and valued in the outer world, therefore suspect in the inner one as well.

> Sure there are things I like to do, but I've always felt rather directionless, as if I were a dilettante because I don't really ever get engaged in anything or committed to anything.[11]

Not "engaged in anything," not "committed"? Words and ideas expressed repeatedly by women who literally have given their lives to their families, women who have committed themselves almost wholly to the well-being of others. To me, it seemed odd, hard to believe that women could say such things about themselves. Yet, as I turned the words over in my mind, there also seemed something true about them. For in the process of making such commitments to others, they generally had abandoned important parts of themselves. Whatever personal ambitions or interests might have stirred in them over the years were systematically stifled as they sought to meet the obligations and responsibilities of wifehood and motherhood. This is the only serious commitment, the only vocation, for which they had been reared, the only one permitted to them without question or censure.

Indeed, husbands and children often want wives and mothers all to themselves, complaining—sometimes quietly and covertly, sometimes noisily and without restraint—if the woman of the household becomes occupied or preoccupied with activities or interests outside the house. One man who claimed to be liberated from such traditional male desires and supportive of his wife's efforts to train herself for a career, nevertheless put it thus:

> I don't mind what she does during the day. But a woman has to be sensitive to how her husband feels when she comes home talking about things he doesn't know anything about. No matter how excited she is about what she's doing, she's better off to tear that page out of the book and come home quietly without saying much about it.

The rule about her interests, then, would seem to be: Limit involvement only to the times when he's not around, and keep it quiet. With such advice, a woman would find it difficult, indeed, to be comfortable with the flowering of sustained and consuming interests. In fact, in such circumstances, the stirrings of interest can be experienced as endangering her primary commitments, therefore also as an aberration, an unwelcome, guilt-producing intrusion that keeps her from devoting all her energy and attention to what she has been trained to regard as the main tasks of life.[12]

Thus, although women study, learn, and do many things, these activities are kept at a distance—defined as not *really* central to life, not *really* important to definition of self, not even *really* a serious interest. That way, they threaten no one and nothing. That way, a woman doesn't have to take herself and her interests seriously, nor does her husband. He may think it's cute that she keeps taking courses, a nice way for her to keep busy. Despite her expanding knowledge and skills, she colludes in that definition—denying her accomplishment, dismissing her commitment. All too soon, she isn't just calling herself a dilettante, she's believing it.

Is it any wonder that I can't write a book about women without reference to men? In so many ways, women's lives—the quality, the character, the choices they are permitted, whether early in life or late—are dominated by their relationships with men. Of course, women play an important role in men's lives as well. But that's precisely the difference: They play a *role*. Men are not dominated by those relationships, almost determined by them, in the same way that women are.

There are, for example, among the women I met, some with professional degrees taken in their youth and never again used after marriage or the birth of the first child. Most were in traditional women's fields—teaching, social work, nursing. But a half dozen were lawyers, research scientists, a medical doctor—male-dominated professions that, especially in that generation, surely required a high level of interest and an enormous effort of will and determination to enter. Yet, when the time came, these six gave up their work just as their nonprofessional sisters gave up jobs as secretaries, bookkeepers, clerks, and the like. Asked about regrets, a lawyer says:

> It was marriage or a career. It didn't seem like much of a choice. I always knew I wanted to marry and have children, and by the time I was twenty-five and not married, I had no more illusions that I could have both.

A doctor says:

> Of course, I've regretted it some. But it's not a great thing beating at my innards.

They all had reasons for giving up a hard-won profession. Nothing dramatic, nothing big, just the requirements of daily life: small children who needed care—*their* children, *her* responsibility; a husband's career that kept them moving for the first years of the marriage; or simply conflict between wife and husband about her work. Whatever the reasons, they add up to conflict between his needs and hers, between his career and hers—his needs, his wishes, his career, his interests taking precedence over hers.

Even those few women who went back to their professions when the children were still relatively young, made job choices that put husband, children, home first. Faced with two jobs—one higher paying, more stimulating, more desirable in every way than the other except that it is thirty minutes further from home—a woman will almost always choose the one closer to home.[13]

> It never felt like I had a *real* choice. It just seemed like the right thing to do, you know, to take the job that was nearer even if it wasn't as good. That way, I would be more available for stuff around the home—for when the children or Gary needed me, or even just to have fun with them.[14]

Small wonder, then, that women feel a lack in themselves—a lack of engagement, of commitment, of interest. Theirs is a lifetime of muting or denying any strivings that might require a serious commitment to anything outside the family. It is precisely those interests which might have engaged them most profoundly to which they feared making a commitment, those interests which are most deeply related to self that they subdued and suppressed. By midlife, it feels as if they never existed. Too often, however, women are so mystified about the matter of their interests that they believe this is something in which they are inherently deficient, something for which they are blameworthy—a personal failing to be viewed with contempt.

> Gary would never have made the choice to take the less demanding jobs as I've always done. I suppose that says I never

made that kind of serious commitment to my work. Disgusting, isn't it, to be so frivolous?

Not "disgusting," not "frivolous," but a way of life to which women are carefully bred, their self-denial and passivity not a cause but a consequence of their gender, of the role assigned them at birth. A lifetime in which they have been taught that to find fulfillment they need only marry the right man, breed and raise the perfect children, simply does not prepare them for the internal search, for the kind of commitment to self, that the full-blown development of serious interests requires. Consequently, women can be bewildered about how such interests happen, often speaking as if they expect to find them somewhere outside themselves.

> I've never had anything come down and strike me like George has had in his life. I've never had that kind of calling.[15]

But George wasn't called any more than she was. He was just born male and complied with the expectations that go with his gender just as she did with hers.

Being born male means living in a different world from anything most women know, anything they will ever know. It means not having to define oneself vicariously through the lives of others. It means having work to do, a reason to get up every day, a place in the world that's visible. It means also never having to answer questions about one's future by talking about someone else's.

It's true that even men who do work they love may come suddenly to question its meaning, to realize at midlife that they're stuck in a rut. But at least they know what the job is. It's true that they may have reason to lament the predictability of their lives. But at least they know with some certainty that they'll be doing something. It's not until retirement, at around sixty-five, that most men must wonder what they'll be doing in the years to come, or whether they'll be doing anything at all. It's not until then that they'll ask themselves, "What am I going to do with the rest of my life?"

Still, one might argue, men also face problems with the midlife transition. They, too, often hate what they do each day, often feel the world has rejected them, passed them by. Most men also have severely limited options for growth and self-development, so consumed are both their time and energy with the need to support the household.

It's true, and it's also beside the point. One indignity doesn't excuse another; one kind of oppression doesn't erase the other. In a society that distorts human life—female and male —we need not measure whose sadness is greater; both have more than they need. Still, there's a particular sharpness to the deprivations a woman experiences at this time of life because of the nature of the choices, the limits to the options, that were hers until now.

At forty or forty-five, her job is gone, not out of some failure of her own, but because, as one woman said, "Motherhood self-destructs in twenty years." She doesn't know what she'll do tomorrow, still less the day after. She wakes up wondering how to keep busy, whether she can fill up the time, what meaning it has if she does.

> There are all kinds of things I like to do. I work in the garden; I have friends over; I go to the women's club at church twice a month; I love to make bread and cook and sew. And I read. [Softly, as if to shield her ears from her own words] But somehow, that's not enough to fill up a life. It doesn't seem to add up to a whole, real person.[16]

Often a woman anticipates this stage of life, even looks forward to it eagerly. But unless she has also prepared well for it, she usually finds that the years, the demands of family life, have taken their toll—paid in the erosion of self-confidence; in the fears that she is undisciplined, incapable of commitment, without real interests; even in her failure to know whether she "adds up to a whole, real person."

All this says, then, that when it comes to wanting something for themselves outside the home as well as in it—to thinking about their lives and to making plans for living in some autonomous and independent way—women bear the limitations and restrictions that come with their gender, a fact of birth that settles their future, almost without question, on the day they are born. Not for them the dreams of conquering new worlds, of high adventure, of exciting and stimulating work. Not for them the chance, however slim, of transcending the limitations, whatever they may be. Not for them—not because of class or color, not because of lack of capacity—but because they were born girls. *Because they were born girls*—transcendence, if it comes at all, commonly will come through a good marriage, a good catch. *Because they were born girls*—they'll live vicariously through their men and their children, rarely inside and through themselves.

But that was yesterday, some will say, the world is different today. Is it? A conversation overheard recently in an enlightened and liberated nursery school suggests, at the very least, that the future is not yet here.

JOHNNY: When I grow up, I'm going to be a sea monster.
SUSIE: And I'll be your mommy.

No parent, no teacher within earshot thought the conversation was anything but natural. No one suggested to Susie that she, too, might enjoy the excitement and adventure of fantasying herself a monster. No one told her that, like it or not, she'll be mommy for only a few years. Then, life will require some-

thing else if she's to remain vital, healthy, alive in some mean-
ingful way. Then, she'll have to ask herself that agonizing
question, that question that dominates the thoughts of midlife
women, that question uniquely theirs: "What am I going to do
with the rest of my life?"

6

"What Am I Going to Do with the Rest of My Life?"

It's unbelievable when I think of it now. I never really saw past about age forty-two, where I am now. I mean, I never thought about what happens to the rest of life. Pretty much the whole of adult life was supposed to be around helping your husband and raising the children. Dammit, what a betrayal! Nobody ever tells you that there's many years of life left after that. He doesn't need your help any more, and the children are raised. Now what?[1]

Now what? What can I do? Where do I go? How can I get there? These are the questions that plague midlife women. Now what? How do I start? What do I know? What do I like? What do I dare even dream about? Question upon question upon question. Plenty of those, but very few answers.

I keep asking myself questions all the time. "What do I want?" "What do I like to do?" I figure if I can answer that I'll know where to start. But, my God, it's like being fifteen again.

"What am I going to do with the rest of my life?" The question women didn't ask at adolescence returns to haunt them at midlife.

After twenty-five years of raising children, it's like I'm back to being twenty again—maybe only fifteen—and I have to start all over again. Only I'm more scared now than I was then. When you're a kid, you still think you own the world. But I'm not fifteen, I'm forty-five, and I know better now.[2]

At forty-five, she must face the fact that she's caught between an outgrown past and an uncertain future. And she's scared—scared because she's not fifteen but forty-five, because those thirty years make quite a difference.

For the fifteen-year-old, there's nothing but the future. For the forty-five-year-old, the past stakes its claim. Forty-five years carry a history—well-established ways of being in the world, of relating to people and to self, ways that long ago set the patterns for life and foretold the expectations from it, ways that don't yield easily. At forty-five, she knows she doesn't "own the world," knows instead how much of her it owns. Children, husband, parents—they all claim their shares, indeed, jealously guard them.

> There's always someone wanting something from me, and someone there expecting my time and attention. You can't just go off and do what you want. They're always right there. It's like they're waiting in the wings, always needing me for something.[3]

For the fifteen-year-old, the task, with all its complications, is clear—to move from childhood to adulthood. If the child is male, that means he's expected to develop a strong, differentiated, independent sense of self; to become a competent, masterful person who stands as a psychologically bounded entity, never again to be merged with another as he was in infancy. And if the child is female? She's not expected to resolve the dependence-independence struggle of adolescence, not expected to develop a bounded and well-integrated sense of self. In keeping with what *is* expected, she exchanges dependence on parents for dependence on a husband at the earliest possible opportunity.[4]

Thus, although the forty-five-year-old wife and mother long ago reached chronological adulthood, in important ways she remains like a dependent child—unable to make her way alone in the world, wholly or largely dependent upon her husband for the most basic of life's necessities. At forty-five, the core of her personal identity still rests with others. She still is located in the world as Joe's wife, John's mother, still defines herself vicariously that way all too often. Listen to these words from an intelligent, competent forty-four-year-old mother of three as she explains why she married her physician husband.

> I guess I married him because in a way he had the drive that I would have had if I were a man. I was even glad he wasn't fully established when we were married. I wanted very much to be part of his growth so that it would be my accomplishment, too. You see, it was very important to me that he be successful—very successful. It was like my husband was representing me as a person, so it was very important that he be the kind of person who could really represent me.

"My husband was representing me as a person." Words that say she exists only through him, is counted and counts herself in the world only in relation to him. Yet, until the recent women's movement came along to call attention to the human waste and tragedy that is the price of such a definition of self, most of us didn't think there was anything wrong with it, probably didn't even notice it.[5] Indeed, so natural did it seem that, until the last half dozen years, sociologists, whether women or men, didn't consider the possibility of developing a measure of women's social status independent of the men in their lives.[6] No surprise in that, however. They are, after all, also products of this culture, blinded by the same values, myths, and shibboleths that obscure the vision of the rest of us.

If it's not a husband, then an achieving son may stand in for her as well, helping his mother to fulfill her own lost dreams, providing her with a connection to life in the world outside the home.

> I've been fortunate enough to be able to experience things through David that I could never experience on my own. Being David's mother adds a luster to my name and my reputation, and to my life.[7]

Certainly, a man might be equally proud of a talented, successful child—especially a son. Certainly, he might speak his pride, boast of his child's accomplishments. But a man isn't likely to live through his son, isn't likely to be defined by him, no matter how talented, brilliant, or successful. A man has his own work to do, his own achievements to count, perhaps his own failures to regret. Not for him the experience of living through a child. Not for him, because at his core is a personal identity that rests, not on the glory reflected from others, but on his own life and what he has done with it.

By the middle of life, such a vicarious identity is not enough for most women either. The same woman who, until now, has lived through her son says:

> For a long time it seemed okay that David was the center of my life. And, you know, I'll always be grateful for what he's given me. But I'm coming to understand now that I need more than that to feel like I'm really alive. I don't know whether it's the time of life that makes me suddenly want more or whether it's all the turmoil and talk about women these days. I'm not a women's libber, you understand, but some things they've been saying force you to sit up and notice. They force you to ask some questions about your life that maybe you didn't dare to ask before, or maybe you didn't want to ask. I don't know. Maybe it doesn't make any difference, anyway. All that counts, I guess, is the questions, because they're hard.

At the middle of life—and just now asking, "Who am I?" At the middle of life—and just now thinking, "What can I do?" At the middle of life—and just now wondering how to "start all over again." There's anguish in that for most women . . .

> People say it's time to live for me now. But what happens if you don't know how after all these years, or if you're not even sure who you are?[8]

. . . even when there's also excitement, a sense of adventure, dreams stirring that seemed to be forgotten long ago.

> When I'm not busy being afraid, it can feel exciting. There's the possibility my life will open up, and that it'll finally be mine. Isn't there?[9]

"What am I going to do with the rest of my life?" At any age, a frightening question; for midlife women a particularly troubling one—partly because it requires such difficult shifts, not only for her, but for those around her as well; and partly because her struggle for independence, her pursuit of an internally grounded personal identity, goes on without much social support, indeed, until very recently, against all social expectations. That means that, despite a decade of feminist challenge, she still suffers guilt and discomfort when moving toward a life of her own, still has doubts about what her rights are, still is unsure about what she can ask of her family, what she can demand for herself. And it means also that, too often, the behavior and attitudes of important others in her life nourish those doubts and sustain that guilt.

Ask a woman who is trying to change her life and, with it, her way of being inside the family to talk about her experiences. Even today, some have stories of the overt and direct assault on their attempts, of the adamant refusal of husbands to tolerate any change. But much more often, women tell what sounds like two different stories—one that speaks of the family's support, the other of their covert subversion. Both are true, reflecting the ambivalence family members feel when mother begins to attend seriously to something besides them and their needs.

Thus, a husband says, perhaps believes, he's pleased to see his wife involved in school, but his resistance makes itself felt in ways more compelling than words.

> Since I've been taking these classes, I've been excited and happy, and he's been testy and angry. When I tell him, he denies he's being different. But I know.[10]

And teenage children tease with pride about mom's good grades. But let her be unavailable to fix the kind of meals they're accustomed to, to take her sixteen-year-old daughter shopping for a new dress on the very afternoon she's dying to go, or to drive her fifteen-year-old son across town to a basketball game, and their pride fades to a pout, while mother's pleasure is exchanged for guilt.

> The kids were used to having things pretty much the way they wanted them, and it's not always that way now. So they grumble that they don't get a decent meal around here any more. You know, there's nothing that can make me feel worse than to hear that. I have to remind myself that I cook a nice, full meal most nights. But if I miss once in a while, or if I don't have something done for them just the way they like it, they grouse and grumble that things are changing in the family.[11]

Parents, too, do their share to sabotage her efforts as they wonder aloud what she's doing, why she doesn't visit so much any more.

> It's hard for my parents to understand why I worry about what I'm going to do, and why I'm going to school again. They're

sweet, and they don't mean to criticize me or anything like that, they just keep asking why I'm doing it. They're getting old and they're lonesome, and I guess they'd just like for me to be around more. And I feel guilty when I'm not.[12]

But it's time women asserted themselves, the argument now goes, it's time they started to live for themselves. They must learn to speak up, to value themselves and their skills, prepare to take risks. Reasonable words, but to many women they seem to be unreasonable injunctions—unreasonable, not because they make no sense, but because they're experienced as injunctions; because they're often heard as exhortations that fail to understand both the internal and external constraints that inhibit a woman's ability to act; because implicit in such injunctions seems to be the suggestion that it is the internal psychology of women that impedes change. A forty-nine-year-old wife of a business executive, married twenty-eight years, speaks angrily about just this:

Every time I hear one of those talks, I get mad. I know they're supposed to be helpful, but they always make me feel as if it's my fault my life turned out this way. They don't know anything —nothing. What do they know about how hard it is? Nothing! The world makes it hard, not me. Tell them that, will you? Tell them!

Another woman, aged forty-two, married twenty-five years to an electrician, speaks more calmly even though ironically:

What a joke those conferences on women can be—I mean, what a bad joke. There was this young man—maybe thirty-three, thirty-four—who came to talk about the job market and where we could fit in. He was a charming young man, but I'm not sure he's too in touch with the real world. Here's this young man with nine years of college and a Ph.D. telling us middle-aged ladies who barely graduated from high school that education wasn't necessary, and to go out and create our own jobs.

Such facile words and absurdly oversimplified accounts of women who have dramatically changed their lives now abound on the lecture platform and in the media. And the distortion of the feminist message implicit in them is shameful indeed. But most women don't know that. They hear the lecture, and they cringe. They read the article, and they're filled with uneasiness, wondering if their worst fears about themselves aren't really true. And they respond angrily—sometimes because they feel unjustly criticized; sometimes because they "hear" criticism that's never intended; sometimes because the words stir longings for autonomy and independence that frighten them; sometimes because the language of the discussion seems without connection to the realities with which they live; and sometimes simply because they feel stuck and have no other target for their anger.

> Words, words, words! I'm getting so's I hate them. Those people who run around talking like that don't understand what it's like. They don't have any idea how hard it is for a woman to be aggressive. It's like they don't live in this world and don't know how awful it feels to be looked at like an aggressive woman. Oh, I know, I know—aggressiveness isn't the same as assertiveness is what they say. I've heard the line. But in my world, nobody seems to notice that there's a difference.[13]

In her world, whatever moves she makes to change her life—to disengage from the family-first orientation—seem to her to threaten the very existence of the family to which she has devoted her life. For if she really means finally to take care of herself—to hear her own inner voice, to respond to its message—she must deal with the fear, also grounded in the reality of modern life, that her marriage will founder.

Divorce—climbing with unexpected rapidity in long-term marriages.[14] Whether perceived as a threat or a promise, it's a fact of social life that has become a part of personal accounting—there to be weighed and measured, a possibility to be taken into account when facing major life decisions.

We're getting divorced—words heard so often it begins to seem as if everyone is doing it. *We're getting divorced*—no longer something that happens to alien people, those who are not our kind. It's all around us. There's Joe's partner, Mary's sister, Cynthia's cousin, Fred's neighbor, our own best friend —all married twenty, twenty-five, thirty years, and suddenly: "We're getting divorced."

We've all seen it, felt it, looked at it uneasily—aware that the very people who make up the divorce statistics today would have remained silently, uncomplainingly on the marriage rosters yesterday. Whether we will it or not, it's hard not to be both frightened and fascinated by the frequency with which we see divorce around us—frightened, as we wonder, "Could this be me?"; fascinated, as we ask, "Would I want it to be?" "Would I be better off or worse?"

Divorce—it's an issue that preoccupies women as they search for comfortable ways to live out the rest of their lives. Some toy with the idea, touching it warily, gingerly.

> [Referring to the character in Ibsen's *The Doll House*] Nora looks more and more appealing all the time. I wonder where women like that get the nerve to strike out on their own.

Most fear it.

> Lately, it seems as if every day someone else announces they're getting a divorce. It's like a frightening, communicable disease. I'm not the only one who's scared either. All my friends who are still married are worried and frightened.

Either way, it's never far from consciousness. Either way, it needs to be reckoned with.

For midlife women, reckoning with divorce means, among other things, seeing friends go from rich to poor, from a life of relative comfort to one of deprivation. More than 20 percent of the women I met are divorced. Some had been married thirty-five years, some thirty, most just over twenty. A few divorced earlier, after eight, ten, twelve years of marriage, when the children were still young. For women who had lived in professional middle-class marriages, divorce meant going from an average family income of $45,000 a year to $14,000; for those from working-class marriages, from $19,000 to $7,000.[15] And the prospects that things will get much better financially are not good for most women who divorce after many years of marriage and financial dependency. One woman, divorced three years and trying valiantly to prepare herself for financial independence, speaks bitterly of the lack of economic opportunities:

> I'm fifty-two years old, and I was brought up to be Betty Boop. I was married thirty years, and all of a sudden, my husband left me. Now what am I going to do with my life? So I'm a junior in college and I'll get a B.A. in two years. Who's going to hire a fifty-four-year-old woman, and for what kind of a job?

Such realities alone could account for women's fear of divorce, for the fact that so often they give up their own needs at seemingly slight pressure from their husbands. Indeed, these income figures alone could explain why women often seem so powerless to shape their own lives. If money talks, these figures shout. The message is clear: Be careful. Don't take on a fight you're not prepared to finish—one whose outcome you can't predict, whose loss could have life-shattering consequences.

My husband doesn't really like me to be involved in anything. He wants me to be ready and available for anything he wants to do any time he wants to do it.

And how does that feel to you?

Oh, I don't know. I don't mind too much, I guess. Well, to tell you the truth, I guess it makes me mad. But what can I do? After all, he's the one who makes the living for us.[16]

It isn't only money that dictates caution, however. For midlife women are acutely aware that their social options as well are sorely limited, their chances of remarriage very slim.

As far as I can tell from what I see around me, being divorced means you're poor and you're lonely. At least that's the way my divorced friends look to me. Oh, not the men— the women, I mean. The guys make out all right. There are plenty of women around for them—young ones, too. So why would a man take a fifty-year-old when he's got thirty-year-olds hanging around?

Indeed, less than a quarter of the divorced women I met have an ongoing relationship with a man. And those who do are much more likely to have been divorced in their thirties or very early forties rather than later. One woman, divorced at thirty-three, remarried at thirty-nine, speaks about that difference:

I was never sorry I got divorced—scared sometimes, but not sorry. But I want to say it's a lot better being divorced at thirty-three than at forty-three. Then, there were still plenty of men around for me to have relationships with. Now, I see my friends who are over forty and just getting divorced, and I feel sorry for them. It's a lot harder because, at this age, there just aren't any men around for them.

Another fourth of the divorced women have casual sexual experiences once in awhile, generally speaking of them with ambivalence.

> I get kind of desperate sometimes, so I go to bed with some guy. But most of the time it doesn't feel very good. I guess I do it because I need some validation about myself and my sexuality. It works—sort of. I mean, sometimes it makes me feel better right at the moment, but I'm not sure it's worth the other feelings I get. I just don't think I'm very good at casual sex. Maybe the younger women are, but I don't think it works very well for women of my age—at least, not from what I hear from the other divorced women I know.

The rest—just over half—say they very seldom have the opportunity to date a man or to get to know one well enough even to consider a sexual interaction.[17]

> There don't seem to be any men around for women our age. Maybe if you're younger it's different. But when you're forty-six, it's really hard to meet men and to get to know them. I'd like to have a relationship with a man, but first you have to get to know somebody, don't you?

Still, that's not all there is to be said about the experience of women in divorce. For while almost all speak of the problems in divorce—the dearth of money, the lack of male companionship, the fears of a lonely old age—theirs are not lives of one long lament. Indeed, very few pine for the marriage that's gone regardless of whether they left or they were left.

Of those who initiated the divorce, most left under some severe stress—an alcoholic husband, a violent one; a man who was coldly, cruelly rejecting, a sexually withholding one. A few left in search of self—to get away from what one woman called "the grinding nothingness," and another characterized as "neither good nor bad, neither rejecting nor accepting, just an insipid pale blue relationship." Others were left—suddenly, unexpectedly, quite without preparation either emotionally or financially.

Whichever way it happened, most women are not shattered by divorce once the initial shock of adjustment passes. One woman—forty-four years old, divorced three years—recalls:

> It was hard at the beginning. My husband left me for someone else and that was a terrible shock. I sat home for ten months just trying to figure out what happened to my life. Then I started to look for a job. It wasn't easy because I didn't even have a high school degree and I had never worked in my life. But after awhile, I got a job as a counter girl in a hot dog place, and that started me coming out of my shell.

And what's your life like now?

> It's not everything I dreamed of, you can bet, but I'd rather be where I am now than in that miserable marriage. I knew it was horrible even then, but I didn't ever let myself realize just how horrible it was until it was all over.

They may be short of money and shy of sex, but most women find at least some comfort in an autonomous life, some relief in daily living that's not fraught with unwanted compromises.[18] A forty-eight-year-old, divorced five years, speaks:

> Even though I was the one who wanted the divorce, there was an initial shock. The first months were a time of taking stock and of dealing with my fears of being alone. But very soon after we separated, I knew without doubt that I had done the right thing. It was as if I'd awakened from a bad dream. It's really not a bad life at all, at least not the way people think it is. In fact, in many ways, I feel as if I escaped from a burning house.

An interesting comment: The life of divorce is not a bad one, "at least not the way people think it is." And it raises an interesting issue: If that's true for so many women, how is it that their friends, neighbors, sisters don't know it? Partly that's because many women who remain married in spite of strong discontents don't want to see any evidence that divorce can have some positive consequences as well as negative ones. A forty-six-year-old woman, divorced only months before we met, spoke with some bitterness about this:

> I was prepared for a lot when I decided to get divorced, but the amount of criticism I had from people I thought were my friends was shocking. Of course, I know that they were furious at me for having confronted them with the questions and deficiencies in their own lives, and for stirring up all their anxieties about their own marriages. But knowing that didn't help any. I was simply not prepared for the intensity of their responses.

Hearing those words took me back to my own divorce almost twenty years ago. They reminded me that my friends, too, reacted with shock, that they, too, were thrust into an unexpected and unwelcome appraisal of their own lives by the news of my divorce. Some people dealt with their discomfort by speaking to me pityingly, some angrily, most somewhat defensively. One friend unquestionably spoke for many when, in surprise at hearing the news, she burst out: "You can't do that. Your marriage is no worse than mine."

But something else goes on as well. For in addition to what they don't want to see, it's also true that married people often don't get a chance to see the lives of their divorced friends at close range. It's no news that those who want to remain married are threatened by a divorce in their circle of friends, no news that often the married want to isolate the divorced, to separate themselves as if from a dread disease.

It's less commonly noted, however, that even when married friends remain sympathetic and welcoming, divorced women soon find they have less and less common ground on which to continue close ties with old friends. When the divorcee begins to build a new life, she also develops new friendships with people who share both her freedom and her new interests. Thus, the contact between divorced women and their married friends is likely to be most frequent in the period immediately following the separation—when the divorcees are most needy, when the shock and pain are felt most keenly. And it's in that condition that they are most likely to be fixed in memory, therefore, to be thought of as desperate or tragic figures.

However it happens—whether from isolation and inexperience with the more positive aspects of divorce, or because of the objective difficulties divorce presents—most married women regard divorce with apprehension, if not with outright fear. Most back off quickly from any undertaking that might engender a husband's serious disapproval. Indeed, many women speak openly of their fears for the marriage, of their unwillingness to take a risk no matter what the personal cost. Thus, a woman with a master's degree in child development taken five years ago while her children were growing up, now speaks about the future anxiously:

> I know I just better do something. I need to make some plans for what I'm going to do with the next twenty-five years or so. But I don't know, I just don't know.

You recently completed an M.A. in child development. Couldn't you do something with that?

> I don't know. It's hard.

What did you have in mind when you took it?

I needed to keep busy, so I did it. Gil works nights a lot, and after the children were in bed, there was nothing to do. Besides, it was a useful thing to take because I was raising four children, and the things I learned came in handy.

Well, why is it so difficult to figure out what to do now?

It's just hard, that's all. [Sitting very still, almost rigidly] Gil really wants me around. He says he wants companionship in marriage. He doesn't want two people doing their own thing and living together side by side. And if my work were to conflict with his, I don't really know what would happen. I just don't know, and I'd worry about it if I got a job.

Doesn't Gil worry about you when you're so clearly upset?

Oh yes. He would be absolutely delighted if I would keep busy because he knows I'd be happier. He'd love for me to do something like crafts or something like that, something that would interest me but that I could do here at home. But he wouldn't want me to take a job.

How do you know that?

We've talked about it. His vacation is really terribly important to him, and he says he'd insist that my vacation schedule would have to match his. And maybe that wouldn't be possible if I had a job with my own responsibilities. That could really be tragic if it didn't work out. I mean, I wouldn't want to do anything to risk my marriage.

I guess he must have a pretty long vacation for it to be such a big issue.

It's not that long—three weeks in the summer every year.

I was stunned. Had I heard correctly? I repeated the words back to her. *"Three weeks in the summer every year?"* "Yes," she assured me, "that's right." Silently I said the sentence to myself as I tried to grasp the full impact of the words. "Three weeks in the summer every year." That means she gives up forty-nine weeks each year so he can do exactly what he wants and when for three.

A dramatic story, unusual only in its fine detail, not in its capacity to illustrate a common process. For it underscores the point made repeatedly by the women I spoke with that the ability to make a serious commitment to a life outside the home is contingent on a husband's approval, if not his encouragement—especially in families where there is no compelling financial reason for a woman to work.

A common point, and also a puzzling one. It seemed to me there had to be something more than a husband's approval at stake—something related to a woman's view of herself in the world. I thought about it, worried over it, turned it over and over in my mind. My thoughts carried me back to my own experience some years ago when I faced just these issues.

For years, I had dreamed of being an attorney, pined for the opportunity missed. Then, certain in my mind that I would fail it because, at the time, I didn't yet have a bachelor's degree, I took the Law School Admissions Test.[19] Three months later, I was astonished to find I had done well enough to be admitted —astonished and frightened. "Now, surely," I whispered to myself, "they'll find out you're a fraud. Now, surely, they'll know that you're just glib, superficial—that the inside doesn't match what they see on the outside." Painful, fearsome thoughts, these—difficult to acknowledge to self, almost impossible to say aloud to another.

My husband, from whom I am since divorced, had his own

problems with the prospect of a wife who might become a lawyer. He voiced a series of objections to my entering law school as a full-time student. Who would take care of our daughter? Who would see to things in the house? Sure, he'd be willing to help sometimes, he said, but there was, after all, his career. And that came first. In any case, he traveled a lot and couldn't really be counted on consistently.

We fought bitterly, ending the battle with my insistence on a separation. I told myself—I told the world—that the rift came because he wouldn't support my aspirations. I believed it then. And perhaps, if I had pushed the issue all the way, I might have found out that was true. I'll never know. By forcing the separation at that moment, I also left myself in a financially vulnerable position from which it was impossible to undertake a three-year commitment to school.

I refused the appointment, blamed him, suffered over it for months. Then, when the immediate possibility of entering school was moot because the new academic year had begun, I agreed to a reconciliation. Chastened by the brinkmanship I had engaged in—fearful that I had damaged my marriage beyond repair—I gave up the idea of law school and tried desperately, if not always successfully, to play out the role of dutiful wife, charming hostess, perfect helpmeet to my husband's blossoming career.

Looking back, I think even then I knew, in some corner of myself where knowing is not always conscious, that I had engineered the crisis because I was afraid—afraid to take the risk of becoming a law student and finding out that I was wanting; afraid, paradoxically, to take the risk of finding out that I was not. For either way, it seemed to me then that I would lose. If I found myself unable to do the job, my already damaged sense of self-esteem would suffer a deadly blow. If I found that I *could* do it, it seemed likely my marriage would not survive. With options like those, who wouldn't be relieved to retreat to safety?

But these are retrospective reflections, undertaken at a time when it's safe to think such thoughts, when, in fact, I have gone on to another life. I didn't really understand these things then, surely could not have articulated them. I knew only in some vaguely intuitive way that it was something more than my husband's objections, that there was also something inside me that was responsible for the events that led me from that law school door.

So it is, too, with the women I met. They may be restless and discontent, but they're also frightened and unsure. They know they need to be doing something, but don't know what it is, what they might be capable of. Indeed, after a lifetime of gaining approval for muffling, if not outright denying, their intelligence, capabilities, and strengths, they have a very tenuous relationship to those capacities at this stage of life. Small wonder, then, that the idea of testing them out—especially without the support and approval of their men—would fill them with fear.[20]

Still, something troubled me. The things the women were saying suggested that they believe it is they alone who must bear the burden of holding the marriage together, their needs alone that must be set aside in the interest of marital stability. Yet, these were all long-term marriages. It seemed reasonable to assume that there was something in these relationships that the men, too, needed—something important there to keep them tied for so many years. But many of the women seemed to have trouble believing that, many more had trouble acting upon it. I expressed my puzzlement, asked for their help.

You live your life as if you're the only one who values this marriage. Yet, your husband has lived in it for the same twenty-odd years. Don't you think he values it enough to make some accommodations to your needs at this time?

A surprised, confused silence generally greeted these words. One woman said her "mind was blown," another that she was "thunderstruck," many that they have "never thought about it like that before." About 20 percent said calmly, quietly, painfully that, in fact, they do believe they value the marriage more than their husbands; that they are, indeed, fearful of putting it to the test. Some tell of having tried over the years to find something of their own, perhaps to build a life that would include work outside the home, and show the scars of a battle lost. Listen to the story of a forty-eight-year-old mother of three, married twenty-four years to a professional man:

> Twice in our marriage my husband had a serious involvement with another woman, and both times it was when I was trying to do something for myself. The first time, I had been trying to write. I was close to the end, all I needed was another week or so, but he just couldn't seem to stay out of my hair. Normally he's so busy and involved in his own work, you have to make an appointment to see him. During that period, though, he seemed to be hanging around all the time, always pestering me. He's a man who doesn't like to go out much, and practically never makes a suggestion to go anywhere or do anything. But that time, he was all filled with ideas for fun and games all of a sudden. I was really into what I was doing, though, and I desperately wanted to finish. So finally, I went to stay at a friend's beach house for a week to get away from his pestering me and so I could write.

Did you finish the piece you were working on?

> No. Before the week was out, he was calling and letting me know things weren't as they ought to be.

What do you mean?

Oh, just dropping hints about how tired he was, or how late he'd been out. Or suddenly, the name of a woman he works with kept cropping up in his conversation. I got upset and wasn't working very well by the end of the week. So I just came home. It was then I found out that he was having an affair with that woman.

What did you do?

Nothing. I put that manuscript away and never looked at it again. I'm not dumb; I got the point. He was getting back at me for being so interested in something else, and he was telling me what to expect if I continued. So I quit.

Was that the end of your attempts at writing?

Yes, but I did try one other time to make something out of myself. A few years ago, my husband took on a very important job that kept him busier than ever. So I decided that was a good time to go back to school and get a master's degree in psychology. By the time the first term was over, things seemed to be going downhill at home. Carl seemed snappy and angry. He worked even longer hours than before, and was almost never home. Then, in the middle of my second term, I found out he was having an affair. I was just devastated. The message was very clear for me. If I didn't devote all my attention to him, there would be another woman in the picture.

What did you do then?

I finished out that quarter, but I never went back. I've thought about it a lot, and I have to believe it's more than coincidental that the only times he got involved were when I was doing something else that really engaged me, not just supporting him. You know, I don't even think it's deliberate and malicious. I think it's totally unconscious. He just feels lonely and needy when I'm not available all the time, and it's as if he just gravitates to someone else to give him that feeling that the world revolves around him.

Did it occur to you not to quit and see what might happen?

[Almost snorting with irritation] Occur to me? Of course it occurred to me. It's often occurred to me that I had a choice. I could get a master's degree and a divorce, or I could stay married and not get the degree.

Another dramatic example, certainly. But it's in just such drama that the issues and conflicts are given their clearest expression. For while the story may be dramatic, it is not unique. The details may change, the drama may not be so intense or apparent, but such stories can be, and are, told many times over. Even when a woman hasn't had the experience in her own life, she usually has a horror story to tell about some friend, family member, neighbor, or acquaintance. Indeed, the culture of midlife women abounds with such stories. They warn each other. And in doing so, remind themselves of the dangers. They worry aloud about what will happen to a friend's marriage. And in doing so, explain to both listener and self their own inability to act.

Joe came to dinner the other night by himself because Marian had to study for an exam. How long will he put up with that? Let's not kid ourselves. There are plenty of women around who would be glad to keep him company.

With such currents in the culture, women don't need the personal experience. The vicarious ones can fill them with fears aplenty, especially if they are among those who do, in fact, believe that they value the marriage more than their husbands do.

You live your life as if you're the only one who values this marriage. Yet, your husband has lived in it for the same twenty-odd years. Don't you think he values it enough to make some accommodations to your needs at this time?

The majority of the women became restless and uncomfortable on hearing the question, most of them unwilling to agree with its premise. Some spoke defensively, rushing to assure me, perhaps themselves as well: "Of course, he values the marriage as much as I do, maybe more."

Why, then, I asked, are they unable or unwilling to confront their men with an assertion of their own needs, with a clear statement about their wish to expand their lives? Why don't they expect some accommodations to be made in the marriage to enable them to meet those needs?

Most deny that they're fearful of making demands of their husbands, presenting evidence to buttress their words. One determined the kind of vacation they took last year, another fought for a child to go to the school of her choice. Others get taken out to dinner when they want, watch the television programs they prefer, choose which films they see, set the tone if not the tempo of social life.

These seem small things. Yet, such activities do color the quality of life as it is being lived, giving it the woman's stamp in noticeable ways. Still, the answers left me unsatisfied. What is it women in this position get? What is it they give? The answer—so simple once it's understood, so elusive before—is found in the women's own words. One, after speaking at length about the blocks her husband put in the way of her engaging in some serious interest outside the home, puts it neatly:

> I don't mean to complain, though, because he's really very, very sweet. I can't imagine anybody who's sweeter and more sup-

portive, and generally easier to live with on the whole—except in the matter of my work. Other than that, I have things pretty much as I want them.[21]

In return for remaining in the role of traditional wife, she gets some concessions on how they live the shared part of their lives—concessions he may be glad to give for the freedom of doing his work unhampered and the comfort of keeping his home life unchanged. But it's an uneven exchange for the woman at home. For her, there remain all the hours of the day —long hours between waking and nightfall in which to think of such things as which film to see that night, which restaurant to dine in.

You live your life as if you're the only one who values this marriage. Yet, your husband has lived in it for the same twenty-odd years. Don't you think he values it enough to make some accommodations to your needs at this time?

Some women argue that a man has a right to expect a wife to be at home, to be available for him when he wants or needs her. A wife—a good wife—understands that, they insist, understands that that's the way of the world, and wants it that way, too. For them, they explain, the problem is not a failure of self-assertion, but guilt—guilt because they fear they ask too much, because they feel they aren't good wives, because they aren't able to *want* to do what they believe they *ought*.

Anachronisms? Holdovers from an age long gone? To write such women off this way is to underrate the power of socialization processes that for generations have trained women for such self-denial and prepared them to carry such guilt when the repressed parts of self return to demand a hearing.

The fact is that the women who spoke thus were speaking also for large numbers of their sisters. Perhaps many would

not put the matter so simply or so crudely. Perhaps they struggle against the belief that men have such rights to service and
sacrifice from women—sometimes using the language of the
new feminism to combat those attitudes which lie deep within
themselves. But change in consciousness lags well behind
change in language, and the inner conviction to back up the
words is another matter. Thus, even when women have
modified the old beliefs to include some rights of their own,
and even when men agree, most women (let alone most men)
have not discarded the belief system that makes their needs
and desires—the very development of self—ancillary to those
of their men. They simply have shifted it a bit to make some
space for themselves within the established system of values.
Indeed, the lives of most of the women I met offer compelling
evidence of how much they honor such belief. Honor it, but
also suffer it.[22]

Even when it couldn't be said directly, it was apparent in the
interaction between us—in their reluctance to end our meeting, in their curiosity about how I manage my professional and
personal life, about the costs of the decisions I've made. After
hours of talk, after I had clearly concluded the business for
which I had come, after I had shared with them some of my
own life experiences, more often than not they invited me to
stay for more—for lunch, for dinner, to enjoy a glass of wine,
to come back another day. Some women offered their services
—typing, interviewing, library work—not for money, they
hastened to assure me, but because they thought the work was
important, because they wanted to remain connected, wanted
to feel useful.

When none of that was possible, they often forestalled the
moment of parting by walking with me to my car, continuing
the conversation the whole time, ending it only when the
engine was already running, and only then—when they knew

we probably would never meet again—said the words that spoke to the missing parts of their own lives. "My God, you're a lucky woman!" "Oh, how I envy you!" "I wish I had been able to do what you've done, but I couldn't, I just couldn't do it." "Just once before I die, I'd like to know what it feels like to be a success—just once."

That doesn't mean that most women actively regret traditional choices made in the past. They do not. With all the difficulties, with all the pain, there have been pleasures—the pleasures of close, intimate relationships, especially with children . . .

> The years I gave to the kids, especially those early years, are precious. I wouldn't have wanted them any other way.

. . . for the more privileged, the pleasures of life not bound by a time clock, of time for activities that enhance personal growth.

> There were good things and bad—both. I had the wonderful opportunity to grow along with my children. I mothered them and they changed me. Tied down as I was, in some ways they were also years when I was free. I was lucky enough to be able to hire someone for a few hours a week, so I had time to explore who I was and to develop some parts of me I hadn't known existed.

"There were good things and bad—both"—an assessment with which few women would disagree. When they think of the good, they'll speak from that side of the equation; when they think of the bad, they'll come down on the other. But almost always they're enough in touch with both sides so that they don't usually dream about doing it wholly differently if they had a second chance at those choices in life.

What, if anything, would you change in your life if you had it to do over again?

Those without college, or what they consider adequate preparation for the world of work, all agree that they wish they had been better prepared before marriage. Others wish they had worked longer, had their feet on a career path to which they might have returned earlier while skills were still current. Still others talk longingly about independence—a wish to have lived on their own for a while, to have traveled, to have had more experience in the world before they exchanged parental protection for husband's. But when these things are said, the reality of the context in which their choices were made comes to the fore. Fantasies are set aside, and a realistic assessment of other alternatives is made—their possibility and their cost.

What, if anything, would you change in your life if you had it to do over again?

A forty-seven-year-old homemaker who gave up a musical career for marriage and motherhood twenty-two years ago says:

> I don't know. I certainly wouldn't have wanted a career if it meant giving up what I have. In my time, that was the choice, you couldn't have both. Maybe now it's possible. But even now, with all the talk, I'm not sure. Somebody has to take care of the children. It's all right to talk about liberated marriages, but there's no such thing as liberated parenthood. Kids need care, and as far as I can tell, mothers are going to be doing that for a long, long time. I don't even know if I'd want to give it up. Hard as it was, it was the best part in some ways.

"What am I going to do with the rest of my life?"—a difficult, baffling question, one women engage with caution. The reasons, as everything I have been saying at such length suggests, are complex—products of both past and present, of external constraints and internal, and an ongoing interaction between the two.

There are the risks to the marriage of which these last pages have spoken—risks not to be denied. It's hard to risk what *is* for what feels like an ill-formed, half-baked dream of what could be.

> I guess I'd be willing to fight it out with him if I really knew what I wanted to do. I've thought about going back to school, but what would I be going for? Could I get a job, or have something I care about doing when I'm finished? Who knows? Anyway, I wouldn't know what to do. I've never had anything that really grabbed me; you know, I mean, nothing I really wanted to be involved in.[23]

Then there are the conflicts women experience at this stage of life—the conflict around identity, around the need suddenly to develop new and unknown parts of self; the conflict around their changing role, around the difficulty of seeing the road ahead, of not knowing how much will change, how much will remain the same. There's anger, too—anger at the violation of the expectations of a lifetime, anger at the realization that they were sold a myth and an illusion. And there's fear —fear, because they're confronted with so many changes in their lives and so many demands for change in themselves; fear, because it's always thus when the need for change threatens to upset existing ways of doing and being. And there's more. For, just as the message was mixed and muddy in their earlier years, the demands for change at midlife are equally unclear and equally ambivalently expressed. The world, husband included, complains if midlife women are bored and depressed—enjoining them to be mature, to adjust to reality, to develop interests and commitments outside the family. But let a woman take that advice seriously, and her attempts are likely to be subverted from all directions—inside the family and out. Recall the woman who says of her husband:

> He'd love for me to do something like crafts or something like that, something that would interest me but that I could do here at home.

And another who snaps:

> I could get a master's degree and a divorce, or I could stay married and not get the degree.

Just two of many who said such things; just two of many who found the conditions so difficult they gave up trying.

But even when a woman has worked through some of those conflicts—even when she's willing to put her marriage at risk —the world outside the home is less than welcoming. There, she faces a youth-oriented culture that looks at her as if she's over the hill. If she's lucky enough to have any specific job skills, she'll find they are of small value because they're either too rusty from disuse or too shiny from inexperience. If she doesn't, she faces a labor market that offers little to women whose organizational and administrative skills are discounted because they were developed in the context of home and family.

Still, some will say, doesn't everything that's been said until now demonstrate that women are, at least in part, complicit in building their own prisons? Doesn't all this show that it is their unwillingness to risk confrontation—their lack of courage and daring, their passivity—that keeps them there? Before we reach for explanations that blame the victim for being victimized, there are some fundamental social facts that must claim our attention. Foremost among these are the power relations between women and men.

It's true that women and men don't usually think about their relationship in terms of power. It's too discomfiting, too at odds with the romantic myths that surround marriage and the family. But whether they *think* about it or not is irrelevant. It's there, and they know it. Who doesn't know that women are relatively less powerful than their men in marriage, divorce, the job market—in fact, in most of the institutions of social life, in most of the ways necessary for survival in this society? Surely not women. Surely not the men with whom they live. Both know it—even if not always allowing the knowledge into consciousness. And both act upon it—even if not always aware that they're doing so. Thus, men send sometimes subtle, sometimes not-so-subtle signals about expected and desired behavior in their women. And women—their antennae ready always to pick up the nuances of communication, verbal or nonverbal—get the message and struggle to adjust behavior accordingly.

In this sense, women play their part. They behave in ways that are cautious—careful always not to upset the balance in the relationship, not to push beyond the limits of what their men will tolerate. In this way, the knowledge of their powerlessness becomes also a prophecy. Husbands don't need to inhibit their actions; they do it themselves.

But that is precisely the nature of the relationship between the powerful and the powerless—a threat implied in every request, sometimes intended, sometimes not. It doesn't matter. For so long as the threat is possible, so long as one person has the power to deprive another of important life supports, the powerless one experiences request as demand. That is the psychology that accompanies powerlessness—indeed, is born of it. Whether among women, racial minorities, the poor of any color, even between parents and children, that psychology of powerlessness turns the relationship between the powerful and the powerless into a vicious circle from which escape is extremely difficult—possible perhaps only for the heroic and privileged few.

Indeed, we often point to these privileged ones to support the myth that equality exists, that it is some failure in the nature of the individual—or of the entire group—that is responsible for the deprivation we see. These exceptions, we say, prove the rule that we are a nation of equal opportunity for all, prove that competence, not color or sex, counts. In truth, such tokenism serves an important social function by taking the heat off the society and putting it on the individual, by providing us with the rationale whereby we continue to blame the deprived for their deprivation.

For women, their powerlessness is the fundamental fact upon which attitudes rest, upon which behavior grows—the fact that dominates their lives, whether consciously or unconsciously. For them, also, it is an especially piercing fact of adult life, replaying as it does their earliest experiences in the family. There, parents meet a girl child's earliest struggles toward independence with greater ambivalence and more constraints than they do a boy's.[24] There, girls learn that efforts to separate can be dangerous—that there are powerful others who block the path. Sometimes it's overt and direct—punishment, censure of one sort or another; more often it's covert and indirect—disapproval, withdrawal of affection. Whichever the mode—one, both, or some combination of the two—they are effective tools for sending girls scurrying back to their place, properly chastened, properly subordinate and dependent.

These early experiences consign women to a lifetime of conflict around dependence-independence issues, of struggle to develop firm, separate personal boundaries, of primary involvement with relationships and relational issues.[25] But it is not simply that women carry these issues of separation, individuation, and independence from childhood into adulthood. It is also that their adult lives and relationships replay these childhood ones—the same objective conditions, the same subjective ones.

A girl child *could* develop a clear, bounded, and differentiated sense of self if she were raised in a culture and a family that valued her for it—that didn't make her fearful for her very survival whenever she moved in that direction. Just so, a woman could struggle successfully against the dependency and passivity for which a lifetime of being female has groomed her if the outcome of the struggle didn't threaten to doom her to a lifetime of loneliness and poverty.

As it is, adult life is a remarkable reenactment of childhood —the interaction between her powerlessness, dependency, and need for emotional support essentially unchanged. That leaves her with the old conflicts around independence, separation, and individuation acutely, painfully alive.

She may rage, rebel, nag, become depressed. But each threat of withdrawal from a husband replays her earliest childhood fears when her moves toward separation and independence were met with similar responses from parents. Such interactions may leave her confused, frightened, perhaps angry, but, as in childhood, they bring her back—albeit ambivalently—into compliance with the wishes of those on whom she must depend.

With all this, what is remarkable is not that so few women have a ready answer to the question, "What am I going to do with the rest of my life?" but that so many dare to look for one.

7

"There's Got to Be More to Life Than Hot Flashes and Headaches"

> Twenty years of kids and doctors and chauffeuring and PTA
> and bridge and all that talk, talk, talk about nothing is enough.
> I got so I knew I couldn't stand another afternoon of that kind
> of talk. Enough! There's got to be more to life than hot flashes
> and headaches.[1]

Enough! A cry that rises up from deep within a woman's soul
—the voice of anger, despair, outrage. Sooner or later, most
women think such thoughts even if they don't utter the words.
Sooner or later, most women make some move to act upon
them, to move beyond the bounds of home and family, of
volunteer activities, of bridge and chitchat and shopping expe-
ditions. Sooner or later, most women want to find out what
that "more" is.

The two most common starting places are the job market
and the local college.[2] Whichever the choice, it's a big one for
a woman at forty. If she has never before been to college, it's
a struggle at first to climb over the fears that she knows too
little . . .

> In school, I'm an absolute infant and I feel dumb, dumb, dumb
> —like an intellectual basket case. I don't know how to do a term
> paper; I didn't even know what a term paper was. I don't really
> know how to use a library and all its reference sources, and how
> to pull out the material I need.[3]

. . . that she's too old, will look too silly . . .

> I think about taking some classes, but I'm so afraid of taking the first steps into something like that—you know, just knowing that people are looking at you and thinking you're too old, and they're wondering who does she think she is to be starting something like that at this time in her life.[4]

For women who live in working-class families, the whole idea of college applied to themselves generally is a new one, the institution itself experienced as alien—a place that's above them, to be looked at respectfully from a distance. They have wondered perhaps what happens there, yet, until now, never believed it would be possible for them to know. When they find themselves on a college campus, then, they confront a mix of feelings. There's disbelief and excitement, it's true:

> My God, I barely finished high school. Who would ever have dreamed I'd be on a college campus one day.[5]

But foremost, until they begin to believe that this is a place that's rightfully theirs, until they find out that they're not really dumb, there are all the fears and anxieties that go with the feeling that they may be stepping out of their proper place, that they will find themselves in over their heads.

Let it be clear, however, that the fear, the insecurity, the sense of inadequacy of which I speak are not given to working-class women alone. Any woman who enters a degree program for the first time in middle adulthood feels similar anxieties. Perhaps the institution itself doesn't seem so alien to the wife of a professional man because she has lived closer to it, perhaps she doesn't feel so out of place in that environment, perhaps the idea of a college or professional degree is not so distant from her dreams as it is for so many women who live in working-class families. But she is likely to be equally unsure about her intellectual capacities, and to speak almost as often about the discomfort she feels in this undertaking.

I don't know exactly why I'm doing this. I sometimes feel a little silly being on campus with all those fresh-faced children. I feel as if I'm everybody's aged grandmother. I don't mean that the kids aren't nice to me, they are. They're respectful and polite, but there's also a way in which we all know it's inappropriate. Sometimes, I wake up in the morning and think, "What the hell am I doing this for anyway?"[6]

"I sometimes feel a little silly being on campus"—words that found their way to an old wound inside me, reminding me again of those years when I also felt silly, when I also felt fearful and unsure. By the time I stepped onto a university campus as a freshman, I had lived as the wife of a middle-class professional man for some years, even had done interesting and rewarding work in both volunteer and paid capacities for most of those years. Still, I was unsure and anxious as I began my college career—unsure of where, if anywhere, it would lead; anxious that I was somehow overreaching myself, that the deficiencies I feared were mine would be found out. For the whole of the four years of my undergraduate work, every time I walked onto that campus, I found myself struggling with the eerie feeling that somebody else had stepped into my skin, found myself trying to restrain the impulse to look over my shoulder for the real me who would come up from behind to claim this body which was doing this untoward and overambitious thing.

Off the campus, I felt awkward as well, and more than a little self-conscious to be an undergraduate in a social circle where nearly everyone else had a college degree, where the man who sat next to me at dinner in the home of mutual friends was as likely as not to be a professor on the same campus where I was a sophomore.

Even for women who have had some college, even for those who earned a B.A. in their youth, going back to school after twenty years or so usually is no small challenge. They may know what a university library looks like, they may remember that once they wrote term papers and even got A's, but the years at home have been paid for with their sense of self as an intellectually competent person.

> After so many years of not reading about anything critically and of not thinking very deeply about anything, I was sure I couldn't compete with those smart kids in my graduate program. They all seemed so bright and self-confident, and they knew more than I did at their age. I was really afraid that I'd find out that I just wasn't so smart any more. All those years of being just a housewife don't help the self-confidence any, I guess.[7]

In fact, it's not just her internal fears, not just a crisis of self-confidence or an inability to value and assert self properly. Being a student after so many years is a difficult, demanding task. The woman with a B.A. must reclaim lost skills, the one without college experience must learn new ones. My own career as a student started less than brilliantly. Never having been to college before, I, too, knew nothing of how to write a term paper; I, too, found myself almost immobilized by the complexity of the university library. Consequently, my first attempts at writing in freshman English were graded with C's and D's—enough to validate my worst fears about myself, nearly enough to convince me that the whole enterprise was a gigantic mistake.

It's true that those women who persevere usually find that they know more than they ever suspected, often turn out to be much better students than their younger classmates. But it takes a great deal of support both in the family and out to hang in long enough to find those things out—support that many women never get.

Larry and the kids laughed at me when I went back to school. He said he thought it was silly, what did I need it for. He used to tease me and say that he had enough problems helping the kids with their homework, he wasn't ready for the four of us. It made me feel bad, all that laughing and teasing. But then, I couldn't help thinking he was right, too. It did seem kind of silly—a grown woman doing her homework. So I gave it up.[8]

Given all those pressures, many women decide not to enter a degree program. They take classes, but not for credit or grade. It's a useful way to keep busy, they say, to relieve the restlessness they feel. For some, it works; it's just enough to take the edge off their days, to keep them feeling some active engagement with life—at least for awhile.

I have no purpose in going to school in order to get a degree so I can do something. It's purely because I find it gratifying. I've gotten so much out of it because it makes me feel more alive to be using my mind.[9]

A few years of taking courses without any direction, without any goal, however, is about as much as most women can take. Then, the restlessness sets in again, the sense of the emptiness of daily life returns.

At first, after I got over feeling scared that I'd seem not too smart, I loved just taking classes with nothing in mind. I didn't need to feel as if I was going any place or planning to do anything. It was enough just to go and be stimulated and excited. But now it's not enough any more. I want to do something with what I know. I don't think it makes sense at my age to go after a degree; it would take too long. But I don't know what I can do. After all these years of keeping the family running and organizing the household and taking classes, you'd think there would be something interesting I could do. But

> what? When I talk to people about it, they just say, "Well, you
> don't have any experience. What can you do?"[10]

Such words reflect quite accurately how the world sees
her, what the possibilities are to use the education and
skills gathered over a lifetime, as almost any midlife
woman who has tried to enter the labor force can testify.
Perhaps the most compelling examples of the difficulties
confronting those who would make this shift are found
among the women who are the "super-volunteers"—
women who hold important jobs in the community, jobs
that require the development and exercise of administrative
and executive capacities, yet are performed without pay.[11]
These are the women who are spared the worst of the feelings of inadequacy, the worst of the fears about their capacities and their worth. They respect the skills they have
garnered through the years. They know they're good at
what they do. But they also know that the possibilities for
shifting to paid work in a job that requires the use of
equivalent skills are slim indeed.

> Sure, I'd like to get paid for what I do. But I also know
> what's available out there. I know that if I went out looking
> for a job, I wouldn't find anything nearly as interesting or
> exciting as the work I do now. And on top of that, I
> wouldn't even make very much money. So why would I do
> it?[12]

Among the women I met, three of the twenty-four who held
these high-level volunteer jobs have made the shift to paid
work at an equivalent administrative level. But not one earns
a salary that is anywhere near commensurate with her skills
and duties. Torn between bitterness and understanding, one
woman, working for $10,500 a year at a job that paid her male
predecessor $24,000, tells the story for all:

I've been very successful on this job, and I believe I've contributed a great deal. And I know they do, too. But I'm obviously underpaid because they know they can get away with it. I always have the feeling that they're thinking that I used to do the job for nothing so I ought to be delighted with whatever they pay me. And it's true that I was when I first started to work for a salary. But after a while, you begin to want to earn what you're worth and what you know they'd be more than willing to pay to a man. So now I'm beginning to get resentful.

There's something else, too. This is an agency whose cause I believe in, and they're always short of money. They know that I don't need the money because my husband does very well financially. So it's hard for me to argue with them about money, and they take advantage of that.

Still, in some important ways, these super-volunteers are the most privileged of the women who do not work at paid jobs outside the home. They're privileged because volunteer work done at this level keeps them active in and connected to the world, privileged also because it keeps them in touch with their skills and competencies. These are the women who—especially if they already have a bachelor's degree earned in their youth and live in middle-class families—are most likely to return to graduate or professional school at thirty-five or forty and forge a new career.

When I was doing volunteer work all those years, I began to realize that I was intelligent. And I began to know in a profound way that I have a very deep ability to get along with people and an exceptional capacity for getting a job done. That was the beginning for me—the time when I began to know I had some exceptional qualities and that I could do something else with my life.

But these are only a small fraction of all women, these super-volunteers; and until now only a minority of them have taken serious steps toward a career—fewer still with any real success.

Nothing wrong with that if they don't want a career in paid work; nothing wrong if they're not interested in that kind of success. What's wrong is that so many of these women *do* want such a career, so many *are* interested in the tangible, worldly rewards such success brings. But it's not available to most of them—first, because they're women; second, because as soon as they want to trade those unpaid skills in for paid ones, they're downgraded by the people who would do the paying.

> I was hearing all the time how important I am and what wonderful work I do. Everyone was always saying the program couldn't run without me. And I believe it. But, you know, it all evaporated when I began thinking I'd like to get paid for some of this work. Suddenly, they began talking about how short of funds the program was. Then they hired this young man in one of the administrative posts. He does half the work I do and gets paid $22,000 a year. When I let them know I was angry, they explained that I didn't have the credentials for the job. Imagine! Credentials! Sure, he has a couple of fancy new degrees. But what about all the years and all the experience I have? Don't they count? All of a sudden, when I wanted to get paid for the work, I wasn't Mrs. Wonderful any more.

In fact, the years of criticism of volunteerism have made their mark. Most of the women I met speak of the personal benefits gained from volunteer work, it's true, but they also understand the costs. They know that volunteerism exploits them and their skills, that it helps to reinforce their second-class status by relegating some of the most talented among them to unpaid jobs that have little power and prestige. They know that their unpaid labor has been a gift to society—a gift responsible for large economies in both the public and private sectors. And they know, too, that their gift has been poorly appreciated, inadequately repaid.[13]

Consequently, the majority of the women I met in these volunteer jobs are getting restive and uncomfortable in them, most are giving some thought to the possibility of making the shift to paid work even while understanding the difficulties all too well. But if these highly skilled and capable women find the job market an inhospitable place, imagine how much more severely limited are the options for women with less experience, fewer skills.

> Three dollars and twenty-five cents an hour—that's what I'm making. Forty-four years old and I can't get a job that'll pay more than they pay the kids. You know, that's what seniors in high school get—$3.25 an hour. They promised me if I did all right, in three or four months I'd get a raise. But even if I get it, what'll I be making—$3.50 or $3.75 at most. Big deal![14]

Angry words, spoken by a woman who left a job as a telephone operator at nineteen when she gave birth to her first child. Now, four children and twenty-six years later, she goes back to an even more poorly paid, lower-status job. What was she doing in the interim? Besides the usual tasks and responsibilities inside the family, she was a girl scout leader, raised money for her sons' Little League, held various offices in the local P.T.A., and continues to be active in her church. Asked what she did with her life through those years, however, she shrugs dismissively and says, "Nothing. I was just a housewife."

"Just a housewife"—words spoken often by versatile and accomplished women, words that deny their experiences and devalue their lives. Because of that depreciation, at the same time that this woman speaks angrily about being exploited in the labor market, she speaks with equal force just moments later about the positive meaning of her new job in her life.

> It may not be much money, but it feels wonderful to know that somebody's willing to pay me for working. It says that some-

body outside the house values you and thinks you're important for something, even if it's only sorting and delivering the mail and little things like that. I wouldn't want that feeling ever taken away from me again. No matter what anybody says, there's just more status involved when you're working and earning your own money. Yep, it feels a lot better that I don't have to say I'm a frumpy housewife when somebody asks me what I do. I say I work, I have a job, and it feels good.

For her, as for so many women, the money may be poor, the work itself even more routine and less creative than a day as a housewife. Yet, the experience is different, offering as it does the increased feelings of independence that come with a paycheck . . .

I don't have to ask if I want to buy a new dress or something nice for one of the grandkids. I carry a $50 bill in my purse now, and it's just for me to do what I want—no questions asked.

. . . and a sense of enhanced status and validation in the world outside the family.

But this is one area of women's lives where class makes a difference. "I work, I have a job, and it feels good." These are words more likely to be heard from wives of working-class men than from those in the middle class, more likely to be heard from women with a high-school education than from those with a college degree. For while close to half of all the married women I met work outside the home, the figures look very different when broken down by class. Then, it turns out that two-thirds of the women in the labor force live in working-class families, only one-third in middle-class ones.[15]

It would be easy to write off this gap to differences in economic need in the families—easy, but inapt. Indeed, the large literature around now explaining that women work because they must speaks only to a partial truth and only about some women—usually those who are at an earlier stage of the life cycle, who head a household, or whose husbands are unemployed or underemployed. As for the midlife women I met, they may have been driven into the labor market at some earlier period in their lives by economic need:

> I didn't go to work because I wanted to but because both my kids needed braces and we couldn't have afforded it otherwise.

But by the middle of life, they stay in it for a variety of other reasons, none having much to do with the family economy.[16] The kids, after all, are gone now. Those heavy expenses— whether for braces, illness, education, or just the care and feeding of a growing family—are no longer an issue.

For some women, there's a giddy sense of liberation just to be out of the house.

> I started out to look for a job because we needed the money. But I have to admit, going back to work for me was like going on a vacation. I loved every minute when I first went back. And I still like it. I like getting up and out. I like getting dressed every day. And it's interesting to be there in the office. I just like it all.[17]

Others speak with exhilaration about their newfound sense of competence and self-confidence.

> There's really something very special in going to work every day and feeling like a good and valued employee. I get excited every morning when I'm getting ready to leave. After so many years of staying home and feeling like I was a nothing, it's absolutely wonderful to respect myself again and to know others respect me, too.[18]

And then there are those who talk about the work itself—the intrinsic qualities in the job that make it satisfying, that make them feel useful.

> I work as a medical receptionist and I love it; I just love it. I've found myself for the first time. I've found something that's interesting and important to me, and it's just wonderful to know I'm doing something useful. When people call me up and want to make an appointment to see the doctor, they're ill and often they're not on their best behavior. And it's a challenge to me to be able to overcome their mood, and to make them a little happier—you know, to make them feel a little bit better for having talked to me.[19]

Whatever facet the women happen to focus on at any given moment, it all adds up to the fact that the experience of working outside the home brings with it a profoundly different sense of self. All speak of some of these differences—the unaccustomed sense of freedom, independence, competence, and confidence, the heightened sense of their own value; many speak of them all. They tell of their conviction that they're now more interesting both in the family . . .

> If I hadn't gone to work, I'd be a complete bore today. What's there to talk about if you've been home all day? Is a man interested in who his wife talked to on the phone, or what she watched on TV? I used to think I was so boring, I never said much. Now, I have as many interesting things to talk about as he does.[20]

. . . and in the world outside as well.

> Before, nobody was interested in what I had to say. I couldn't blame them, even I wasn't interested. Now, when I go to a party, I can talk about my job and what I do, and people listen to me as if I'm a different person.[21]

Substantial benefits, these; substantial reasons why women remain in the work force long after economic need is pressing. But why would class make a difference? Surely these reasons would fit college-educated middle-class women as well. Indeed they do. But the problem of finding their way into the work world, and the problem of what they'll do when they get there, are considerably more complicated for them than for most high school-educated working-class women. For the college-educated wives of professional men, educational background and class position come together to create a different set of situational and psychological realities.

For the working-class wife, there generally are economic pressures that initially push her into the labor market—sometimes against her will, almost always against the resistance set up by her fears. Not so for the woman in a middle- or upper-middle-class family. She may, usually does, suffer the same fears and doubts as her working-class sister, but there is no external necessity or motivation to overcome them. Just the opposite, in fact. The economic security in the family buffers her from the need to confront the inner doubts even when she acknowledges them. "Why should I when I don't have to?" she asks herself. "I'm lucky I don't," she tells me. Perhaps she shouldn't; perhaps she is. I'm not sure. I *am* sure, however, that the privilege of asking the question carries with it costs as well as benefits. For the cost is high indeed if, in return for financial security, a woman never gets to test herself, never gets to know what she can do. It may not be worth the price if she never gets to push the boundaries of who she is, never gets to experience herself as an autonomous, independent, competent adult capable of making her way in the world outside the home.

The economy of the family makes a difference in other ways as well. Because of economic necessity, a working-class husband is forced to come to terms with his reluctance to see his wife go out to work. He may gripe and complain; he may remind her that she has a first obligation to home and children; he may insist that it's only temporary—just until this particular crisis has passed. But he knows there's a crisis as well as she does. He knows, as well as she does, that the children need braces, that the car needs repair, that medical bills are piling up, that there's no money to pay the property taxes due next month. And he stands aside as she sets off to find a job.

> My husband never wanted me to go to work. He thought that was the man's job, and that I had my job—you know, to be home and take care of the kids. But we didn't have a choice when I first started. I just had to, and he had to let me. There was no choice.[22]

Similarly, his wife is forced into a confrontation with her guilt and fears—guilt about her restlessness and boredom at home, about her wish to get out and do something in the world with other adults; fears about her competence in the world outside the house, about what will happen to her half-grown children if her watchful eye is not upon them every moment they're home.

> I felt like there were two of me, like these two parts [balling her hands into fists and bringing them together in a gesture of confrontation] were at each other like this. I was guilty because I really wanted to go back to work. And I worried about what would happen to the kids if I wasn't here when they came home after school. And, you know, I was scared about what kind of job I could get, and whether I could hold onto it, and things like that. But like I said, we didn't have a choice. I had to go to work, and that was that.

Scared or not, guilty or not, they needed the money. So she went to work. And in doing so, she found out things about herself, her needs, her capabilities that she had perceived only dimly, if at all, before.

In families where choice is not cut off by economic need, it's different. There, a husband's wishes about whether his wife works or not are more likely to control. Without the financial reasons to confront them, a wife has less leverage, less ability to oppose his will. When he says, "You're lucky you don't have to," she knows there's truth in that—a truth for which she is, in fact, grateful. When he says, "The children need you; it's your job to be here with them," he taps into her own guilt that she may not be the perfect mother, her own fears that she may not raise the perfect children. But unlike her counterpart in a working-class family, she has nothing with which to rationalize acting on her restlessness and discontent—no compelling other interest in the form of bills to be paid that would require wife or husband to fight it out either inside themselves or with each other.

Still, many women who live in middle-class families would be willing to confront these issues with their husbands and themselves, many do consider the possibility of entering the work force. The question for them is what they would do there that would be appropriate to their class position and consonant with their educational background.

Three-fourths of the middle-class women I met have at least a B.A.; of those, almost 45 percent have advanced academic or professional degrees. Compare that with the working-class wives where only two are college graduates. An enormous difference—one that, in another context, I would point to as documentation of the privilege of class. And indeed it is just that. But in this context, it is something else as well. For given the social organization of the family—the roles women are expected to play there—this particular privilege carries within it a contradiction of grievous proportions.

It's true that, whether for use in the labor force or not, the opportunity for advanced education carries with it important advantages. It affords a stimulating environment in which to learn, to think, to hear new ideas, to embrace or discard old ones. It allows some years between adolescence and the assumption of adult responsibility in which to seek, test, and expand self. In short, it provides the atmosphere and opportunity for intellectual and personal growth. No small advantages over the working-class young who generally go from high school to a job, then quickly into early marriage and parenthood.

It's also true that, for men, advanced education generally means the opportunity to do work that's intrinsically more interesting and financially more rewarding than the average job. But for women? For women who have these educational privileges, there is a profound disjunction between the kind of consciousness they develop as a consequence of their education and the structural realities within which they will live out their lives. Listen to one who, with a near Ph.D. degree in biophysics, worked in research at an elite eastern university until the birth of her first child:

> I worked in the lab at Yale until Karen was born. After that, I had to do something else. George was still in medical school then, and we were poor. So I did all kinds of odd jobs after the baby came. I took in other people's babies, I did sewing—all kinds of things like that.

Think of the cost of exchanging that lab coat for an apron. Consider the absurdities of a system of social organization that systematically requires such self-abnegation from one group of people simply because they happen to be born female.[23] For she's only one of many millions—women who are sent to college to develop both the social and intellectual skills that are the necessaries of their class position. But once having acquired them, they're expected either to put them away or to limit their use to family and family-related spheres. They're expected to be informed, literate, intelligent, but only as adjuncts or accessories to their husband's career. They're expected to take their place in the community, but only as unsung and unpaid volunteers—Lady Bountifuls who pay the social dues for the whole family, whose services buy off the family's guilt for its privileged position.

All these activities, while confining in some ways, also require the continued development of the social and intellectual skills these college-educated women brought with them to the family. In the years between youth and midlife, they often remain intellectually and socially active. They read the current books, keep up with the latest ideas, serve in high office in community organizations, even take classes—although, until the recent upsurge in adult college attendance, usually not for credit or for a grade, usually not in a competitive situation in which they might be judged and found wanting. But with the children going or gone, with the ferment among women now making itself felt in all sections of the population, all that no longer seems quite right for many of these women—not quite enough for a full life, not quite enough to feel like, as one said, "a whole, real person." Where do they turn then? Not to the labor market, where most women find that—regardless of past education, regardless of skills accumulated over the years—the crucial question they'll have to answer is, "How fast can you type?"

Those who have some particular talent or skill may begin to devote themselves more seriously to their artistic development, spending many hours a week at easel, potter's wheel, loom, typewriter, sculptor's tools, sketch pad, or sewing machine.[24] But so long as they remain outside the paid work force, their way of life is very likely to be trivialized, treated as insignificant, irrelevant, something that's nice to do, but certainly not consequential.

Right now, I'm working in clay and really enjoying my own development in that medium. I don't know, maybe I'm just kidding myself that I could be happy with what I'm doing now and nothing more. I'm not really sure. The problem is that I feel as if I'm never taken seriously. [Stopping to search my face] Even though you're not saying anything, I don't think you're taking what I do seriously either.

And what about you? Do you take yourself seriously?

[Quickly, defensively] Sure, of course I do. [Then, more thoughtfully] Well, I mean, *I* do, but it's hard to do that all by yourself, isn't it? I mean, it's hard to keep taking yourself seriously when nobody else does.[25]

In one form or another, this conversation was repeated with every woman who is trying to make a commitment to her own artistic development. No matter how hard they try, no matter how defensively they protest about the meaning in their lives, about their satisfaction, they're left with questions because "It's hard to take yourself seriously when nobody else does." There is, of course, deep pleasure for them in the creative process, but not enough to erase the conflicts they suffer or their fears about the future. Thus, a woman whose impressive artistic talent is displayed on every wall in her home says:

After all these years, I finally believe I have a real talent, but it's hard to keep believing that without some feedback from the rest of the world that would validate my belief. It would feel a lot different if only I could bring in a steady flow of income. It's not that we need the money, or that it would change anything really, but after awhile you begin to feel like a parasite or like you're still a child or something. And God knows what would happen to me if my husband weren't here to support me. I'm forty-eight, unskilled, and unemployable.

Oh sure, I could go out and get a job as a saleswoman, but I mean I couldn't get something I'd enjoy and could feel good about doing.

Indeed, whether artists or not, most well-educated women can't be satisfied with such work. Their class position alone makes these jobs, in their view, unseemly. "Why," asks the wife of a doctor, "would I go to work in another doctor's office?" The man she would work for is probably her husband's colleague, might be her dinner partner at the home of mutual friends next week—a situation altogether too awkward for anyone to tolerate comfortably. And anyway, if she's going to do something like that, she thinks, she might as well work for her husband who has been complaining about having trouble getting good help. Sometimes she does that. More often, such work, even for her husband, seems dull, menial, too routine—in a word, beneath her sense of herself and her capacities, beneath what her education, background, and these twenty years or so of experience have led her to expect from a job. Thus, no matter what the deficiencies of life as a homemaker, for two-thirds of the middle-class women I met, it seems preferable to such jobs.

This is no simple matter, however. It's true that she makes the choice because the homemaker role offers more flexibility, more possibility for self-development than the dull jobs she might be able to get. It's true that it seems preferable also because it's more in keeping with her image of herself as a literate, cultured person than some tedious office job would be. But it's also true that the years of housewifery and mothering have eroded her confidence so that she's often afraid to take the first step into the world outside, afraid even such small jobs will prove to be beyond her. So she's at war with herself —one side shouting, "You're too good for that job"; the other, "How do you know you could even do *that?*"

Moreover, remaining a homemaker at midlife has its own problems and carries its own costs. For unless a woman makes an effort to keep active, to get out, once the children are gone, she is relatively isolated from sustained daily contact with the world outside her house. With time, that isolation has a profoundly important effect on her sense of self. With time, the war grinds to a halt. The side that believed in her skills and abilities loses. She may finally find some peace from the conflict, but the cost is high indeed—the toll paid with her belief in herself, however ambivalently held, as a skilled and competent person.

Thus, while life at home may, in fact, be preferable to most of the jobs available to midlife women, it's a choice, not between a good and an evil, but between two evils. For the reality of the life of the midlife homemaker, the struggle to keep busy through seemingly endless days, is difficult and painful. Indeed, the distress can be so great that many women deny it, warding off their depression with a rush of words.

> Oh-I'm-so-busy-all-the-time-I-can't-possibly-tell-you-what-I-do-all-day. I-ran-into-a-friend-last-week-and-she-asked-how-I-keep-busy-and-I-swear-I-couldn't-tell-her-I-just-couldn't-think-how-I-spend-my-time.   All-I-know-is-that-I'm-very-busy-all-the-time-very-busy. [Stopping for a breath, then continuing more slowly] I can't tell you exactly what I do, but I just know there isn't enough time to do it.

Could you say what the "it" is?

> Just all the things I do all the time. I never stay home. I have to be doing something every day, and I make sure I am. I never stay home for a whole day; I find something to go out of the house for.[26]

Others are much more in touch with the emptiness of their lives, live much closer to the despair.

> It's too hard to think about the rest of my life, or the next thirty years, or anything like that. I can only stand thinking about one day at a time. What I ask myself every morning is: "What am I going to do today?"[27]

"One day at a time"—the credo of those for whom each day is a trial, for whom the possibility of a future filled with such days is beyond endurance. "One day at a time"—an unending succession of days, each just like the other, each requiring her to "find something to go out of the house for," each bringing with it the question, "What am I going to do today?" These are the women who remind themselves that they ought to feel lucky, ought not complain. Still, they can't help complaining. They're intelligent, sensitive women whose daily life is largely taken up with trivia. They're accomplished and complicated women who, because they followed the mandates of the culture, are as likely as not—more so if they're middle class than if they're working class—to be consigned to a life of preoccupation with hot flashes, headaches, and the activities of others.

An odd twist, isn't it, that some of the issues that made the earlier years in working-class marriages so difficult also are the very ones that make the midlife transition easier for many women in those families than for their sisters in the middle class.[28] At thirty, the financial stress was agonizing in many of these working-class families. Economic necessity often thrust the women into the labor market when they were unsure and unready.

But out of those very difficulties, new strengths are wrought. At forty and forty-five, two-thirds of the working-class women I spoke with are in the labor force, most having made their way there for some years. At forty and forty-five, most have developed skills and competencies unknown before, and a self-confidence that one rarely sees in women of that age who have never earned a paycheck. For even when they work at what middle-class women consider relatively low-level jobs, these are women who have had a chance to expand their horizons, to test themselves, to develop a sense of mastery in the world.

This is not to say that all working-class women are satisfied with the work they do. The point is simply that, for a variety of reasons—some related to the work itself, many not—being out in the work world offers advantages not to be found in traditional roles inside the home.

Indeed, regardless of class, many women are restless with the low-level challenge to their innate talents and abilities that most jobs pose. Still, they tolerate such jobs with relatively few complaints—certainly less than I have heard from men in similar positions. Partly that's related to the different expectations with which women and men are raised. Because they're women, they have learned to expect less of the work they do outside the house, to count it as less important than men do. And partly it's due to present realities as well. For one thing, unlike men, whose core identity rests with their work, women have an alternate identity—wife and mother—that is central to definition of self. If, therefore, the work is dull, routine, even demeaning, it is not a statement about who they are, only what they happen to be doing. For another, many of the tasks of the homemaker are as tedious and repetitive as the worst job while at the same time being performed in lonely isolation inside the house. For many women, then, almost any job looks good so long as it offers the possibility of getting them out of the house and into social interaction with other adults. But for all the reasons I have set out here, there are many fewer college-educated middle-class women in the work force at midlife, therefore many fewer have the opportunity to experience whatever intrinsic and extrinsic gratifications they might find there.

On the one hand, then, it's a privilege not to have to work. On the other, for women, at least, that privilege is not without its costs. It means that they are more likely than those who are not so privileged to live a daily life about which they are, at the very least, highly ambivalent. It means, also, that they are more likely than their working-class counterparts to remain wholly dependent, less likely ever to confront either the internal fears or the external mandates that keep them from developing a grounded sense of their own capacities, of their efficacy in coping with the world outside the sphere of human relations. It means that for too many life will be a daily struggle to find ways to keep busy, an unending round of bridge and lunch and shopping and talk of "hot flashes and headaches."

8

"I Know I'm Taking a Big Chance!"

> It's frightening, sure. If my husband decides he's had it, I can't make it on my own financially yet. Maybe I never will, I don't know. I know I'm taking a big chance, but it's the only way. There's no stopping me now. I keep telling my daughter, "Do it now; don't wait until you're forty-three. It's harder to take chances then." [With a deep breath that straightens shoulders and pushes head high] I know the risks are great, but I'll take them because I have to. There's nothing less than my life at stake.[1]

Vivid words, and fitting as well. They speak to the clamor inside her, tell of the struggle between her need for safety and security as it clashes with her restless yearning for self-realization, for autonomy, independence, mastery—a struggle, until now, won always by the side demanding safety.

Repeatedly, women comment about the risks: "I know I'm taking a big chance." Repeatedly, they speak of their determination: "There's no stopping me now." But what chance is taken? Who's stopping them?

Hasn't it already been said that about half the women I talked to have active lives outside the house—engaged either in the paid work force or spending an equivalent amount of time in volunteer activities? The critical issue here, however, is not just whether a woman is active outside the house, not just whether she goes to school or has a job, but what level of commitment she makes to that activity, how important it becomes in her life.[2] It's one thing for her to find ways to keep busy, even to earn enough money to make life's comforts more readily accessible, another for her to invest any significant part of herself outside the family. This is the tricky one to negotiate in a marriage, the one most likely to demand daring and determination, as the testimony of most of the women who take the risk shows quite clearly. It's the amount of emotional energy a woman gives to her work that generally is the source of conflict, rather than what she does, how much time it takes, or even how successful she may be at it. Indeed, it's not unusual for a husband to take a certain pride in his wife's achievements, speaking of her activities much as a proud parent does of a child who is doing well.

> When I first started in school, neither one of us took it very seriously. In the beginning, I did whatever I had to do in terms of school so that it wouldn't interfere with my being Tony's wife, the children's mother, and my mother's daughter. He was very proud of me then, very proud of what I was doing and how well I was doing it. He used to take my grade cards and show them around to everybody.[3]

It's when those achievements begin to require her attention in ways that interfere with his needs or with their accustomed way of life that the trouble begins.

> His initial reaction was one of indulgence, which is his reaction to all my behavior. It was as if he were saying to himself, "Some wives play tennis, some wives play bridge, and my wife is going to school." It only began to bother him when I started the Ph.D. program. That meant a lot of hard work and a very real and very different kind of commitment. Then it was a whole different ball game.[4]

That "different kind of commitment" means that, even when she still takes care of the physical needs of family and household, she may not be so readily available to manage their social and emotional needs as well. It means that she can't entertain so often because she has work to do.

> The resentment began when I could no longer be the charming companion all the time. It's true, our life has changed; it's changed a lot. We used to entertain a great deal. I was always the perfect hostess. But I just can't do it and write my dissertation.

It means that she doesn't want to go to a movie because she's studying for an exam.

> I tell him to go to the movies himself. After all, you can't talk there. So why can't he go sit in the dark by himself. Why does he need me for that? But he won't. He just hangs around and sulks, and then I feel so guilty I have a hard time studying anyhow.[5]

It means that she may be too preoccupied with a conference tomorrow to want to have sex today.

> It takes a lot of preparation to make a staff presentation—I mean, not just preparing the material but psyching myself up for it. When that happens I can be quite withdrawn, and it's true I'm just not available for much—not sex or anything else. That's always a sore point and a trouble spot.[6]

One woman, divorced from her salesman husband ten years ago, compared her life as a student during marriage and after.

> Let me tell you, it's much easier to go to school when you're divorced, even when you have children, than it is when you're married. Maybe that sounds a little crazy to you, but it's really true. At least it was for me. I couldn't possibly have gone to school seriously—I mean for a degree—when I was married. When you're divorced, you just have much more control over

your own life and your time. You don't owe anybody anything; nobody's standing around, sort of hovering over you and waiting for something.

I don't understand. You had three children living with you when you were first divorced and went back to complete your education. Surely they needed things from you.

Of course, I don't mean that I didn't have to be concerned about the kids. But it was different. I could plan my life the way I wanted to without having to worry about what he would be thinking or saying or complaining about. If I didn't feel like cooking, we had hot dogs for dinner, and that was fine for the kids. We'd make sandwiches and go out in the yard some nights, and it was fun for them, like having a picnic. When they were littler, they'd go to bed at eight or nine or so, and I'd have the rest of the evening to study—nobody to tell me I shouldn't, or be irritated or upset or angry. [Pausing to reflect] It wasn't even as if he got overtly angry or anything like that. It was just that the whole atmosphere became oppressive and it was impossible to do anything.

Still, it must have been difficult financially once you were divorced.

Yes, that's true, it was hard—very hard. You have to be willing to be poor to get divorced and go to school. But I don't really think I had a choice. The only jobs I could get paid very badly and were boring as hell. So if I was ever going to do anything I cared about, I had to go and get some training.

No celebration of divorce, this. The issues women face when divorced are difficult indeed. But it reminds us that there are problems either way—that some choose one resolution, some another, and that neither is without cost.

In fact, when, for the first time in a couple's life, *her* work, *her* interests interfere with *his* life, it's an especially troubling shift for him—which, of course, means for her as well. For him, the difficulty starts because the change seems alarming—alarming because it upsets the existing state of the relationship, because he can't know where it will end, what the outcome will be. From being alarmed, he moves to being angry—angry because there seems to be a new set of rules he had no part in promulgating, rules he doesn't always understand. He tries to reach back for the old ways, to seduce her with things that would have kept her happily in the house a few years ago. But, much to his consternation, they no longer work.

> It's hard to explain to him that my priorities have changed. Five years ago, all I wanted was to redecorate the house. I would have been out of my mind with joy if I could have done it. But I couldn't. Now, he keeps talking about how we should redecorate, but to me it just seems like one more thing I'd have to do that I don't want to. Now, it would be a burden, not a pleasure.[7]

Over and over, that's the story. Husbands offer goods their wives once cherished only to find them rejected now for reasons the men don't clearly understand.

> He used to complain because I was too extravagant. Now he complains because he doesn't get any bills for clothes any more. But I don't really want clothes any more. I only bought them before because I didn't have anything else important to do with my life.[8]

They offer entertainments the women once valued, only to find they're considered an imposition now.

> It used to be a big treat to take me out to dinner. Now it's all different. He's the one who wants to go, and for me, it doesn't feel like a favor any more. I need most of my evenings to get

my schoolwork done. I try to go with him one night a week, but it's hard to sit there and look like I'm having a good time when I'm really feeling antsy to get back home to work.[9]

Interesting shifts, these—difficult ones in a marriage. A woman once obsessed with her appearance now says, "I don't really want clothes any more." Another, once preoccupied with the state of her house, feels "it would be a burden" now to redecorate it. A wife who before nagged to be entertained, now entertains herself, indeed, is so deeply engaged in her own interests that she complains about his attentions.

For husbands, there's bewilderment. And there's rage—both born of a new sense of precariousness in the family, a fear of being out of control in a world they thought they knew. "Isn't that just like a woman?" men storm. "Now that I'm doing what she always said she wanted, she's not interested. How the hell can you win at that kind of a game?"

They can't, if it's a game. But the women I am speaking of are not playing games. They are not engaged in the kind of manipulative power plays so common on both sides of a marriage relationship, not retaliating for past hurts.

It's not that there are no past angers and hurts to repay, not that the women are unaware of the potential shifts in the balance of power in the marriage, not even that they don't like the prospect of such shifts. Of course, those issues are there —sometimes consciously, sometimes not. But these are not the motivators of the behavior that cause such confusion and difficulty for the men. Rather, the women reject their husband's offers and attentions because they are in the process of change. And those things, formerly so important to them, no longer are needed. For the clothes, furniture, entertainments were not just pleasures, they also were needs—needs born of an ill-formed sense of self, of the fear that deep inside there's nothing but emptiness. To avoid dealing with the fears of that inner void—with the terror that there's nothing of substance on the inside—people turn to fixing up the outside.

I say *people* because this is not characteristic of women only. Men who have these feelings of emptiness and incompleteness, who lack a firm and secure identity, do the same. The difference is only in the substance of their preoccupations. Without inner guidelines, both women and men look like caricatures of the social stereotypes that define masculine and feminine. Thus, men strive ceaselessly to become more and more powerful, to own bigger and better cars, to conquer the most beautiful women. And women struggle endlessly to fix up their faces, their bodies, their homes. All to no avail. For the problem they're trying to alleviate, the pain they're trying to compensate, lies inside, not outside. And no amount of patching on the outside will give anything but a brief respite, temporary surcease from the restless strivings that drive them.

Real rest, and the inner peace that makes it possible, comes only when the focus shifts from outside to inside. Then, the desires that once seemed urgent and insatiable—the search for the best car, the perfect outfit—become irrelevant. Then, it's just a car, just a dress—more or less attractive, more or less appealing, but not connected to the definition of self.

So it is with the women I'm describing here. It's not that they're no longer interested in their appearance, not that they don't enjoy an evening out any more. It's that these things have a different meaning in their lives now that they have begun to attend to the inside instead of the outside. Until now, they demanded their husband's attentions in the hope that it would make them feel good about themselves—sometimes even as a reminder that they existed at all. But it didn't work. Until now, they dressed themselves in finery in the hope that the attractive image in the mirror would distract them from the emptiness and despair inside. But it didn't work.

Now, finally, they know, albeit not always consciously or articulately, that these involvements with externals have served to keep them distant from both their deepest fears and most profound yearnings. Now, finally, they are engaged in activities and commitments that will still the fears and fulfill the yearnings—activities that foster the development of a strong inner sense of self, commitments that facilitate the belief that there's a solid core inside with an identity that's bounded and an integrity that's firm.

There's exhilaration in that—a joyous, almost wondrous, response to their own unfolding. And there's a sense of freedom to test and explore self in ways not known before. Powerful experiences, these—especially heady because they come late, in the middle of life, therefore not to be given up lightly.

But the pressures are harsh on a woman who dares not just to want something for herself but to reach out and take it— pressures both internal and external, pressures from a psychology and a society that long ago came together to keep her in her place. Thus, she suffers from guilt and anxiety over the course she has set, over the consequences to her family. She blames herself for anything that goes wrong with the children —from dirt behind their ears . . .

> I had to learn that if my teenage kids went to school dirty, somehow they would survive and I would survive. I was guilty as hell, but I had no choice. It was stay home and nag about such things, or attend to my own life.[10]

. . . to a serious accident or illness that might befall them.

> My youngest son had a terrible accident when I was halfway through school. I knew it could have happened even if I had been at home all day, but I blamed myself anyway. [Shaking her head as if to ward off the painful recollection] But it wasn't just

me, everybody around me blamed me, too. Even if they didn't say it straight out, their disapproval was made clear—my mother, my sister, friends.[11]

Yes, even when she can deal with the internal pressures, she must face the external ones—wrought by a family and a community that are threatened by the challenge her activities pose to stereotypic conceptions about what and how a woman, especially a mother, ought to be.

Some women persist. Perhaps because they have an especially high tolerance for conflict and stress. Indeed, the personal freedom they seek may well be attainable only in proportion to the amount of stress they can tolerate. For stress is the necessary accompaniment of the deep inner struggle required for the quest for freedom.[12] Until now, they could hold onto some belief in security, some hope of certainty. Now, if they are to pursue the goal, certainty—or at least the illusion of it—must be exchanged for ambiguity. For any of us, a hard bargain; for most, perhaps an impossible one.

Who dares to try to overcome such difficulties? It takes a high order of courage, perhaps a special gift that has not been crushed by the weight of years, by the need to serve others before self. Who dares to risk the pain? Perhaps only those who believe "There's nothing less than my life at stake."

> My daughter was sick for a long time, for months. I was so guilty and anxious that I felt like I was suffering the tortures of the damned. But it just wasn't possible for me to leave school. I was getting such ego gratification from it—so much that I never knew I could even feel—that I just couldn't leave. Maybe you'll think it's odd, I don't know. But I felt as if I would die if I had to give it up.[13]

And what of those who can't go on "suffering the tortures of the damned?" What of those who desist under the burden of these obstacles? They give up the search for freedom, the struggle for self. But oftentimes it is so difficult and hurtful a loss that it can only be done when their bodies make the decision for them.

> I had just been offered a promotion that would have put me into a management position. I was already feeling a little guilty about working by then because we no longer needed the money, and my husband was very doubtful about my continuing. But I had been very restless at home, and I enjoyed my job. Then one of my children got sick with what we thought might be meningitis. Obviously, I was scared and worried, but I kept on working because I had responsibilities there.
>
> A few days later, a couple of my neighbors dropped in, supposedly to find out how Timmy was. But in the course of the visit, they told me without mincing words that they believed he was sick because I was working and not taking proper care of him. I was just stricken. It's a classical story from there on; you don't need to be a psychologist to figure it out. Within twenty-four hours I had a severe attack of ulcerative colitis—my first but not the last—which put me in the hospital and resolved my dilemma about working.

There we have it—two women, each making a difficult choice; two choices, each carrying with it significant costs. For the one who drops out? She'll be relieved of her guilty burden, it's true. But at what price?

And for the one who pushes on, who dares to hold onto the dream? She'll probe new levels of self, perhaps find gratifications not dreamed of before, it's true. In exchange, guilt, fear, anxiety will be her companions—painful misgivings to be wrestled with daily. For her, also, there is the prospect of a continuing, almost relentless, assault. Family, friends, colleagues, the institutions within which she would make her way, all place formidable barriers in her path. And, not surprisingly, the more successful she becomes, the more the pressure will build, the more likely she'll feel the backlash, both inside the home and outside.

On the outside, there's prejudice, discrimination, and hostility—tales so often told, facts so well documented, they need little further discussion here.[14] Still, there's one story that's worth telling—partly because it's so typical of what women face; and partly because this particular woman acted with the kind of high courage and grand humor that is an inspiration for us all.

Married to an automobile mechanic for twenty-six years, this forty-three-year-old was the first woman ever elected to the city council in her city of residence—an election that sent shock waves through at least some part of that conservative, male-oriented community.[15] Almost immediately after she took her seat on the council, the discomfort and hostility of her male colleagues became apparent to her.

> I thought male chauvinism was just words those women libbers used until I won that election. But I sure learned my lessons quickly. Things change fast when a woman steps out of line. There's no reason for them to be chauvinistic or treat us badly if we stay in our place and they're in theirs. But just try walking over into their place and see what happens.

Give me some examples of the kind of thing you're calling "chauvinistic."

> [Thinks a moment] I'm trying to decide which of the many to talk about. I assume you don't have all week to listen to all the stories I could tell. Oh, here's one. It happened right after I was elected. We needed to have an extra meeting, and my colleagues decided to have a breakfast meeting at 7:30 in the

morning. I said to them, "You can't do that. I have a family to take care of at that hour of the morning." They replied, "We're sorry, but that's the most convenient time for us to have extra meetings. If you can't be at the meetings, then maybe you shouldn't be serving on the council." I was fit to be tied, just outraged, but I didn't know what else to say.

Well, the morning of the meeting, I got up very early and got everything all together. I got the family off—or at least ready to go off—and then got myself ready. I dressed fully, but over my clothes I put on my bathrobe and I left my rollers in my hair. I walked into the restaurant where they were meeting looking like some kind of an apparition, I guess. They turned red and gasped when they saw me come through. At that point, I marched up and gave them a lecture that everybody in the restaurant could hear. I said to them, "Listen, you men have somebody who gets you out of the house every single morning—somebody who makes your breakfast, who keeps your house in order, and who sees that your clothes and you are ready to go. Well, I don't have anybody like that. In my house that somebody is me. I'm the one who has to get four kids and a husband out the door every morning. I'm the one who has to pack their lunches and make their breakfast, see that their clothes are ready and in order, handle all kinds of crises, and get all five of them out the door on time. And with only one bathroom in the house. So from now on, we're going to have meetings at some reasonable time when a woman with four children and a husband can make it. I was elected just as you were, and from now on, I'm your colleague whether you like it or not."

What happened?

They were floored. They stuttered and sputtered. And while they were doing that, I took off my bathrobe and took the rollers out of my hair so that we could get to work. They couldn't look at me for a while, but it was the last breakfast meeting we ever had.

I, too, was astonished—not just by her courage, but by my own inner reactions. For I knew as I heard her that I wouldn't have dared to take such a bold step. I would have argued, pleaded, reasoned. And when I lost, I would have set my sights on being superwoman—always there, always on time, always trying to prove myself an equal by striving to be better; always, in sum, the "good girl" seeking their approval and acceptance.

A painful recognition, not one I'm particularly proud of. Intellectually, I know there's no victory my way. So why would I continue to do it? For the same reason a slave hides his rage under a bowed head and an ingratiating smile. But, we keep hearing, slavery is dead, and women are free. Lovely words, but not yet wholly true. For many of the institutional forms of oppression remain alive and all too well. And if, in fact, they really were dead? It would still take more than these few years to change the consciousness of those who have suffered them.

"I know I'm taking a big chance." Who takes it? There are plenty of theories around, few explanations.

Some say women who take that big chance are more likely to be only children, others that it's those with no brothers. Some say it's women whose fathers supported their competence, others that it's those whose mothers modeled nontraditional ways of being. Some say it's usually first children, others that the last one has the best chance.[16]

Take a pick—any or all of them. Among the women I met, there's no sense, no order, no clear association with any of these family patterns. They are first children, only children, last children, with brothers and without. They are women with passive fathers and aggressive ones, with no fathers, with supportive fathers, with authoritarian ones who demanded that everyone in the family play out rigidly sex-stereotyped roles.

They are women with dominant mothers and submissive ones, with mothers who worked outside the home and mothers who didn't, with mothers who were content with traditional roles and those who were not.

Maybe we don't know much about *who* takes the chance, but the problems that beset women who do are there to be seen by any who would look.

Inside the family, women repeatedly complain that, while they get verbal encouragement for their efforts to make a life outside the home, no action backs up the words.

> I have a terrible time structuring my time so that I can get everything done that needs doing. My family is very verbally supportive, but something is lost in the translation from words to doing. We're all adults living here now, and I'm ready to give up the supermom ethic. But everyone else is a little reluctant to let it go. I guess I can't blame them. They've had it pretty easy all these years.

Just what do they do to take some responsibility around the house?

> [With a dismissive wave of her hand] What are you talking about? That's just the point! They don't take responsibility at all; *that's all mine.* Oh, their words are great, and we keep talking about needing new systems—always at my initiation, of course. We even keep setting them up. When it works, it's fine. The problem is that it doesn't often work. I mean, if it fits in with their own needs, they'll help out. Otherwise, forget it. In the final analysis, either I do it or I become an angry, shrewish nag. Not much of a choice, is it?[17]

It may not be much of a choice, but it's the one most women are stuck with.[18] Why are those the only choices, though? Why can't a woman step back from her traditional household role and let the chips fall where they may in the family? Why, indeed? Because a lifetime of training for just that role makes it almost impossible for her to do so without enormous guilt. Why? Because a sixteen-year-old who has to fix his own school lunch, maybe even put his clothes in the washing machine, looks at her with a mixture of anger and sadness and says, "I don't understand what's happening around here. I thought you *wanted* to be a mother." Why? Because even when a husband says he doesn't care what the house looks like, just let the dishes pile up or his shirts go unwashed, and she'll either hear an angry roar or face a subtle withdrawal.

Sure, he knows better these days than to complain directly about the dishes or the shirts. After all, he's liberated enough himself to want to support her efforts. Doesn't he tell her so all the time? So he starts a fight over some real or imagined slight that in another moment would go unnoticed. Or he builds a wall of hostile silence around himself. No, he'll assure her when she asks, he's not angry about anything; everything is really okay. He understands she's busy with important things just as he is. It's just hard to be in a house where he can't even find a clean cup. Besides he's preoccupied with an important case tomorrow, and he just happened to notice he doesn't have a clean shirt. It's all right, he assures her, he understands. He'll do the laundry when he finishes writing this brief; it's just that it'll be very late.

Long before the litany of complaint and justification is through, she has taken care of the laundry, tidied up the kitchen, brought him a fresh cup of coffee. She'll stay up later preparing for an exam, getting a lecture ready—perhaps feeling frustrated and angry. But she's used to it, she tells herself. She can do both things more easily than he can.[19]

Maybe all that's true; maybe that's the way it goes in most families most of the time. But isn't it only part of the story?

one might ask. Isn't it also the case that women have some trouble giving up control in the only domain in which their expertise has been recognized consistently? Maybe. But I suspect that's an explanation much overused—another of those seductively clever formulations that appeal precisely because they blame the victim for being victimized while letting the victimizer off scot-free.[20]

Perhaps women who have no other expertise to claim will be reluctant to give up control of the household. But I'm speaking here of women who do have other expertise. Perhaps at the beginning of the transition period some will want to keep one foot in each world. But, at best, that means only *one* foot, not both. Perhaps there will be some period of conflict for them as they recast their lives, reorder their priorities. But not one of the women who works outside the home would agree that the core of the problem lies inside her—in her inability to give up doing dishes, making beds, or cooking breakfast. In fact, whether in resignation or anger, all speak of their struggle with husbands and children around this issue of dividing the household labor more equitably. Even women who agree that it was once difficult to give up control over the household cast the issue in a different light:

> The whole business of how to organize things and who did the organization was one of the most difficult issues. I could get them to do things—I mean, chores—but it was always at my insistence and with me organizing it all. Eventually, I came to understand that part of that was my reluctance to give up being the overseer of it all; it was hard for me to stop being in control of all of that. But I can assure you that I'm quite able to give it up now; in fact, I'd be deliriously happy to. But there's no one to give it to.

Have you tried to see what happens if you don't either do it or organize it?

> Certainly I have. And it's better than it used to be—much better. But in point of fact, I'm still the overseer in important ways. On the less important things, I don't oversee, but they also don't get done most of the time. And on the important things, I still have to be the one.[21]

There's little doubt that most women are willing to give up being overseer and organizer, willing even to give up having everything in the house exactly as they'd like it. Partly that's because it's too difficult a burden to carry when they're trying also to build another life. But there's another, perhaps more important, reason. These are women who already have their minds on other things, already have the beginnings of an alternative identity. They no longer need to hold on so tightly to the housewife-mother routine because, in fact, there's something they'd rather do, even—although they may dare say it only in a whisper—something they'd rather be.

> It used to be a very prideful thing for me that I was an excellent housekeeper and a fine cook. But I'll tell you, it wouldn't be hard to give that identity up if the world would only let me. Oh, I might have a few twinges once in a while (I still like to cook elegantly every now and then), but you can be sure, I'd suffer them gladly.[22]

Too often, however, their attempts to give up both the tasks that go with the job of housewife and the identity are thwarted by others in the family who are threatened by the impending changes. Thus, at the very moment mother gets involved, a teenage child acts up, gets into trouble, in one case, even runs away. Found and brought back, she weeps to her mother,

"You're so busy these days, I didn't think you'd even miss me." "Is it true?" I ask. "Have things changed that much in the family?"

> Well, I'm a lot busier than I used to be, and I'm not here every minute like I was before. But no, it's not true; things haven't changed that much. I'm still here every evening and some afternoons, and I make sure nothing interferes with my being available for her when she needs or wants me. The truth is that I could have been part of the furniture before, so little did she seem to care whether I was here or not. I just think it's hard for everyone in the family to get used to the idea that I have something to do besides taking care of them—something that I want very much to do.[23]

If it's not a child, then a husband may subvert his wife's efforts even while denying that he's doing so. A woman, just finishing her first year in a tough graduate program, tells of the subtle pressures that make her wonder about her capacity to handle the life she's set for herself, that undermine her determination to continue.

> My husband keeps saying he's really very happy to have me back in school. He says all he cares about is that I should be doing something that makes me happy. But when I worked so hard studying this year, he kept telling me he was worried about me, you know, that I didn't seem to be happy. He said he was concerned about me because I seemed so preoccupied a lot of the time. And I guess I was. He keeps commenting that I don't seem happy and asking me if it's really what I want to do. I find it confusing to have these conversations with him. I begin to wonder if it really is what I want to be doing. Then, when I get away from the conversation, I begin to get angry and wonder what he really wants to say.

Do you ask him?

Sure, but he keeps insisting he's only worried about me, not himself.

Small wonder she's buffeted from one side to the other. These are mystifying conversations—difficult to handle because the latent message doesn't match the manifest content. Such covert and murky communication is common in families, taking place most often around issues that threaten to provoke conflict either within the individual, between family members, or both.

This is not to suggest that this husband, and others like him, consciously plan to confuse their wives and confound the issues. Rather, at one level, this man probably sees and hears his wife's need for testing and developing herself in the world outside the family. Perhaps he wants to, perhaps he even does, encourage it in some measure, in some ways. But at another, deeper level, he feels a vague, unspecified anxiety—anxiety born of his internal conflict. Somewhere inside him, fear gnaws—fear about what the change will mean in the family, how it will affect his relationship with his wife, whether his needs will now be sacrificed to hers.

But all this very likely lies far outside awareness, because the acknowledgment of those feelings threatens to reveal his inner conflicts and to provoke conflict with his wife. Consequently, he only knows he's discomfited—suffering diffuse feelings of tension and anxiety, perhaps a free-floating anger that distresses him precisely because it feels so global and irrational. In that state, he fastens on his wife's anxieties about her school performance, projecting onto her some of his own, and begins to wonder aloud whether it's good for her to be working so hard, to be so involved, so preoccupied. Partly because it touches some of her worries and conflicts about the path she's taken, the one thing his wife hears with relative clarity out of his mixed and muddy message is: He wants me to quit.

Listen to the story of another woman who has worked for almost two years as a medical receptionist—a job that caused few problems in the family. She worked only part time; she didn't bring her work home with her; she was always available for her husband. Recently she was offered the opportunity to manage the office of a busy group of doctors—a job that not only promised a substantial salary increase, but one that would put her into a position of some consequence and responsibility, and, of course, would require a full-time commitment. Her husband, she reports, did not overtly object to her taking the job. But he was withdrawn and uncommunicative for weeks after the offer came. Their sex life, until then an active one, almost overnight became practically nonexistent. After weeks of pushing him to talk, pleading with him to tell her what he was troubled about, he grudgingly said that he was worried about her health, fearful that she was getting too thin. Since she was easily thirty pounds overweight, I expressed surprise. She replied:

> You have to understand that until two years ago I weighed three hundred pounds. At first, Ed liked it that I lost weight. But lately, he doesn't seem comfortable with it, especially since the new job. He moped around for a long time and wouldn't say anything, and finally, would you believe it, he told me just the other night he wished I'd never lost all that weight, and that he liked me better the way I was before.

And how do you understand his feelings about that?

> Well, losing all that weight *has* changed my life. If I were still fat, I wouldn't be doing what I'm doing. I know that he's

worried that I won't be the same person if I keep going this way. And I guess I can even understand that because in a lot of ways I'm not. [Tearfully] All I can say to him is, "I love you, but I can't go back to being what I was. I can't do that for anybody." I finally feel that I'm a person with something to offer the world. I'm not going back to what it was like before for anything—no matter what.[24]

For too many women, however, such pressures corrode determination and erode confidence.[25] And they give way. Some do it unconsciously. They fail their preliminary doctoral exams, can't write a thesis, have trouble passing the bar exam after having done very well in law school, fall ill with some malady that effectively stops them in their tracks.

I didn't know it then, but I know now that I failed my prelims because I had such tremendous anxiety about what I was doing and whether I had any right to be doing it. It was already clear that there would be terrible problems in the family if I continued. [With a tight, sad laugh] Well, I solved those problems, didn't I? But in my whole life nothing ever hurt so much; I've never experienced such pain.

Others act with more awareness.

It got too hard, both physically and emotionally. I was guilty and tired and afraid all the time. Nobody dared to complain out loud, but it was clear that my husband wasn't happy with the way things were. So I quit. [Her voice devoid of feeling] It's better with him now. For me, I don't know; I just don't know.

Whether conscious or not, the outcome is the same. They go back into the house—chastened, often worse off emotionally than they were before. For now, in addition to the other strains and discontents they suffer, they live also with the knowledge that they failed in their attempt to change their lives. True, they often say the right words. "I didn't want to do it anyway." "It wasn't my personal failure; I had lots of help." But their eyes, their voices, their every gesture give another message—a message of discontent with the world and of disappointment with themselves.

Most women, however, take a path somewhere between the determination to take the promotion no matter the price and quitting outright. Most carefully count the costs to the marriage as they weigh their alternatives, their calculations usually leading to a decision to put a checkrein on ambition. They leave law school and become instead a paralegal; they settle for the smaller, less responsible job—the one that pays less money, the one that requires less time and energy.[26]

Some speak of being fearful of earning more money than their husbands—a concern so common among women that it's mentioned often even where it's most unlikely. But whether it will ever happen or not, the fact that so many women think about it tells us how deeply embedded is the belief that, for a relationship between a woman and a man to work, he must be more and better than she, always her superior.

> All I ever wanted to do was to earn enough so that my income would make a difference in the family. And I do that now. Now he's got to respect my working because our lifestyle depends on my earnings. But that's enough. I don't ever want to be in a position where I might earn more than him. It would never work. It just wouldn't be worth it.[27]

To make sure it will work, she takes care to dim her luster. But that's not the only cost of these absurd social definitions of masculinity and femininity. For her husband carries the burden from the other side. He's stuck with having to be the "big man" at all times—the man for all seasons, for all occasions. He's stuck with having to prove his superiority every day, every hour—stuck with having to shine like a star, even when he doesn't believe in it, even when he doesn't feel like it.

Other women don't speak of money. They say instead that they don't want the additional responsibility. But if we listen carefully to their words, it's never quite that clear. There's always some conflict, always some sadness, always some regret at not being able to go as far as their capacities will take them.

> It was a hard decision not to take that job offer. But we decided finally that I didn't want to have to be that involved. It's not worth it; there are other things I care about. [Pausing, then continuing defensively, as if wanting to convince both of us that her choice was the right one] Besides, if I allow myself to get as busy as my husband is, then we'll never be able to do things together any more. Oh sure, sometimes I have fantasies about making waves, about going all the way—really doing something big and important. But I know it's not real at this point in my life. And I'm not complaining, not at all.[28]

Interesting words: *"We* decided finally that *I* didn't want to have to be that involved." So what's wrong with that? Nothing, providing she also has the same rights in deciding *his* future, *his* degree of involvement in his work. Interesting, too, is her concern that they would have less time for shared activities. A legitimate concern—crucial for the maintenance of a relationship. But why is it always the woman who takes responsibility for it? Why is it always she who gives up some part of her life, her needs, her desires, to ensure that it's possible?

Over and over, women speak of their fears for the marriage relationship if they climb too high, go too far.

I just couldn't take the promotion. I was too afraid it would cause too much distance between us for me to have a job that has more prestige than his.[29]

Over and over, they speak of their determination not to surpass their men—sadly, even when it already has happened.

I'm not ever going to let my husband feel that I'm more intelligent or more educated than he is because I know how damaging that is to the male ego. I worry about it a lot though. When we were married, I looked up to him as if he was an intelligent god. And he was then, too. Now, after twenty-two years, he hasn't changed or grown much. I don't mean in his work; he's successful enough there. But that's where all his energy has gone, not much into his own growth and development. Even before I went back to work, I had grown and changed a lot—just from reading and being in school, and even from raising my children. You have to be prepared to grow and change if you're going to keep up with your kids.[30]

Proud words, "I've grown and changed a lot." Sad words, "He hasn't." Sadder yet that she diminishes herself, yokes her ambition so as not to damage his fragile ego.

Then, there are those women who speak of none of these things, indeed, who speak of almost nothing at all. They can't confront the risks directly, so they act—covertly, indirectly, but they act.

When I was out there in the world relating to people, I felt like a whole person for the first time in years and years. Then my kid got into trouble. And everybody said it was because I wasn't home when he got home from school and I wasn't meeting my responsibilities as a mother. It was hard to have to go back inside those four walls again. So hard! I felt miserable, but I did it. I had no choice.

Then I guess I rebelled in my own way. I seemed to be tired

all the time. I slept a great deal during the day. In fact, most of
the time I was in bed asleep when the kids came home from
school and when John came home from work. I didn't seem to
be able to do anything but sleep and sit. I couldn't keep the
house up. I stopped doing any real cooking. The main reason
I was there was to supervise the kids, and I hardly even knew
when they were there or not. I slept and I sat. I didn't even
watch TV much—just slept and sat.[31]

"I rebelled in my own way." Interesting words, fascinating
in their implication. She describes depression—"I didn't seem
to be able to do anything but sleep and sit"—and calls it
rebellion. A provocative notion, this: *Depression as a form of
rebellion.*

We hear a lot about depression in women, especially in
midlife women. There are biological, psychological, and sociological explanations of depression—each offering some
clues, none wholly convincing by itself. Women are depressed, we are told, because they're too passive, too dependent, too narcissistic, because they have too much to do when
the children are small or too little to do when they're grown,
because there's a sudden profusion of roles or a sudden loss
of them, because their bodies are manufacturing too many
hormones or too few.[32]

Since the rise of the most recent wave of feminism, something new has been added. Depression in women is explained
also as a response to the helplessness and dependence that are
the central features of their social role.[33] The argument, in
brief, is that since young girls are socialized to be helpless,
dependent, and unassertive, grown women have little capacity
to assert self and needs directly. Rather, they respond to their
angers and discontents in the passive mode to which they have
been trained. They become depressed.

In that context, then, depression is seen as a by-product of the social situation of women—the depressive symptoms consonant with their learned helplessness and passivity. A reasonable explanation, one that certainly speaks to the social reality within which women live their lives. But it doesn't go far enough, precisely because it accepts without question the stereotypic image of women as helpless, dependent, passive creatures. *And they are not.*

It's true, that's one side of women. It's true, also, that it's the side most often seen. But that's only because it's the side that most readily meets with social validation and approval. Indeed, in the relationship between the powerful and the powerless, one of the greatest injustices is the fact that the powerful provide the socially approved definition of the powerless. That definition, then, becomes a self-fulfilling prophecy as it sets the boundaries of permissible behavior. Thus, the slave knew to present to the master the face of the compliant, carefree, innocent child. And women know to look prettily helpless and languidly dependent. The slave knew to hide his intelligence, anger, and pain because they didn't fit the caricature. And so do women.

But what does this say? Is this *only* a public face? Unfortunately no, because such definitions become the accepted truths of a society—extremely difficult to dislodge from either social or individual consciousness. Unfortunately, the public face eventually also becomes at least partly assimilated into the private one as well. But the crucial word here—the word not to be missed—is *partly.* For such social definitions rarely *wholly* transform an individual's sense of self. Thus, even when the outward demeanor fits the world's image exactly, even when people play their socially prescribed parts perfectly, something else usually goes on inside. For most women, that something else is the residue of the ambivalence of their early training—those mandates that taught them at once to be intelligent, yet to hide it; to be competent, yet to look helpless.

While it's true, therefore, that women are dependent, their emotional dependency is often overstated as a defining characteristic, while the economic dependency they suffer is understated. Just so, the economic *in*dependence of men often is mistaken for emotional independence. As for women, they may *act* passive, dependent, helpless because it's expected of them; that's the price of their economic dependency. But inside, they know better; they know they live with an outside and an inside that don't always match.

A lifetime of such contradictions between social definitions and expectations and the inner sense of self could itself be an explanation for the prevalence of depression in women. Seen this way, depression could well be a response to the dissonance between those cultural mandates and the reality of a woman's being. For the need to deny the assertive, independent, masterful parts of self brings with it both conflict and rage—an emotion so socially unacceptable when it appears in women that it is internalized to reappear only in its passive mode, depression.

> I tried to be what they all wanted. I tried to be what I knew my husband wanted me to be. But it always backfired. I could never quite do it right. I always felt like I was being torn in two, and I just became more and more confused and more and more depressed. I know now that I was angry, too, but it took years of therapy to understand that. What a price for trying to shove myself into the correct mold! What a price—for everybody, not just for me, for everybody.[34]

But what about depression as a form of rebellion? What about the woman presented earlier who says she felt miserable, but left her job because she had no choice? How else can she legitimately express her anger at the ways in which life as a woman confines her?

She can't refuse to be home when the children return from school, especially when one already has gotten into trouble. Doesn't everybody agree that's her primary responsibility? Isn't it what the school counselor said? Isn't it what the social worker at Probation said? So she's there—at home, right where she's supposed to be. But she's asleep.

Similarly, she can't refuse to keep the house in order. It's her job, isn't it? So she doesn't refuse. But she's so depressed she can hardly move, can barely stay awake long enough to eat something, let alone to cook it. "I slept and I sat." Who can criticize her if she's too sick to do anything more?

But, one might say, that's self-destructive behavior, maybe even masochistic. Perhaps so. But the labels are less important than understanding that such depression may indeed be a rebellion—a pained and painful cry for the right to live for herself, for at least some shred of autonomy.

All right, one could retort, but it's not the most functional mode; it certainly doesn't get her what she wants. Doesn't it? At worst, she doesn't passively step back into the old traditional role she performed so well before. At worst, she has complied on the outside, but some inner core of self remains relatively untouched. At best, family, friends, even her doctor, begin to worry. Perhaps the doctor advises that she needs to do something to keep busy, to get her out of the house. Eventually, as with this woman, she may go back to work.

> It got so bad everybody was worrying about me, and they finally decided I should try to go back to work. That was the most remarkable thing. I got this job and I just perked up right away. My confidence came back. All of a sudden, I had energy again.

> I did more in the house in one evening after work than I did
> in a month when I was moping around at home. It was like a
> miracle.[35]

Not a miracle, but a victory won, the rebellion ended.
Unfortunate, it's true, that depression is the only mode of
rebellion available to so many women. But that's the emotional cost we all pay for the socially defined characteristics
that make up woman.

These, then, are more of the tragic costs of the socially
structured division of roles in the family. In theory, each is
supposed to complement the other. He takes care of what
social scientists call the *instrumental* side of life; she tends to
the *expressive* side. That means, he brings home the bacon; she
cooks it. He fixes the plumbing; she, the psyche. In reality, he
has spent his life trying to pretend he's all-knowing, all-compe-
tent, all-masterful; she has spent hers trying to pretend she
knows little and can do less. In reality, he's been buried in a
job all his life; she's been buried in the house. But the differences in the worlds of their burial are profound.

His task is to become more and more skilled at what he
does, more and more expert. Too often, that means he
becomes progressively more narrow as well. Recall the
woman who said, "I looked up to him as if he was an intelligent god. . . . Now, after twenty-two years, he hasn't changed
or grown much."

His wife, meanwhile, lives in a world where she's not expected to be expert at anything. So she becomes what she calls
a *dilettante.* But stand back from that word for a moment; stand
back from its pejorative implications. Then we see that it
means she has moved in a direction opposite from her husband. Her interests have broadened, her world widened.

Add to that the fact that she has spent much of her life trying to mute her instrumental capabilities, he suppressing his expressive ones. The result, too often, is two people whose interests and experiences—their inner psychological experiences as well as those in the outer social world—are so disparate that they can barely communicate with each other about anything but the most mundane and superficial matters.

There are other consequences as well of these stereotypic role assignments—consequences and complications that make the midlife transition inordinately difficult. Because he has spent his life in the work world, he knows its limitations. Even if he enjoys his work, he's beginning to slow down, to look for other interests, to experience the shallowness of his interpersonal relationships. In her life, it's just the other way around. She knows all about those things he misses. She has spent her life developing emotional closeness with others, honing her interpersonal skills to a fine edge. That's where she's most expert. For her, the time has come to test her competence in other ways. She goes to school or gets a job—fearful perhaps, but also filled with excitement, the promise of adventure filling her fantasies. For her, the world often seems shiny and new.

> Every day I go to work is a thrill. I love walking into my office, closing the door, and getting at the things on my desk. I feel like a kid who has a new toy to play with every morning when she gets up. [Slightly abashed at what she's just said] I hope you won't think that's too silly.[36]

In fact, her excitement about her life is anything but silly; it's a refreshing delight to see. But again, it often means new problems in the family. Sometimes they're felt immediately because he's ready to slow down at just the moment she's accelerating her investment in a new career.

> After all these years, my husband is taking things easier—you know, taking more time off—and he'd like me to be more

available. But I just can't be. He tries to be understanding, he really does, but it's hard. It's ironic, isn't it? All those years that's what I wanted him to do. I always thought that's what would make me happy. Maybe it would have before. But now I have my own things to do.[37]

Sometimes the issues are in the future—the stirrings already felt now as husband and wife begin to negotiate a life that will include his retirement.

I don't know what will happen when Mel has to retire. He's looking forward to it in some ways; he's ready for a change in his life. I don't blame him; I would be, too, if I were him. It's just that I'm not ready for that. He wants to make plans for buying a ranch up north or something like that. But I'm just not ready. I just got started doing something I love, and I'd be devastated if I had to give it up. Honestly, I don't know what I'll do when we have to face that; I'm just not sure.[38]

She has just made her new beginning. Change is the last thing she wants right now. But for him? Thirty-five years on the job—any job, even one he likes—is enough. For him, change is long past due.[39]

Difficult problems, these—and so many of them. Painful problems—with no pat answers, no simple solutions. How will they end? Who will suffer the risks to continue the search for self despite the anxieties it generates; despite the guilt, fear, and pain; despite the redoubtable obstacles the world continues to put in her way? Perhaps only those who say: "I take the risk because I have to." Perhaps only those who feel: "It's the only way." Perhaps only those who believe: "There's nothing less than my life at stake."

Afterword
"Tell Them, Will You— TELL THEM!"

It has been months since I wrote the last word of the last chapter of this book—months during which I revised it, polished it, picked at it; months during which I sent it off to readers and waited with agonizing impatience for their response. And through it all, the recurring questions: What more do I want to say? What more do I *have* to say?

I find myself thinking about my own life, about the choices I've made, about the years of struggle for my career. I'm grateful—grateful that I live in this age when such options exist; grateful for the presence of a women's movement to support my efforts, to let me know I was not alone. I heard such sentiments from many women—women who spoke of their sensitivity to the currents in the culture around them, women who took courage from those currents and from each other.

> As much as anything, it was the women's movement that made it possible for me to consider making a serious commitment to a life aside from my family. It isn't that I belonged to anything, or that I considered myself a part of it in any organized way, but it seemed to be surrounding me, and it made all kinds of choices possible that didn't even exist a few years ago.

Once again I go over in my mind the main themes about which I have written. I realize that some will quarrel with me, insisting that this book reflects the bias of the path I've chosen;

that, with its focus on the world of work, it suggests that I value the world of men, respect what they do, more highly than the world of women. And I object! For it's not *I* who imposes those values, it's not *my* bias; it belongs to the world —to the society we live in, the society whose values are, whether we like it or not, a part of our being. We may struggle against those values; we may wish to cast them aside. But words alone—no matter how compelling, no matter how often reiterated—won't accomplish that. Indeed, no matter how loudly I have ever shouted that a woman's world is more beautiful, more desirable, than a man's, I was never wholly convinced; the ache inside me never quite stilled.

I know what's positive in my woman's world; I know its value. It's more humane, more fully human in the best meaning of that word. I have always known, always said—even when I was still a small child—that I would never change places with a man. Nothing in my experience has changed that sentiment. But I also have known always what this society values; I also have seen clearly what earns its most respected rewards. And it is not the life that women have traditionally lived, not the qualities and attributes that belong to the world of women, that take the richest prizes.

It's a wonderful feeling now to be able to earn some of the rewards that I was taught were "for men only"; a remarkable experience to have found a part of myself I didn't know existed; a source of unending joy to be able to believe in my competence, in my worth, in myself—not unequivocally, not without guilt and struggle, not without doubt—but still, to believe.

Of course there are costs. A commitment to a career means at least some compromise of the other things I hold dear. I'm less available now for the human relationships and relatedness that have been, and remain, so important a part of my life. It's a loss—a profound one—to have less time for friends; to be unable sometimes to give my family what they would like, what I would like. As I move through this new life, I have come to understand at least one reason why men who are committed to a career so often abandon those other values. It's hard to do both—very hard. The temptation is there for me, too, sometimes to seal myself off from the world in order to do my work. But, because I'm a woman, I can't, I don't, I won't. Because I'm a woman, I'll struggle endlessly with what a friend and colleague called the "competing urgencies" in my life.[1]

I grapple with these thoughts and the feelings they stir—wondering anew about the choices we make, wishing again that there were some easy way out of the dilemmas they pose. I remember the women whose lives are at the opposite end of the spectrum from mine.

> Yesterday I was picking up some clothes to put them in the washer, and suddenly I realized that I was doing the same work now that I was doing twenty-nine years ago when I first got married. *It's like never growing up.*

And I think about those who are somewhere in between.

> I'm happy with what I do. I know now that I can do more, and that I'm just beginning to find out about my capabilities. But I also know I can't go too far with that without jeopardizing other things I value; so I just won't do it.

I know that each of us must answer for ourselves which is the "right" way. But let it be an answer based in an understanding of the possibilities—an answer based in clear knowledge about how much really is our individual choice, how much was defined for us long ago, on the day we were born girls. For without that knowledge, we suffer in isolation, as if the issues were ours alone; without it, we blame ourselves, each of us thinking this is our unique and personal deficiency; without it, we have no basis even for a fantasy about what changes are necessary in the structure of our social world so that not only we, but our men as well, can live more fully.

I think these thoughts, write these words. Good words, I say to myself. But, I ask, are they enough? Or is there something more the women I met would ask me to speak for them? The question lingers, following me through my daily routine, nagging even while the rest of my work goes on.

Then, one day, a patient asks if I will meet with her and her mother to help them deal with some issues between them. Of course. A few days later, I walk, hand outstretched, toward an attractive fiftyish woman sitting with her daughter in the waiting room. "Hi, I'm Lillian Rubin. It's a pleasure to meet you." Rising from the chair, she extends her hand and says, "I'm Joan's mother. I'm glad to meet you, too."

I stand quietly, waiting. Will she tell me her name? The silence grows awkward. "I'm sorry, I didn't catch your name." She glances about as if to see whether I'm speaking to someone else, flushes slightly, then, seeming surprised that anyone would care, "I guess I didn't say it."

I stand there, listening to the message in what she says, hearing also what she doesn't say. A woman who has no name. How many have I met like her?

Days flow into weeks—busy days, restless ones. I pick up a novel read some time ago, looking for something in it, something that connects to these thoughts churning round inside me. I flip the pages, seeing passages I marked off long ago.

> My favorite question that is asked only of women is "What do you do with yourself all day, now that the children are in school?" . . . "I write. I paint. I meditate. I masturbate." "Re-

ally," they say vaguely. "That's nice. At least it keeps you busy."[2]

I remember how often I was torn between laughter and tears as I read this book.

So the question is, if masochism is out as a way of life; if it is no longer a worthy calling; if, in fact, it is nothing but a sickness —then what do I do with my years of training? I'm not really fitted for any other kind of relationship. I'm not even convinced there is another kind.[3]

Funny-sad words, with an edge that cuts deep. But why *this* book; what is it here that keeps calling to me? I turn more pages, recapture more passages. Suddenly I see. She has no name, the heroine of this novel. *A whole book about a woman who has no name.* She's one of us; and she's all of us—all the women we have known for so long; all of them who have been John's wife, Stephanie's mother, the Barnetts' daughter; all the women who, until now, have had no name.

She still exists, this woman who has no name. She's not yet gone from our world, not yet absent from our lives. She's the woman who lives in the house down the street. And the one who lives on the hill. But whoever she is, wherever she lives, she's beginning now to be aware of the loss, beginning now to count up the cost. And from the pain she's finding deep in her soul, the words well up in a shout:

The world makes it hard, not me. Tell them that, will you— TELL THEM!

Appendix
About the Study

The material for this book is taken from interviews with 160 women who range in age from 35 to 54. Median age of the women is 46.5 years; of the men to whom they are or were married, 51.5.

Since I was interested in women who, earlier in their lives, had taken marriage and motherhood as their primary life tasks, all have been married and all have borne and raised children. Median length of intact first marriages, 25 years. Almost 7 percent were in second marriages ranging in length from 1 to 31 years; median, 16 years. Two women were in third marriages, one of 4 years duration, the other, 5.

Almost 22 percent were separated or divorced after a marriage that had lasted, on the average, 19.5 years. Two of the 35 divorcees (almost 6 percent) were in nontraditional living arrangements—that is, living with a man to whom they were not married. One was in the process of discovering herself a lesbian after having been married for 22 years. The rest were living alone or with whatever children remained in the home.

Widows were systematically excluded since, for them, the midlife transition is complicated by the need to deal with death.

Because I was concerned about the ways in which women cope with the period in life when the requirements of motherhood no longer dominate, none had any children under thirteen left in the home. That age was suggested by the fact that this is the year when children leave elementary school for junior high—a major step in the developing independence of the child, and a time when women often experience a sharp diminution in the demands of the mothering role and function.

Median age of the children of these families was 21 years; median number of children per family, 3.

This project was designed and carried out as a cross-class study. Although an adequate specification of class is a matter of some dispute in the sociological literature, there is general agreement that class status is closely correlated to level of educational attainment. My earlier work on families rested on that assumption, and class was defined therein by a combination of education and occupation. But indicators of class that work more or less well in research on *families* become problematic indeed when the research focus shifts from families to *women.*

The class status of a woman in the American society has traditionally been determined by her husband's place in the occupational structure. While that method has come under attack recently, there is yet no alternative status-ranking system that satisfactorily reflects the realities of the social status of married women.[1] Therefore, in specifying the requirements for the sample, I decided that, regardless of whether she held a white-collar job or a blue-collar one, a woman would be counted as working class if she had no more than a high school education and was married to a man with a similar educational background who was working at a blue-collar job. A middle-class woman was defined as one who had a college education or more, and was married to a man with a like educational background who worked in one of the professions or at a managerial level in business or industry.

But even that relatively straightforward definition had to be revised very soon after the gathering of the sample had begun. It quickly became apparent, for example, that the educational attainment of a married woman (especially in that generation) was not necessarily an indicator of her class position. Just over one-third of the women who were married to highly educated professional- or management-level men never completed college; almost one-fourth had no more than a high school diploma. Yet, the most elementary common sense demanded that these women be assigned to the class position of their husbands—for at least as long as they remain in that marriage.

Other problems came into view with equal rapidity. For example, to which class would I assign a woman who completed her high school education at thirty-five, went on to get both bachelor's and master's degrees, and now is the assistant director of a program for reentering women at a community college, while she remains in a twenty-six-year marriage to a warehouseman with a tenth-grade education? Or by what criteria would I make a class assignment to a woman who was divorced from a professional husband earning $70,000 a year —a woman with a master's degree in biochemistry who had not worked for the twenty years of her marriage and, when we met, was living on $9,000 a year in spousal and child support.

These are, of course, extreme examples, especially so among working-class women, where few who start with a high school education or less ever move to such heights of achievement in adulthood. Nevertheless, it is by looking at those extremes that the depth and dimension of the problems of defining the class status of married women become more visible.

In some instances, a husband's status still clearly determines the wife's; in others, it clearly does not. Those are the easy ones. But that leaves the cases where there is no clarity. Then the investigator stumbles in the dark, hoping the evidence in the empirical world will be compelling enough to facilitate a reasoned and reasonable class assignment. In this research, that task was made somewhat easier by the fact that I had before me the life history of each respondent along with data about each member of the families of origin and of procreation. By examining that broader picture, it was possible to assign a respondent to a given class with some assurance that the conceptual category and the empirical world were a reasonable fit.

It would have been possible, of course, and, according to some social scientists, perhaps preferable, to set up class categories in advance that would have remained inviolate. No doubt people would have been found to fit those categories. Enough criticism has been made of such reification of the categories of analysis that it is unnecessary for me to do more here than to signify my agreement with the critics. Better always to let go the analytic categories with which we come to the field than to distort the empirical world in the interest of making it fit our conceptualizations.

With that caveat about the looseness of the class categories that follow, I can now say that the composition of the sample is: working class, 45 percent; middle-middle class, 24 percent; professional or upper-middle class, 31 percent. While some investigators undoubtedly would have made different decisions about some of the marginal or difficult cases, I am confident that there would not be significant deviation from the proportions I have given.

In any case, perhaps the most important statement this study has to make about class is that, when looking at married women, gender transcends class as the major determinant of the quality of their lives. That does not mean that there are no important differences in the particulars of life depending upon class. But the overall sweep of the problems midlife women face—their concerns, their hopes, the nature and rhythm of their lives, even the language they use to speak of all these— cuts across class, the similarities becoming more compelling than the differences, as the data show so forcefully.

Fifty-four percent of the women were Protestant, 19 percent Catholic, 14 percent Jewish, and 13 percent claimed no religion.

Because the life experiences of black and white are so different on so many important dimensions both inside the family and out, it seemed to me it would confound the study to have women of both races. Therefore, only white women were included.[2] During the course of the work, however, I did speak informally with some black women at the same stage of the life cycle, and some have read all or portions of the manuscript. Their collective response does indeed suggest that, while similarities are to be found, many of the issues I have dealt with in this work would be experienced quite differently by black women; others, touched on only lightly here, would be central—a potentially fruitful area for comparative research.

Except for eleven (almost 7 percent) who lived in Southern California, New York, Massachusetts, or Pennsylvania, the women all lived within a 150-mile radius of the San Francisco Bay area—all of them in urban or suburban areas. The women in working-class families were much more likely to be native to California than those in the middle class—62.5 percent compared to 33.0 percent—suggesting much greater residential mobility among the more highly educated families of that generation. But even among the nonnatives, most were long-term residents of the state: 24.5 years on the average.

The women were drawn into the study by the snowball method of sampling. I started with a few women known to me whose characteristics fit those required by the research. After each interview, I and my two research assistants asked for referrals. Sometimes we got one, sometimes a list of twenty. From these names I made the interview assignments for the three of us, always choosing the next person to be interviewed on the basis of her having the most distant connection—both geographically and emotionally—from the respondent who referred her. Thus, if there were eight to choose from—some close friends, some acquaintances, some who lived in the neighborhood, some a hundred miles away—the choice was always in favor of the woman who lived at a distance and was a casual acquaintance. These precautions assured that the study would not be biased by being composed of friendship networks.

Although I exercised the same care throughout the research, by the time a third of the interviews had been completed, it was no longer necessary. For I had, by then, almost two hundred names on file from which to draw respondents —women who came from such distant places and different referral sources that there was little likelihood of getting caught in any small network or circle. In fact, after the completion of the study, I had in my files the names of three hundred women who had not been interviewed.

The success of this method in securing a relatively unbiased sample is evident in the fact that the women in this study match the national population on such characteristics as age at the time of first marriage, number of children, length of marriage, proportion divorced, proportion in the labor force, and the kinds of jobs they generally hold.

All interviews were focused, in-depth discussions lasting no less than three hours, often as many as ten, and sometimes requiring more than one visit. All included a life history of the respondent.

In style, the interviews lie somewhere between a research instrument and a clinical hour—a technique that serves the goals of flexibility and adaptability, and that facilitates the emergence of unanticipated data. At the same time, the fact that it is focused prevents aimless wandering, assures that all interviewers will cover the same basic ground, and gives the interviewer the basic structure with which to remain in control of the interview situation.

Such interviews are best done by people who have some training in clinical work. Clinical skills are invaluable for extracting the maximum data because (1) they enable the interviewer to establish quickly a facilitative, nonthreatening, neutral atmosphere that frees respondents to share their thoughts, feelings, and perceptions; (2) the interviewer is capable of sorting out and grasping the dynamic underlying the responses she gets; (3) the interviewer is in a position to judge when she is meeting resistance or denial, when to push for more data, and when to back off because she runs the risk of threatening or alienating the respondent; and (4) clinically trained persons are not only attuned to the dynamic processes of the other, but have learned to attend to their own in order to minimize countertransference effects. That means that they are more capable of controlling their own tendencies to projection, thus more able than most to "hear" and perceive the perspective of the other, even when dealing with highly emotion-laden material.

Accordingly, the two research assistants who shared the interviewing task with me were graduate students in clinical psychology. Together, these two women completed eighty interviews, while I did the other eighty.

One of the standard criticisms of this method of interviewing is that it is all but impossible to maintain consistency across interviews and interviewers. My experience in this and prior research suggests that the criticism has little merit *providing* the interviewers are well trained and carefully supervised. While such training is a difficult and demanding task for the director of the research, when properly carried out it assures that the data from different interviewers will be highly consistent and congruent.

Training and supervision in this study were carried out very much along the lines of the clinical model, with both group and individual supervisory sessions. We listened to field tapes together, discussed the strengths and weaknesses of each interview, explored the problems of the interviewer, and sought ways to overcome them. While supervision continued throughout the data collection, the frequency and intensity diminished as the interviewers became more accomplished and self-confident. But because the typed transcript in this research was not an exact replicate of the interview in the field, I listened to the tapes of every interview done by my assistants. This enabled me (1) to get the full flavor of the person being interviewed, to hear the voice, to gain some understanding of the *process* of the interaction, to pick up the nuances of the verbal communication; and (2) to compare the typed transcript with the field tape to be certain my assistants were processing the interview adequately and not missing any important data.

Some students and practitioners of the qualitative method undoubtedly will have questions about the advisability of using an edited transcript. As with all research strategies, there are costs and benefits. But I am convinced that the benefit in the ease of data retrieval—an issue on which so much qualitative research ultimately founders—far outweighs any costs. Therefore, a word here about the method of data recording.

In addition to taping, all interviews were recorded by hand on the site—a task that requires that the researcher have some shorthand or speedwriting skills. This note-taking was selective to the degree that we did not record material that was irrelevant to the goals of the research. Everything else was taken verbatim.

Immediately following the interview, the notes were organized in accordance with the conceptual categories previously developed and coded.[3] All material that fell under a particular category was brought together so that ultimately it would appear in one place on the transcript. That means, for example, that even though a woman talked about her experience of motherhood at several points during the interview, the final transcript showed all that material under the heading "motherhood."

Once the organization was completed, the interviewer dictated the verbatim material—both questions and answers—into a transcribing tape recorder. That tape became the basis for the typed transcript from which the data analysis would proceed.

Again, researchers sensitive to the issues in qualitative research may be concerned that, in using this system, some of the context is lost. And to some degree that may be true. But it is possible to minimize that loss by requiring that, when it seems relevant, appropriate, or important to understanding the data, the interviewer record comments about the context that will then appear on the typed transcript.

Indeed, this method of handling the data turns the transcript into a doubly valuable tool. It is, of course, the source of the data. But the need to organize it means also the need to think about it while it is still fresh. And the process of recording it in its newly organized form provides the opportunity for including whatever thoughts the analyst may have about the material. Thus, much of the analysis that is ongoing in the research takes place at that time and in that form. The analytic thoughts stimulated by the process of organizing the interview material are clearly labeled and included in the transcript under the category that is the subject of the analysis. When the time comes for the final analysis of the data, then, all the material on a particular category—motherhood, for example —together with the developing analysis is in one easily accessible place. Thus, much of the analysis of motherhood and the empty-nest issues that appears in this book is a product of that continuing process of recording, refining, and reformulating as the data of the interviews were organized and prepared for transcription.

Other researchers speak of the need to develop research memoranda during the course of the fieldwork in order to develop and refine conceptual categories and analytic themes as they emerge during the course of the study. While I, too, write specific memoranda from time to time, they serve largely to sort out, bring together, and develop the analysis that is already a permanent part of the typed transcript of the interview.

Qualitative research of the type described here has, for some time now, come under criticism and suspicion in the social sciences, much of the argument centering around its lack of representativeness and the difficulty of managing the mass of data it generates in any orderly and systematic way. This brief appendix is not intended as a defense of qualitative research in general or of research based on intensive interviews in particular. That must await a more detailed discussion of the methods of this research and the specific means for controlling the data mass. For now, I am content to offer colleagues in the social sciences a general picture of the sampling, interviewing, and data-recording procedures from which they can make judgments about the methodological adequacy of this study.

But I would also insist that methodological adequacy is far from enough to give legitimacy to this or any other work. In this research, the nonrandom sample may make generalizations suspect in some technical sense. And the anecdotal presentation may raise questions about representativeness in the use of the data. But if, on the pages of this book, the reader has found her/himself in familiar territory, if the empirical world as it is described here has that familiar ring of truth—yet a truth not clearly understood or formulated before—then this work will have achieved its purpose.

For too long now, concern with the method of research has obscured attention to its substance, with the result that social scientists are fast losing credibility and public support. Our quarrels about the value of hard versus soft data are irrelevant to the world and its problems, and unnecessary and distracting for us. Different research methods need not compete with each other; we need only understand that they tell us different kinds of things. Large-scale studies based on statistically representative samples have a place in the social sciences; but it is not the *only* place. They add to our knowledge; but they cannot tap all the knowledge that is potentially available. Such probability studies tell us something about social trends; but they leave us guessing about their effects on the people who must live them. For that, nothing replaces the smaller sample qualitative research based on face-to-face interaction with other humans—research that can capture the fullness and richness of life as it is experienced by those who live it, that can teach us something about the way people interpret the world and give meaning to their lives.

It is true that such research is more difficult to carry out, less easy to control than studies done with what we call the hard methods. Like human life itself, qualitative research often defies neat categories and clear concepts. But such difficulties should not be permitted to blind us to its necessity. Nor should they force us to shrink from one of the great challenges in the field—to describe and analyze human social life in all its stubborn complexity and diversity.

Notes

Chapter 1: Of Beginnings and Endings

1. Mannes (1963): 125.

2. Witness, for example, the millions spent in the attempt to defeat the Equal Rights Amendment or the enormous sums now being poured into antiabortion campaigns.

3. These changes include a steadily increasing life expectancy, changes in fertility patterns due to more effective contraception, a declining number of children per family, an earlier end to the child-bearing and childrearing phases of women's lives, and a growing concern for more egalitarian relationships between women and men both inside and outside the family.

4. Class culture makes a difference in a complex and varied society such as this one. But the difference in the age of marriage between high school-educated working-class women and college-educated middle-class women is about three years, so that generally they still move through the life-cycle stages at close to the same age.

5. Of course, I speak here of modern society where medical and contraceptive advances permit such choices.

6. Since the 1950s, there has been a striking increase in the proportion of never-married women—up from 4.1 to 7.0 in these two decades. But even this dramatic rise leaves the proportion of those who never marry almost 2 percent below the same group in the first decade of the century (Glick, 1977).

7. Ibid.

8. Ibid.

9. Ibid.

10. Women marrying in the 1970s are, on the average, 22.7

years old when their first child is born; in the 1900s, they were 23 (ibid.).

11. Life expectancy at birth in 1920 was 54.1 years; by 1974, it had climbed to 71.9. For women alone, the increase is even more dramatic: from 54.6 to 75.9 years (U.S. Bureau of the Census, 1976b, Table 85).

12. Glick (1977) shows a relatively steady decline over the last eighty years in the age at which women give birth to their last child and their age when that last child marries.

13. Ibid.

14. *Wall Street Journal* (June 27, 1978).

15. U.S. Bureau of the Census (1976b), Table 46.

16. Glick (1977).

17. Ibid.

18. Ibid.

19. U.S. Bureau of the Census (1976a).

20. U.S. Bureau of the Census (1976b), Table 46.

21. U.S. Bureau of the Census (1977), Table 1/2.

22. Ibid.

23. Women between the ages of twenty to thirty-four make up roughly 20 percent of the current female population, all those over fifty-five amount to another 20 percent.

24. This figure is roughly comparable to national statistics that show that in 1973 the percentage of American women obtaining a divorce who were forty years old or more was 18.3 percent, up from 14.1 in 1960, but slightly down from 18.7 in 1970 (U.S. Public Health Service, 1975).

25. Forty-seven percent of the women I met are now in the paid work force—roughly 70 percent in full-time and 30 percent in part-time jobs. Cf. U.S. Department of Labor (1977a), which shows that among married women with husband present and no children under eighteen in the home, 44 percent are presently in the labor force, and U.S. Department of Labor (1976), which reports that 72 percent of *all* working wives held full-time jobs, 38 percent part-time.

Chapter 2: The Empty Nest: Beginning or Ending?

1. Forty-three-year-old mother of four, two of whom still live in the family home. Married twenty-six years to an automobile mechanic, when asked her occupation she says:

> I always feel uncomfortable when someone asks me that. I'm a homemaker, but I also consider myself a bookkeeper.

In fact, as the interview progressed, it turned out that she spends about one day a week keeping the books for her husband's small business; she is a beginning student at a state college; and she is an elected official in her city of residence.

2. Forty-eight-year-old homemaker, mother of three, married twenty-five years to a banking executive.

3. There are some notable exceptions in the work of Deutscher (1969a, 1969b) and Neugarten (1968a, 1968b, 1974); Neugarten, et al. (1968); Neugarten and Datan (1974). Over a decade ago, they showed that most women accept the departure of their children with equanimity if not relief. But these findings have been paid scant attention, probably because they fly in the face of established stereotypes and preconceptions. As recently as 1974, Neugarten wrote: "The notion that [women] mourn the loss of their reproductive ability and their mother-role does not seem to fit modern reality. No matter what the stereotypes tell us, it is not the way women talk when you listen." Yet, so pervasive are notions about the empty-nest depression that researchers continue to express doubt about their own findings when their data contradict the preconception. Thus, Glenn (1975) concluded: "Although the findings of this and similar studies indicate that the so-called 'empty nest syndrome' is not as prevalent... as was once believed, problems of the 'empty nest' may be prevalent enough to warrant public concern...." And Lowenthal, Thurnher, and Chiriboga (1975) heard the women they interviewed say they were looking forward to the children's departure, and concluded that their anxiety and despair about the empty nest were too deep to be tapped by their interviews.

4. Bart (1967); Deykin, et al. (1966); Jacobson and Klerman (1966); Weissman and Paykel (1974).

5. Bart (1967, 1969, 1970, 1971) is an important exception to these comments. Her pioneering work offers a complex and subtle social-role analysis that few others have matched.

6. Over the last few years, other investigators have begun to suggest that, in fact, the departure of the children brings both an increase in marital satisfaction for women and an increased sense of well-being (Fuchs, 1977; Glenn, 1975; Lowenthal, Thurnher, and Chiriboga, 1975; Lowenthal and Weiss, 1976; Maas and Kuypers, 1975; Sales, 1977). Still, these new research findings have received relatively little attention (even sometimes from the researchers themselves; see note 3 above) compared to the old ones, which are closer to the myth and stereotype about the nature of woman and the naturalness of motherhood.

7. Bart (1967); Deykin, et al. (1966); Jacobson and Klerman (1966); Weissman and Paykel (1974).

8. Those symptoms are a profound clinical depression, usually characterized by several serious psychiatric symptoms such as deep sadness and despair; sleeplessness; loss of appetite; loss of sexual desire; retardation in initiative, thinking, and motor abilities; severely low self-esteem and self-confidence; little or no interest in daily life and ordinary affairs; an incapacity to experience pleasure or joy; and an inability to engage in anything that requires sustained effort or attention. Descriptions of such women are to be found in Bart (1967); Deykin, et al. (1966); Jacobson and Klerman (1966); Weissman and Paykel (1974).

9. Harkins (1978) reports some differences in well-being between pre-empty nest, post-empty nest, and women who are in the transitional period. But the differences are slight and disappeared within two years after the event, leaving her to conclude that "there is no effect of the transition on physical well-being and a positive effect on psychological well-being."

10. Spence and Lonner (1971) found that women see themselves as successful or not depending upon the degree to which they view

their children as successes or failures. Even though the children were no longer in the home, the women they studied did not consider their jobs completed if they still had to counsel or function in some mothering manner.

11. Powell (1977) found that, among women whose children were gone, those who were employed outside the home scored significantly higher on tests of mental health than those who were not.

12. Fifty-four-year-old mother of two, married thirty-three years to a dentist. Thirteen years ago, at age forty-one, she returned to school to finish a bachelor's degree abandoned years ago when she married, then went on to a master's degree and a teaching job at a community college.

13. Fifty-year-old homemaker, mother of three, married thirty-one years to a professor.

14. Forty-two-year-old cashier, mother of three, one still living at home, married twenty-three years to a small businessman.

15. Forty-five-year-old homemaker, mother of three, married twenty-five years to the operator of a garage and service station.

16. Forty-two-year-old clerical worker and aspiring student, mother of two, married twenty-two years to a telephone lineman.

17. Weiss (1975,1976) offers a vivid and moving account of the emotional issues that accompany divorce.

18. Fifty-one-year-old homemaker, mother of three, recently divorced from a computer technician after a twenty-nine-year marriage.

19. Fifty-three-year-old high school counselor, mother of two, divorced twelve years from a physicist.

20. Forty-three-year-old receptionist, mother of four, married twenty-six years to a factory foreman.

21. Cf. Bart (1967, 1971); Weissman, et al. (1973); Weissman and Paykel (1974).

22. Rubin (1972).

23. Rubin (1976a).

24. Fifty-year-old homemaker, mother of two, married thirty years to a chemist.

25. Bart (1967, 1971) argues that whether mothers have satisfactory or unsatisfactory relationships with their children makes little difference in their adjustment and suffering around the children's departure. "Role loss is apparently an all or nothing phenomenon . . . ," she writes (1971). While that conclusion may be apt for the clinically depressed population she studied, there is no evidence to support it in this group of 160 women who are coping well and functioning normally.

In a recent telephone conversation with Bart, she suggested that the changed cultural context—that is, the difference between the experience of being a midlife woman in the 1960s and the 1970s after the changes wrought by the women's movement—could also be a factor in accounting for the difference in her findings and mine about the prevalence of the empty-nest depression. While this is certainly a reasonable speculation, it is not enough, since it does not take into account that, even in the 1960s, research findings that challenged the belief that the empty-nest syndrome was a common phenomenon went unattended (see notes 3 and 6 above). Indeed, it is an equally tenable speculation that women in the earlier era blamed their depression on the departure of their children because it was the most socially acceptable and easily accessible response.

26. The point is so well understood in the culture that it needs no documenting. For some recent writers who deal with the issue, however, see Abramowitz (1977), Bernard (1975), Lazarre (1976), McBride (1973), Rich (1976), Russo (1976), Slater (1970).

27. Fifty-two-year-old homemaker, mother of three, married thirty-two years to a construction foreman.

28. Forty-nine-year-old homemaker, mother of three, married twenty-eight years to an engineer.

29. Forty-eight-year-old homemaker, mother of four, married twenty-seven years to an attorney.

30. Sales (1977) notes that, since one of the major requirements of women's role is adaptability to the needs of others, they are constrained from making long-range plans for their own lives. That means that, generally, they are deprived of the pleasure of attaining

goals that require extended time commitments in any area except motherhood. Thus, many women experience long-term satisfaction only in their maternal role and view their children's progress to maturity and achievement as their most substantial contribution in the world, and the most important evidence of their own personal worth.

31. Forty-four-year-old typist, mother of five, married twenty-five years to a maintenance man.

32. Forty-nine-year-old would-be writer and homemaker, mother of three, married twenty-six years to a hospital administrator.

33. For a few recent challenges to that view, see Bernard (1975), Block (1978), Chodorow (1978), Cott (1977), Easton (1976), Lazarre (1976), McBride (1973), Rich (1976), Rothman (1978), Wortis (1974). Cf. Rossi (1977) who seeks to bring a biosocial perspective to the analysis of motherhood, and Stacey, Breines, and Cerullo (1978) for a critical response.

34. U.S. Department of Labor (1977a), Table 22, shows that in 1976, among married women with husband present and children under six years old, 37.4 percent were in the labor force, up from 11.9 percent in 1950, 18.6 percent in 1960, and 30.3 percent in 1970. While also large, the increase in working women, married with husband present and *no* children under eighteen in the home, is considerably less striking—30.3 percent in 1950, 43.8 percent in 1976.

35. There are, of course, often other gains for women who work —gains in self-esteem, in a sense of independence, in autonomy, and in marital satisfaction—which will be discussed more fully in later chapters.

36. See Baruch (1976) for a study that shows the positive relationship between self-esteem and the self-perception of competence among fifth- and tenth-grade girls; also Laws (1976) for an excellent critical discussion of the literature on work aspiration and achievement motivation in women; and Condry and Dyer (1976), Schnitzer (1977), and Tresemer (1976) for recent challenges to the theory that women's relatively limited achievements

in the competitive world of education, business, and the professions is related to their fear of success. In her fine discussion of tokenism and the toll it takes on the person in the token role, Kanter (1977) reinterprets the fear of success notion and suggests that what researchers see actually may be the token's fear of *visibility*—a phenomenon that is not sex linked, but is related to the structural arrangements of the organization and the job, and to patterns of discrimination and stereotyping.

37. Forty-eight-year-old student-homemaker, mother of three, married twenty-five years to a business executive.

The designation "student-homemaker" is used to identify those women who call themselves homemakers but who also take some classes each year even though they have no plans to work toward a degree.

38. Fifty-two-year-old baker, mother of four, married thirty-two years to a machinist.

39. Forty-four-year-old homemaker, mother of two, married twenty-three years to a computer programmer.

40. See Deutsch, vol. 2 (1973), for a psychoanalytic view of motherhood and motherliness; also Bowlby (1969, 1973); Fraiberg (1977); and Mahler, Pine, and Bergman (1975), all authors who put motherhood at the center of their theoretical work on human development. For an alternative theoretical perspective that places motherhood in a sociological framework, see Chodorow (1978) and Dinnerstein (1976). Kagan (1978) and Shorter (1975) look at the historical evidence and show that, in fact, the modern view is a highly sentimentalized, idealized, and culture-bound theory of the meaning of the maternal bond and the mother-child relationship. Cf. Weiss (1978) who examines childrearing manuals in America from 1913–1976, viewing them as mother-rearing tracts.

41. Lessing (1966): 197.

42. Forty-five-year-old homemaker, mother of two, married twenty-six years to a stockbroker.

43. Fifty-year-old clerk, mother of three, married thirty years to an operating engineer.

44. Forty-seven-year-old secretary, mother of three, married twenty-eight years to a bartender.

45. Fifty-one-year-old bookkeeper, mother of three, married thirty-two years to a certified public accountant.

46. Fifty-four-year-old homemaker, mother of three, married twenty-nine years to an optometrist.

47. Forty-six-year-old student-homemaker, mother of two, married twenty-seven years to a sheet metal worker.

48. Fifty-one-year-old homemaker, mother of four, married thirty years to a sales representative.

49. Forty-seven-year-old waitress, mother of three, married twenty-six years to an assembly-line worker.

50. Cf. Glenn (1975) whose findings also suggest that, on the whole, fathers are more likely than mothers to suffer a loss in psychological well-being as a result of the children's departure. Lowenthal, Thurnher, and Chiriboga (1975) give some evidence as well that men have some problems with this transition and that they speak with regret of not having spent more time with their children.

51. Forty-four-year-old stenotypist, mother of four, two still living at home, married twenty-seven years to a plumber.

52. Forty-nine-year-old super-volunteer with three children, married twenty-five years to a dental surgeon.

53. Forty-one-year-old school cafeteria worker with four children, one still living at home, married twenty-three years to an appliance repairman.

54. Forty-three-year-old student-homemaker, mother of three, the oldest a few months away from leaving for college, married twenty-three years to a professor.

55. Fifty-year-old super-volunteer, mother of five, married twenty-seven years to a physician.

56. Forty-nine-year-old clerk-typist, mother of four, married thirty years to a butcher.

57. Fifty-four-year-old homemaker, married thirty-two years to a business executive.

58. Fifty-three-year-old homemaker with three children, married twenty-nine years to a child psychiatrist.

59. Forty-six-year-old mother of two who recently completed a master's degree in social work, married twenty-four years to a psychiatrist.

60. Forty-nine-year-old sales clerk, mother of five, married thirty years to a real estate salesman.

61. Forty-five-year-old homemaker with two of three children still at home, married twenty-two years to an insurance executive.

62. Forty-six-year-old child-care worker, mother of two, married twenty-eight years to a truck driver.

63. Forty-five-year-old artist-homemaker, mother of two, married twenty-three years to an attorney.

Chapter 3: Who Am I? The Elusive Self

1. French (1977): 48.

2. See Chesler (1972) for an intriguing analysis of the sources of madness in women; also Milford's (1970) biography of Zelda Fitzgerald.

3. Forty-nine-year-old reading specialist, married twenty-seven years to a school administrator.

4. See Stone (1977), Chapter 5, for a history of patriarchy and the social degradation of women between the sixteenth and nineteenth centuries.

5. Cf. Rosen and Aneshensel (1976) for a study of the "chameleon syndrome," in which they found this accommodative response to the social environment much more common among girls than boys.

6. De Beauvoir's (1961) early exposition of this process remains one of the most brilliant and beautiful in the literature. See also Lakoff (1975) for a fascinating discussion of the two dialects in the English language—one male, one female—and the implications of this dual language structure for keeping women in their place. In a study of sex differences in self-concept among adolescents,

Rosenberg and Simmons (1975) found that girls are much more likely than boys to be *self-conscious* in the sense that they are much more concerned with self in relation to others, more involved with what others think of them, and more apt to base their self-esteem on their ability to relate favorably. By adolescence, the authors conclude, boys want to do well and girls want to be well liked. In a comparison across race and sex, these same authors (Simmons and Rosenberg, 1975) found that white girls have lower self-esteem and tend to be much more self-conscious than black girls—a product of the fact, they suggest, that black girls are less likely to believe they will be successful in achieving a stable marriage and living the life of a traditional housewife-mother; therefore, they do not direct their attention *exclusively* to the attainment of that goal.

7. See, for example, de Beauvoir (1961), Hunter (1976), Lederer (1968), Millett (1970), and Williams' (1977) brief overview of the history of "mythic woman."

8. See Bardwick and Douvan (1971) for a discussion of the relationship between female socialization practices and ambivalence. Cf. Chodorow (1978) who, while she does not deal directly with the issue of ambivalence, provides the basis for a more psychoanalytic interpretation of its sources in women.

9. Chilman (1974) also speaks of women's tendency to veil their strengths from men "partly out of necessity, partly out of compassion"; and Ruble and Higgins (1976) show that the sex composition of a group affects sex-role awareness and leads to sex-stereotypic responses.

10. As recently as 1963, Norman Cameron, the author of one of the most widely used texts in personality development and psychopathology, wrote (p. 128):

Ordinarily, a greater degree of aggression and self-assertion is required in the male than in the female role. Aggression and initiative are masculine prerogatives in sex relations; relative passivity and receptivity are feminine prerogatives. The man finds his major daily outlets for aggression in his work, the woman in running the home and presiding over her children's welfare and activity.

Cf. Fox (1977) for an interesting analysis of the social control of women through such "nice girl" value constructs.

11. Fifty-year-old super-volunteer, married to a businessman.

12. Forty-one-year-old teacher's aide, married to a longshoreman.

13. Forty-four-year-old attorney who passed the bar just two years ago, married twenty-two years to a real estate developer.

Cf. Rapoport and Rapoport (1971, 1976) for a discussion of the competitive role strains under which married career women live, and the necessity they feel for segregating work and home roles. Indeed, one of their respondents, a much younger woman than those in this study, spoke with almost identical words. "When I'm at work, I'm very authoritarian. I wear a white coat at work and I try to hang up my working personality with it when I leave the office."

14. Forty-six-year-old salesperson, married twenty-seven years to an operator in a steam plant.

15. Forty-two-year-old woman who recently opened a book store, married nineteen years to a writer.

16. Forty-eight-year-old homemaker, married twenty-nine years to an engineering executive.

17. For fuller discussion, see Rubin (1976a).

18. Some few women married to professional men have no more than a high school diploma. But they suffer feelings of inadequacy for lack of it, and seem to spend a good part of their lives trying to make it up in one way or another—that is, by reading a great deal, taking classes, keeping almost compulsively current. Despite their efforts, however, they report feeling very uncomfortable when they must make a public admission of not having gone to college in their youth.

19. Lever (1976, 1978) presents a compelling analysis of how the games children play reinforce the sex-stereotyping of girls and boys. She argues that through the games that are considered sex-appropriate, boys are socialized to competitive public roles and girls to private relational ones.

20. Forty-eight-year-old homemaker, married twenty-five years to a research scientist.

21. Sound statistics on the marriage rate of highly successful career women are hard to come by—partly because there are so few of them. A recent survey by *Fortune* magazine shows that only 0.2 percent of the officers and directors of the country's 1,300 major companies are women. In their study of women in top-level managerial positions in industry, Hennig and Jardim (1977) found only half their small sample ever married, all when they were past mid-thirty, and none ever bore children. For a critical review of that work, see Rubin (1978). On February 20, 1979, the *Wall Street Journal* reported on a survey by the management consulting firm of Wareham Associates that shows that women in executive jobs are far less likely to be married than their male counterparts. Among the women top executives surveyed, 23 percent had never been married and another 31 percent were divorced, compared to the men, almost all of whom were married and very few divorced.

22. Chodorow (1978) argues that the differences in male and female personality are rooted in the structure of the family—in particular, in the fact that women are the primary childrearers. Consequently, the mother becomes the first object with which the infant of either sex identifies. For a girl, that presents few problems in the developmental task of establishing an appropriate gender identity since it requires a continuous and gradual process of the internalization of a feminine identity with mother as model. For a boy, however, such role learning is discontinuous, involving, as it must, the rejection of his earliest identification with his mother as he seeks an appropriate masculine identity.

The argument, then, is that, since a girl need not reject that earliest identification in order to negotiate the Oedipal phase successfully, feminine personality is based on less repression of inner objects, less fixed and firm ego-splitting, and greater continuity of external relationships and relatedness. On the other hand, since boys must repress these same attachments as they shift their identification from mother to father, they come to define and experience themselves as more separate from others and with more rigid ego boundaries. Adult masculine personality, therefore, comes to be defined more in terms of denial of connection and relatedness with others.

23. Forty-three-year-old homemaker, married twenty-one years to an attorney.

24. Fifty-one-year-old homemaker, married thirty years to a city planner.

25. See Millman (1980 forthcoming) for a compelling look at the fat phenomenon in America and the untold anguish it causes so many women.

26. Lowenthal, Thurnher, and Chiriboga (1975) also note that midlife women rarely mention occupational activities when talking about themselves and their philosophies of life, emphasizing instead responsibilities to the family. Indeed, ambitions toward personal achievement were often viewed as incompatible with their primary responsibilities in the family. Only about one-fifth of the women they interviewed mentioned personal achievement or self-fulfillment as their main purpose in life, and those were generally women who were already in one of the high professions, or who were widowed, divorced, or living in a precarious marriage.

27. Most meetings took place in the women's homes. But because of these strikingly similar responses, the wording, sequencing, and meeting place were systematically varied in order to test whether the responses were a function of any or all of these factors. None made a difference.

28. See Adams (1971) for an interesting discussion of what she calls the "compassion trap"; also Chodorow (1971) for a more extended discussion of the being-doing distinction.

29. The age range of these thirty-five men is forty to fifty-five. Believing that a younger group of men might respond differently, one of my research assistants talked with ten more men, whose ages range from thirty to thirty-nine. These are all professional men, all well versed in the language of feminism and the small companion movement among men, all sympathetic to the aims of both. Yet their answers did not differ significantly from the more diverse group of older men. It's true that the younger men may have been more discomfited by their own responses than the older, more traditional

ones, more surprised to find that work was still the first thing that popped into their heads and from their mouths when asked for a definition of self. And it's also true that the intellectual understanding of the narrowness of such self-definition may eventually change consciousness. But it does not seem to have happened yet—at least not on any large scale.

30. See Braverman (1974) for an important discussion about the degradation of work in the twentieth century; Aronowitz (1973) for the ways in which do-it-yourself projects are used by men to compensate for the alienation and degradation of their skills during the working day; and Rubin (1976a) and Sennett and Cobb (1973) for discussions of the impact of work on family life.

31. Forty-eight-year-old secretary, married twenty-four years to an economist.

32. Forty-two-year-old homemaker, married twenty-three years to a foreman in a manufacturing plant.

33. For a psychoanalytic view of this process, see the recent outstanding work in object relations theory by Mahler, Pine, and Bergman (1975); and Chodorow (1978), whose work on mothering makes the link between internal psychological development and the structure of the family. Huber (1972) presents an account of her own experiences as she analyzes the "ambiguities in identity transformation."

34. Lakoff (1975) provides plenty of other such examples, and notes also that, in social situations, women will be asked about their husband's occupation because it serves to place them in a social status. Since a man's status is not derivative, what his wife does is not socially relevant, therefore is not attended to seriously.

35. This explains why the traditional homemakers, as well, more often than the working women (but less often than the volunteers) describe themselves with words that suggest competence. It is not that these women actually view themselves as more capable than do women who work for wages, but that it is more acceptable to acknowledge their abilities given that they are devoting their lives to achieving competence in traditional roles.

36. Sherman (1976a) presents an analysis of the incompatibility between the social definitions of femininity and competence, and argues that we know little about how to rear women to be competent, partly because competence has never been considered an important goal for women. Chilman (1974), on the other hand, argues as I have here, that, since few males can easily tolerate strong, independent females, most women find it the wiser course to gloss over their competencies with a patina of deference. Lowenthal, Thurnher, and Chiriboga (1975) note that, even in this era, the high school girls they interviewed are uneasy about acknowledging such characteristics as competence and self-directedness.

37. See de Beauvoir (1961) and Lederer (1968) for extended discussions of this fear of women; also Millett (1970) for a later, feminist analysis of what she calls "sexual politics."

Chapter 4: "Sex? It's Gotten Better and Better"

1. Fifty-two-year-old homemaker, married thirty-three years to an electrician.

2. Twenty-two percent of the women in this study presently are divorced. At the developmental level, there are, of course, no differences between the divorced and married women. But at the behavioral level, sexual issues for divorced women at midlife are likely to be felt most keenly around the limited opportunities they have for sexual contact and expression with men they consider appropriate partners. See Chapter 6 for fuller discussion.

3. For a similar age group, Kinsey, et al. (1953) show just under 60 percent engaging in oral-genital sexual activity twenty-five years ago.

4. For identification, see Chapter 2, note 15.

5. Forty-three-year-old recent graduate of a counseling program, married twenty-four years to a businessman.

6. For identification, see Chapter 3, note 3.

7. Over 60 percent of the women I met were virgins when they married—a figure that corresponds roughly to the Kinsey, et al.

(1953) data about women of the same generation. Among those in this study, 41 percent of the working-class and 37 percent of the middle-class women had premarital coitus.

8. For identification, see Chapter 2, note 42.

9. Most women also say it only happened once or twice, or a few times at most. Frequently as well, they speak of the accidental quality of the experience, which suggests that even now they need to absolve themselves of responsibility for their behavior either by believing that it was an accident or that they found themselves in the grip of uncontrollable impulses.

10. Forty-four-year-old factory worker, married twenty-five years to a roofer.

11. Forty-nine-year-old nurse, married twenty-eight years to a musician.

12. In general, this is true of both working-class and middle-class men, although it is also true that complaints about a husband's lack of concern for his wife are more often heard from working-class than from middle-class wives. See Rubin (1976a) for extended discussion about sexual behavior in younger working-class families—i.e., where women are on the average twenty-eight years old and men are thirty-one.

13. The popular marriage manuals of the day are quite explicit on the issue of male responsibility for female orgasm. See, e.g., Chesser (1947) and Van de Velde (1930); also Gordon and Shankweiler (1974) for a review of eighteen best-selling marriage manuals in the period from 1950–1970.

14. Fifty-two-year-old sales clerk, married thirty-four years to a shipping foreman.

15. Fifty-one-year-old homemaker, married thirty-one years to a management consultant.

16. Bernard (1976) also speaks to the inadequacy of assertiveness training programs and for some of the same reasons.

17. Kinsey (1953) showed that by the fifteenth year of marriage, only 10 percent of his sample never reached orgasm in marital coitus, and by the end of twenty years of continuous marriage, 47 percent were having orgasm all or most of the time. These figures

comport with the women I studied, where close to 90 percent are orgasmic, over 50 percent more than half the time. For other recent studies showing that sexual pleasure for women increases with age and the longevity of marriage, see Fuchs (1977) and Whitely and Poulsen (1975).

18. For a compelling argument about the physiological reasons for the increase in orgasmic potential after childbirth, see Sherfey (1973).

19. Forty-year-old homemaker, married twenty-two years to a policeman.

20. Several recent accounts of motherhood, written by women who are also mothers, speak to the joys and pains of what Adrienne Rich calls the "institution of motherhood." All make clear that many of the problems experienced by mothers are related to the culture myths around motherhood and the guilt women experience from the internalization of that package of impossible expectations (Hammer, 1975a; Lazarre, 1976; McBride, 1973; Rich, 1976).

21. For identification, see Chapter 3, note 3.

22. For identification, see Chapter 2, note 42.

23. See Hobbs and Cole (1975) for a replication of their 1963 study, which shows that decreased sexual responsiveness in women continues to be a major problem in the transition to parenthood. Indeed, there's plenty of evidence around that marital satisfaction in general suffers a decline with the birth of children and continues until they reach maturity (see, for example, Lopata, 1971; Sales, 1977). Bernard (1973: 70) writes:

The effect may be traumatizing. There is a drop in all indexes of marital satisfaction. Diverging interests—the wife's in her maternal and household responsibilities, the husband's in his professional career—can produce a drop in daily companionship. The marital interaction pattern seems to be muted.

For an excellent article analyzing the readjustments that must take place when couples move from childlessness to parenthood, see Rossi (1968). Rollins and Cannon (1974) argue that marital satisfaction is lowest at those periods in the life cycle when role strain is highest—that is, when a high level of stress is generated by a high number of intense and demanding social roles that place conflicting and/or incompatible demands on the individual. The early child-rearing phase of marriage is just such a period, especially for women.

24. See Miller (1976) for a recent study showing that children tend to decrease the frequency of marital companionship, therefore their presence generally means also a decrease in marital satisfaction.

25. Hobbs and Cole (1975) show that "feeling more distant from spouse" is among the top seven problems women and men experience in the transition to parenthood.

26. Gagnon and Simon (1973) argue that this split between sex and love, this separation of sex from the total relationship, is the hallmark of male sexuality in the American culture. Kuten (1976) holds that a major issue in the sexual relationship between adults is that it replays the infantile symbiotic tie which is both desired and feared. If he is correct, it seems reasonable that the relatedness issue would be more anxiety laden for men than for women because, in the nature of the male resolution of the Oedipal phase, that old identification with and dependence on the mother had to be repressed. The stirring of those archaic anxieties and the need to contain them could explain that male split between sex and love in psychodynamic terms.

27. Thirty-eight-year-old homemaker, married twenty years to a data processor.

28. Westoff and Jones (1977) show striking increases in vasectomy as a means of sterilization in the years between 1965 and 1975. Among white couples continuously married for fifteen to nineteen years, the proportion of vasectomies jumped from 4.4 percent in 1965 to 19.5 percent in 1975. Among those married twenty to twenty-four years, the corresponding proportions are 5.9 percent to 19.5 percent.

29. Forty-four-year-old full-time undergraduate student, part-time bookkeeper, married twenty-five years to a lab technician.

30. Forty-four-year-old clerk-typist, mother of four, married twenty-six years to a machinist.

31. Hunt (1974) compares sexual behavior in the 1970s with the data from the Kinsey studies of the early 1950s to document the sweeping changes in sexual behavior across the generations. See also Rubin (1976a) for data and analysis of the meaning of such large cultural changes in the lives of the people who are trying to live them.

32. Rubin (1976a).

33. Fifty-year-old super-volunteer, married twenty-seven years to an attorney.

34. See, for example, Hammer (1975b), Koedt (1971), Lydon (1970), Millett (1973), Phelps (1975), Sherfey (1973).

35. Forty-six-year-old graduate student, married twenty-three years to a physician.

36. See Slater (1976) who also argues that our preoccupation with orgasm and the techniques for achieving it is a natural extension of the Protestant work ethic in which nothing is to be enjoyed for its own sake except striving.

37. One can see this tension between work and pleasure played out in the public policy debates about unwed mothers where the discussion repeatedly focuses on their alleged "licentious" and "pleasure-seeking" behavior. In reading or listening to these discussions, it is difficult to escape the conclusion that our national rage is directed, not simply toward their sexual behavior, but toward the pleasure we fantasy they take in it.

38. Forty-one-year-old LVN, married twenty-two years to a carpenter.

39. For identification, see Chapter 3, note 3.

40. For identification, see Chapter 2, note 42.

41. Fifty-three-year-old clerk-typist, married thirty-four years to a glazier.

42. For some elaborations of the theory of the dual labor market —one for men, one for women—see the Spring 1976 supplement of *Signs,* edited by Blaxall and Reagan, especially articles by Bernard, Lapidus, Hartmann, and Blau and Jusenius.

43. Forty-six-year-old legal assistant, married twenty-three years to a physician.

44. Forty-nine-year-old homemaker, married twenty-eight years to a cabinet maker.

45. For identification, see Chapter 2, note 13.

46. Forty-four-year-old legal secretary, married twenty-three years to a salesman.

47. Forty-eight-year-old student-homemaker, married twenty-three years to a television cameraman.

48. For identification, see note 11 above.

49. See Rubin (1976a) for discussion of these power struggles as they are seen in younger families.

50. Forty-five-year-old court reporter, married twenty-six years to a fireman.

51. While not wishing to deny other forms of family—in particular the homosexual family—I am speaking here of heterosexual families only.

52. This felicitous phrase is borrowed from the title of Kraditor's (1968) volume of feminist writings.

Chapter 5: Of Women, Men, Work, and Family

1. Lowenthal, Thurnher, and Chiriboga (1975) also note that the middle-aged women they studied indicated only vague and unfocused plans for the additional time they would have available after the youngest child left the family home.

2. For identification, see Chapter 4, note 15.

3. *San Francisco Chronicle,* December 30, 1977.

4. Ibid., November 6, 1977.

5. See Papanek (1973) for a discussion of the "two-person career"; also some of the literature on dual-career families, all of which shows that, even when husbands are supportive of their wives' careers, they generally are given considerably less weight than the husbands' (Epstein, 1971; Heckman, Bryson, and Bryson, 1977; Holmstrom, 1972; Hunt and Hunt, 1977a; Poloma, 1972; Poloma and Garland, 1971; Rapoport and Rapoport, 1971, 1976; Safilios-Rothschild, 1976). Indeed, in her study of

marital partners who are also law partners, Epstein (1971) showed that even the work within the firm tended to be divided along stereotypic sex-role divisions—that is, women were confined to the less visible, less prestigious jobs. Hunt and Hunt (1977a) note that, while discussions of dual-career families generally recognize the barriers that families place in the path of women's achievement, they have failed to assess adequately the supportive role of the family in the achievements of men.

6. Gould (1974):73.

7. Woolf (1977).

8. See Chapter 2, note 34 for labor force data.

9. Forty-year-old homemaker, married twenty years to an architect.

10. Fifty-three-year-old homemaker, married thirty-four years to a building contractor.

11. Thirty-nine-year-old homemaker, married nineteen years to a municipal official.

12. Given these social definitions and expectations and the threat of family disruption that is implied in their violation, it is no surprise that researchers often see women as relatively uninterested in and uncommitted to their work. See, e.g., Lowenthal, Thurnher, and Chiriboga (1975) and Poloma and Garland (1971). My own findings, however, show that midlife women value their work experiences highly and find it an important source of gratification and self-esteem. (See also Ferree, 1976a, 1976b; Gannon and Hendrickson, 1973; and Herman and Gyllstrom, 1977.) But they often are reluctant to discuss their work commitments because of their guilt and discomfort about violating social expectations that home and family come first. Thus, in reply to questions about these issues, they may give the answers that seem to them to be most appropriate, or that are, psychologically, the most readily accessible. Further probing, however, and the development of a trusting relationship with the interviewer, usually reveals that they value working deeply and are reluctant to give it up even under rather heavy pressures from husbands.

Still, this is a complex matter, for, as I shall discuss at length in later chapters, often a woman's high commitment to work threatens her husband and marriage. Therefore, she tends to curb both ambition and commitment in the interest of meeting what she and the world consider her primary responsibilities.

13. See Ericksen (1977) for a recent article that analyzes the meaning of the "journey to work" for women, and shows that women's home-role requirements are important predictors of the length of their journey to work.

14. Fifty-two-year-old social worker who returned to work when children were ten, twelve, and fifteen, married twenty-six years to a high-level state administrator.

15. Forty-seven-year-old homemaker and volunteer museum guide, holder of a master's degree in English, married twenty-three years to a professor.

16. Forty-eight-year-old homemaker, married twenty-seven years to a business executive.

Chapter 6: "What Am I Going to Do with the Rest of My Life?"

1. Forty-two-year-old homemaker, married twenty-one years to a business executive.

2. For identification, see Chapter 2, note 42.

3. Forty-three-year-old student-homemaker, married twenty-four years to a telephone installer.

4. See Rosenberg and Simmons (1975) for the differences in the development of self-concept between female and male adolescents. Also Broverman, et al. (1972) for an intriguing study that shows that practicing psychotherapists (both male and female) hold a different standard of mental health for women and men—that is, the healthy adult and the healthy male are identical; the healthy female is exactly the opposite from the other two. The healthy, mature woman is defined as more submissive, more dependent, less competent, less objective, and less logical than the healthy, mature male. Cf. Cowan (1976) for a challenge to the Broverman findings.

See also Chodorow (1978), whose psychoanalytically based theory connects the resolution of this dependence-independence struggle—or the lack of it—to the structure of the family and the fact that mothers are the primary care givers in the modern nuclear family. While mothers are the first and primary attachment for infants of both sexes, the issue of separation and independence becomes complicated for girls because both mothers and daughters have a more difficult time in distinguishing self from other. Cf. Friday (1977); Hammer (1975).

5. Lipman-Blumen and Leavitt (1976) present a typology of achievement orientations from vicarious to direct. Socialization patterns, they write, elicit directness, agency, initiation, and activity for boys; vicariousness, communion, implementation, and passivity for girls. "The vicarious achievement ethic, when applied to women," the authors note, "implies that marital and maternal roles—largely vicarious in nature—are *the* most desirable and appropriate roles for women."

6. See Acker (1973) and Nilson (1976) for two recent attempts at the development of such a measure.

7. Forty-four-year-old homemaker, married twenty-three years to an administrator in state government.

8. Forty-year-old secretary, married eighteen years to an attorney.

9. For identification, see Chapter 2, note 42.

10. Thirty-nine-year-old student-homemaker, married twenty-one years to a machinist.

11. Forty-three-year-old graduate student, married nineteen years to a newspaper reporter.

12. Forty-six-year-old graduate student, married twenty-five years to an auditor.

13. Forty-one-year-old super-volunteer, married twenty years to a university administrator.

14. See Chapter 1, note 24, for divorce statistics.

15. A U.S. Dept. of Labor study (1977a), Table 39, shows that the median income of divorced women who are full-time year-round

workers is just 64 percent of the income of divorced men—$7,922 for women compared to $12,321 for men. The same source, Table 41, shows that the earnings of married women, husband present, account for only 26 percent of family income. Thus, when the husband leaves, he takes most of the family income with him.

See also McEaddy (1976), who reports that the median income for *all* female-headed families is less than one-half that of husband-wife families. Moreover, among families living in poverty, a much higher proportion are headed by women, and the number of poor families headed by women is rising continuously, while the number headed by men is falling steadily.

16. Forty-six-year-old homemaker, married twenty-five years to an environmental engineer.

17. Williams (1977) also notes that the most important factor influencing sexual expression in older women is the unavailability of partners with whom they might have the opportunity for regular sexual experiences. Fuchs (1977) presents evidence that shows that while there are declining opportunities for sexual expression for divorced or widowed women over forty, when such women do have sexual experiences, they are very satisfying, with a higher incidence of orgasm than when they were married.

18. Long ago, Goode (1956) found that divorced women often felt they and their children were better off as a result of the divorce. More recently, Bequaert (1976); Brandwein, Brown, and Fox (1974); Brown, et al. (1976); and Gillespie (1972) have all written of some of the positive aspects of divorce for women. Bequaert makes an interesting argument against the currently fashionable trend of analogizing the experience of loss in divorce with death and dying. Such psychological notions, she asserts, mask the relief that many women feel. My own findings—both clinical and research— suggest that, while there often is some grief work to be done in a divorce, the magnitude of the loss and the necessity for grieving tend to be overstated for some large and significant number of people— an overstatement that leaves guilt and discomfort in its wake among those who do not feel the "appropriate" amount of pain. In fact, the

emphasis on feelings of loss and grief as a natural consequence of divorce encourages a focus on the grief rather than the relief, thus inviting many newly divorced women and men to distort their own inner experience.

19. California still permits a person to become an attorney by reading for the bar and, at the time I applied in 1956, still permitted admission to law school without a B.A.

20. Heckman, Bryson, and Bryson (1977); Holmstrom (1972); Knudsin (1974); Rapoport and Rapoport (1971, 1976); Sutherland (1978); and Trigg and Perlman (1976) all provide evidence that a husband's support is an essential prerequisite for a successful career for a married woman.

21. Forty-seven-year-old homemaker, married twenty-three years to a judge.

22. Except for a handful—less than 10 percent—who were Born-Again Christians and/or adherents of Marabel Morgan's "total womanhood" philosophy, all acknowledged that they suffer it.

23. Forty-six-year-old homemaker, married twenty-four years to a statistician.

24. There still exists some dispute about whether parents treat boys and girls differently in the early months and years of life. In the most thorough review of the literature to date, Maccoby and Jacklin (1974) conclude that there is little difference in the ways male and female infants and young children are treated. But Block (1976), in a comprehensive and critical review of their work, presents a challenge to the methods of their study that throws this and other findings into question. Even psychoanalysts who, until very recently, have been unsympathetic to the notion that the observed differences between women and men can be traced to early childhood environmental and socialization influences, are looking at the question anew. Thus, a summary of a panel discussion on the psychology of women held at the annual meeting of the American Psychoanalytic Association asserts: "There is increasing evidence of distinction between the mother's basic attitudes and handling of her boy and girl children starting from the earliest days and con-

tinuing thereafter" (Galenson, 1976). See Chodorow (1978) and Dinnerstein (1976) for expositions of how and why these differences occur and their consequences for personality development in women and men.

25. While dealing with extreme cases of psychopathology and not focusing on women alone, the clinical literature on borderline patients is instructive in that it shows plainly the difficulty people with such early childhood experiences have in separating and individuating. See, for example, Bowlby (1969, 1973); Kernberg (1957, 1974, 1976); Mahler, Pine, and Bergman (1975); Masterson (1976).

There is, to my knowledge, no systematic analysis of whether there are more female than male borderline patients, but the case studies more often feature a woman than a man. That, of course, might simply be because more women than men present themselves for psychotherapy. Or it might be that clinicians are quicker to see borderline pathology in women. But my own clinical observations suggest also that there may well be more women who meet the classical borderline definition precisely because of their early and more difficult problem in separating from mother—a problem that is not innate in feminine personality but that arises because the primary parent and survival figure is of the same gender. The implications of that single fact of a girl's life are too profound to be discussed here in a few sentences. At its most simple level, however, that sameness means that both mother and daughter are less able to distinguish the boundaries between self and other, making it extremely difficult for the infant daughter to take the necessary steps toward individuation and autonomy.

These brief reflections are in no way intended to diminish the importance of the work of the socialization theorists who have told us for years now that the differential early treatment of girls and boys is responsible for the typical differences we see in the adult personality of women and men. But those theories tell us what *is,* not why it happens. For that understanding, we need to look at how the structure of the external world interacts with and creates an inner personality structure that is passed on across the generations through the structure of the family.

Chapter 7: "There's Got to Be More to Life Than Hot Flashes and Headaches!"

1. Forty-four-year-old student-homemaker, married twenty-two years to a businessman.

2. See Astin (1976), Gould (1976), Raushenbush (1961, 1962), and Taines (1963) for more extended discussion of the benefits to women who reenter the academic world, as well as the personal problems and the institutional barriers they confront.

3. Forty-one-year-old student-homemaker, married twenty-five years to a welder.

4. Forty-nine-year-old student-homemaker, married thirty years to a furniture upholsterer.

5. Forty-five-year-old student-homemaker, married twenty-seven years to a meat inspector.

6. Fifty-year-old student-homemaker, married twenty-nine years to a research scientist.

7. For identification, see Chapter 4, note 35.

8. For identification, see Chapter 3, note 16.

9. For identification, see note 1 above.

10. Forty-nine-year-old student-homemaker, married thirty years to a business executive.

11. Most of the super-volunteers are upper-middle-class, college-educated women—partly because, without the necessity to work for wages, they are the ones with enough leisure and enough money to buy some household help to free them for activities outside the house; and partly because the Lady Bountiful tradition belongs to the upper and upper-middle class. This is not to say that working-class women do not also volunteer their services to community, schools, church, and so on. The distinction here is between women who virtually make a career out of volunteering and those who do not.

12. For identification, see Chapter 2, note 52.

13. Other criticisms of volunteerism hold that by keeping women in noncompetitive roles, it reinforces their difficulty in engaging a competitive situation; and that, by their voluntary efforts, women collude with the society to apply Band-Aids to serious social problems. For further discussions and analyses of the costs and benefits of volunteerism in women's lives, see Artson (1978), Bardwick and Douvan (1976); Daniels, Joslyn, and Ruzek (1975); Feeney (1976); Gold (1971); Hartman (1976); Mueller (1975).

14. Forty-four-year-old mail clerk, married twenty-six years to a salesman.

15. These figures are close to those issued by the U.S. Department of Labor (1977a), Table 33, which show that, among women between the ages of 35 and 54 who are in the labor force, 64 percent have between one and four years of high school, while only 26 percent have between one and four years *or more* of college.

16. In the first volume of a massive, four-volume study on dual-career families supported by the U.S. Department of Labor (1970–1976), Parnes found that: "Despite rather poor earnings . . . the vast majority (95 percent) of employed women in the sample report favorable attitudes toward their jobs. Indeed, three in every five indicate that they would work even if they (and their husbands) had enough money to live comfortably without working." Ferree (1976a, 1976b) and Rubin (1976a) both found that even working-class women with young children who hold relatively low-level, routine jobs prefer to be in the labor force at least part-time rather than to spend full time in the routines of housewifery and mothering. Cf. Sales (1977) who, after reviewing the literature, concludes that, despite age discrimination and the mundane nature of the jobs generally available to them, married women whose children are grown are most satisfied with their lives if they are in the paid work force.

17. Fifty-year-old secretary, married thirty-two years to a refinery worker.

18. Forty-six-year-old typist, married twenty-six years to a warehouseman.

19. Forty-three-year-old medical receptionist, married twenty-four years to an asbestos worker.

20. Fifty-year-old assistant bookkeeper, married thirty years to a longshoreman.

21. Forty-eight-year-old speech therapist, married twenty-four years to an urban planner.

22. Fifty-two-year-old beauty operator, married twenty-nine years to a maintenance man.

23. In a paper presented to the American Sociological Association in 1976, Mortimer, Hall, and Hill argue that, so long as the structure of occupations remains the same, the wife of a professional man will be under pressure to support her husband's career and abandon the pursuit of her own occupation in a serious, career-oriented way. For further analysis of the dilemmas that women in dual-career families face, see Darley (1976); Epstein (1971); Heckman, Bryson, and Bryson (1977); Holmstrom (1972); Hunt and Hunt (1977a); Poloma (1972); Poloma and Garland (1971); Rapoport and Rapoport (1971, 1976); Safilios-Rothschild (1976).

24. Artistic capacities are not, of course, confined to the middle class, but the *development* of those talents is much more likely to occur in middle-class homes than in working-class ones. From childhood on, middle-class families are more likely to encourage some limited artistic development, especially in girls—partly because it's a luxury they can afford, and partly because the image of the "lady of culture" includes in it some minimal skills in the arts. It is, therefore, accorded at least an affectionate indulgence both for the girl child and the grown woman.

25. Forty-six-year-old sculptor, married twenty-three years to an advertising executive.

26. Fifty-three-year-old homemaker, married thirty-two years to a physician.

27. Forty-nine-year-old homemaker, married twenty-seven years to a business executive.

28. See Rubin (1976a) for a detailed cross-class analysis of these difficulties at the early childrearing stage of family life.

Chapter 8: *"I Know I'm Taking a Big Chance!"*

1. For identification, see Chapter 7, note 19.

2. Mortimer, Hall, and Hill (1976) provide a good discussion of these issues. See Chapter 7, note 23. Poloma and Garland (1971) studied married women in high-level professions—doctors, lawyers, academics—and found that, even when they work, "most married professional women *do not* have careers, but rather professional involvement that is 'occupation oriented.'" They present evidence to show that, although both husband and wife may give the wife's career a high priority early in the marriage, with time, her career takes a back seat to his. Consider the meaning to women of such limitations if, as Maas and Kuypers (1974) argue, a sound and stable personality organization relates not to *what* one does but how *deeply* and *rewardingly* one enters into the various arenas of life.

3. For identification, see Chapter 2, note 12.

4. For identification, see Chapter 4, note 35.

5. For identification, see Chapter 4, note 29.

6. For identification, see Chapter 7, note 21.

7. For identification, see Chapter 2, note 1.

8. Forty-four-year-old graduate student, married twenty-two years to an insurance executive.

9. For identification, see Chapter 4, note 29.

10. Forty-two-year-old recently graduated clinical psychologist, married twenty-one years to an engineering executive.

11. For identification, see Chapter 2, note 12.

12. Cf. Fromm (1941).

13. For identification, see Chapter 4, note 5.

14. For a brilliant and subtle analysis of discrimination in the corporate world, see Kanter (1977), especially the chapter entitled "Numbers: Minorities and Majorities," which is an outstanding analysis of the costs and consequences of tokenism. Cf. Spangler, Gordon, and Pipkin (1978) for a study that tests and affirms Kanter's hypothesis. Comparing the performance of women law students in

two law schools with significantly different sex ratios, they found that performance pressure, social isolation, and role entrapment all operate to diminish women's achievements where they are only a small minority of the student body. Bernard (1976) also presents a recent examination of the more subtle forms of hostility and discrimination against women, especially in the academic world.

The most compelling evidence of sex discrimination, however, is to be found in the statistics of the U.S. Department of Labor (1977b), which show, among other things, that education and training have a significantly lower payoff in the labor market for women than for men. Those figures also show that the male-female earnings gap has widened over the past twenty years. In 1955, women working full time year round earned 64 percent of men's earnings; in 1972, they earned only 58 percent. In 1972, only 11 percent of the women who were fully employed earned $10,000 or more, compared to 51 percent of the men.

15. For fuller identification, see Chapter 2, note 1.

16. The literature on this issue is fraught with confusion and contradiction. Hennig and Jardim (1977), Lozoff (1973), and Walstedt (1977) all argue that fathers who encourage their daughters' competence and autonomy while valuing them as women are the most likely to produce high-achieving daughters, while Helson (1971) found that women mathematicians identified with fathers who were lacking in warmth. Hunt and Hunt (1977b), on the other hand, present an altogether different view, suggesting that girls may grow the strongest in father-absent families.

Rey, Noell, and Woelfel (1976); Rosenfeld (1978); and Tangri (1972) show that whether a mother worked outside the home and what occupation she held both have an important effect on a daughter's destiny, while Altman and Grossman (1977) insist that whether a mother worked or not is less important in influencing the daughter's life plan than whether the daughter perceived the mother as satisfied or dissatisfied with her status. Cf. also Baruch (1972), LaRussa (1977), Lipman-Blumen (1972), Sutherland (1978).

While there is a more general consensus in the literature on birth order and sibling composition, these studies, too, leave questions unanswered. Monson and Gorman (1976), Poloma and Garland (1972), and Rapoport and Rapoport (1971, 1976) present evidence that achieving women are most likely to be first children, only children (what the Rapoports call the "only-lonely child pattern"), or from an all-girl family. There is general agreement among these and other authors that parents' desire for achieving children may be so strong that, in the absence of a son, they will allow a daughter to step into the role of surrogate son and become a high achiever.

My own earlier work among working-class families (Rubin, 1976a), however, suggests that, at best, these are highly class-biased findings. For in working-class families, especially where there are four or more children, it is often the last child—son or daughter—who is likely to be upwardly mobile and to achieve at a higher level than the older siblings. Partly that may be because the last child may already have before him or her a rather grim picture of the lives of the older siblings; and partly because, if she or he is the last child left at home, the family may, for the first time, have the resources to offer financial and/or emotional help that was unavailable to the others.

17. Thirty-nine-year-old full-time undergraduate student who also works two days a week in her husband's business and has two of her three children still living at home.

18. Even in a family that can afford household help, it is rarely enough so that all the organization and the tasks necessary to run a household are done by paid help. Indeed, even among the very wealthy who have a staff of servants (none in this study), much of a woman's time is spent in managing that staff and organizing their work.

19. There are plenty of recent studies to show that there's more talk than action when it comes to reapportioning domestic tasks. See, for example, Araji (1977), Lapidus (1978), Lobodzinska (1977), Pleck (1977), Sokolowska (1965), Walker (1970). Even among unmarried cohabiting couples, household labor generally still is divided along traditional lines, with the women doing far more of it

than the men (Stafford, Beckman, and Dibona, 1977). For a fine article on the "politics of housework," see Mainardi (1970).

20. Enough has been written on the phenomenon of "blaming the victim" that it is not necessary to detail it here. For a classic book on the subject, however, see Ryan (1971).

21. For identification, see Chapter 4, note 5.

22. For identification, see note 10 above.

23. Forty-three-year-old graduate student, married twenty-one years to a professor.

24. In an article entitled "Weight-loss Surgery Might Also Produce Strains On Marriage," *The Wall Street Journal* (July 31, 1978) tells of research reported in the *Journal of the American Medical Association* that found that marital stress often accompanies large weight losses in women because they feel more self-confident, become more expressive and assertive, and are interested in spending more time outside the home. Husbands feel threatened and fear abandonment, the researchers conclude, citing typical words from one man: "She has got it into her head that she's too good for anybody, and that includes me."

25. Smith (1977) writes compellingly from her own experience about the costs to a woman of putting her feet on a career path. Although she says she would do it again, she concludes that she would "never push someone to do what I have done."

26. The literature on dual-career families affirms this point repeatedly (Darley, 1976; Epstein, 1971; Heckman, Bryson, and Bryson, 1977; Holmstrom, 1972; Hunt and Hunt, 1977a; Poloma, 1972; Poloma and Garland, 1971; Rapoport and Rapoport, 1971, 1976).

27. Forty-seven-year-old bookkeeper, married twenty-eight years to a construction worker.

28. Forty-six-year-old woman, married twenty-three years to a professor, who turned down a management position in the firm where she has worked for six years.

29. For identification, see note 27 above. This woman turned down the job of assistant credit manager for fear of damaging her marriage.

30. Forty-one-year-old executive secretary, married twenty-two years to a plumbing contractor. Although she is hungry to return to school to complete a B.A., she has decided against it for fear of the consequences to her marriage.

31. Forty-five-year-old secretary, married twenty-four years to a warehouse supervisor.

32. For an excellent edited volume on depression, see Gaylin (1968); also Weissman and Paykel (1974), Chapter 1, for a brief overview of the literature.

33. Bart (1967), Weissman and Paykel (1974).

34. Fifty-three-year-old substitute teacher, married thirty years to a certified public accountant.

35. See note 31 above.

36. For identification, see Chapter 3, note 13.

37. Forty-eight-year-old school counselor, seven years on the job, married twenty-seven years to an engineering executive.

38. For identification, see Chapter 4, note 5.

39. Lowenthal and Weiss (1976) and Mayer (1969) also note that the long-range goals of women and men at midlife are often in conflict because women look forward to these years in the hope of entering some activity or interest beyond the family, while men look forward to them in the hope of being yet more pampered by their wives.

Afterword: "Tell Them, Will You—TELL THEM!"

1. My thanks to Arlie Hochschild for this evocative phrase.
2. Gould (1974):73.
3. Ibid., p. 180.

Appendix: About the Study

1. Acker (1973); Felson and Knoke (1974); Nilson (1976); Rossi, et al. (1974).

2. For the same reasons, other minorities as well are not represented here.

3. Throughout the process, of course, we remained alert to the emergence of new data that required the reformulation or refinement of existing categories or the generation of new ones.

Bibliography

Abramowitz, Christine V. "Blaming the Mother: An Experimental Investigation of Sex-Role Bias in Countertransference." *Psychology of Women Quarterly* 2 (1977):24–34.

Acker, Joan. "Women and Social Stratification: A Case of Intellectual Sexism." In Joan Huber, ed., *Changing Women in a Changing Society.* Chicago: University of Chicago Press, 1973.

Adams, Margaret. "The Compassion Trap." In Vivian Gornick and Barbara K. Moran, eds., *Woman in Sexist Society.* New York: Basic Books, 1971.

———. *Single Blessedness.* New York: Basic Books, 1976.

Aldous, Joan. "The Making of Family Roles and Family Change." *The Family Coordinator* 23 (1974):231–236.

Altman, Sydney L., and Grossman, Frances Kaplan. "Women's Career Plans and Maternal Employment." *Psychology of Women Quarterly* 1 (1977):365–376.

American Medical Association, eds. *Quality of Life: The Middle Years.* Acton, Mass.: Publishing Sciences Group, 1974.

Amundsen, Kirsten. *The Silenced Majority.* Englewood Cliffs, N.J.: Prentice-Hall, 1971.

Andreas, Carol. *Sex and Caste in America.* Englewood Cliffs, N.J.: Prentice-Hall, 1971.

Applegarth, Adrienne. "Some Observations on Work Inhibitions in Women." In Harold P. Blum, ed., *Female Psychology: Contemporary Psychoanalytic Views.* New York: International Universities Press, 1977.

Araji, Sharon K. "Husbands' and Wives' Attitude-Behavior Congruence on Family Roles." *Journal of Marriage and the Family* 39 (1977):309–320.

Ariés, Philippe. *Centuries of Childhood: A Social History of Family Life.* New York: Vintage Books, 1962.

Arlen, Michael J. "Three Views on Women." In *The View From Highway 1.* New York: Ballantine Books, 1974.

Arnott, Catherine C. "Husbands' Attitude and Wives' Commitment to Employment." *Journal of Marriage and the Family* 34 (1972): 673–684.

Aronowitz, Stanley. *False Promises.* New York: McGraw-Hill, 1973.

Artson, Barbara Friedman. "Mid-Life Women: Homemakers, Volunteers, Professionals." Ph.D. dissertation. California School of Professional Psychology, Berkeley, 1978.

Astin, Helen S. "Continuing Education and the Development of Adult Women." *The Counseling Psychologist* 6 (1976):55–60.

Astin, Helen S.; Suniewick, Nancy; and Dweck, Susan, eds. *Women: A Bibliography on their Education and Careers.* New York: Behavioral Publications, 1974.

Astin, Helen S.; Parelman, Allison; and Fisher, Anne. *Sex Roles: A Research Bibliography.* Washington, D.C.: U.S. Government Printing Office, 1975.

August, Harry. "Psychological Aspects of Personal Adjustment." In Irma H. Gross, ed., *Potentialities of Women in the Middle Years.* East Lansing: Michigan State University Press, 1956.

Babcox, Deborah, and Belkin, Madeline, eds. *Liberation Now.* New York: Dell Publishing, 1971.

Bachtold, Louise M. "Personality Characteristics of Women of Distinction." *Psychology of Women Quarterly* 1 (1976): 70–78.

Bahr, Stephen J. "A Comment on 'The Study of Family Power Structure: A Review, 1960–1969.'" *Journal of Marriage and the Family* 34 (1972):239–243.

———. "Effects on Family Power and Division of Labor in the Family." In Lois Wladis Hoffman and F. Ivan Nye, eds., *Working Mothers.* San Francisco: Jossey-Bass, 1974.

Ballantyne, Sheila. *Norma Jean, the Termite Queen.* Garden City, N.Y.: Doubleday & Co., 1975.

Balswick, Jack, and Peek, Charles. "The Inexpressive Male: A Tragedy of American Society." In Arlene Skolnick and Jerome Skolnick, eds., *Intimacy, Family, and Society.* Boston: Little, Brown, 1974.

Balswick, Jack, and Avertt, Christine Proctor. "Differences in Expressiveness: Gender, Interpersonal Orientation, and Perceived Parental Expressiveness as Contributing Factors." *Journal of Marriage and the Family* 39 (1977):121–127.

Bane, Mary Jo. *Here to Stay: American Families in the Twentieth Century.* New York: Basic Books, 1976.

Bardwick, Judith M. "Middle Age and a Sense of the Future." Paper presented at the Seventieth Annual Meeting of the American Sociological Association. San Francisco, California, August 25–29, 1975.

———. "When Women Work." In Rosalind K. Loring and Herbert A. Otto, eds., *New Life Options: The Working Woman's Resource Book.* New York: McGraw-Hill, 1976.

Bardwick, Judith M., and Douvan, Elizabeth. "Ambivalence: The Socialization of Women." In Vivian Gornick and Barbara K. Moran, eds., *Woman in Sexist Society.* New York: Basic Books, 1971.

Barglow, Peter, and Schaefer, Margaret. "A New Female Psychology?" In Harold P. Blum, ed., *Female Psychology: Contemporary Psychoanalytic Views.* New York: International Universities Press, 1977.

Barker-Benfield, Ben. "The Spermatic Economy: A Nineteenth-Century View of Sexuality." In Michael Gordon, ed., *The American Family in Social-Historical Perspective.* New York: St. Martin's Press, 1973.

Barnett, Rosalind C., and Baruch, Grace K. "Women in the Middle Years: A Critique of Research and Theory." *Psychology of Women Quarterly* 3 (1978): 187–197.

Bart, Pauline B. "Depression in Middle-Aged Women: Some Sociocultural Factors." Ph.D. dissertation. Department of Sociology, University of California, Los Angeles, 1967. University Microfilms # 68–7452.

————. "Why Women's Status Changes in Middle Age." *Sociological Symposium* 3 (1969):1–18.

————. "Portnoy's Mother's Complaint." *Trans-action* 8 (1970): 69–74.

————. "Depression in Middle-Aged Women." In Vivian Gornick and Barbara K. Moran, eds., *Woman in Sexist Society.* New York: Basic Books, 1971.

————. "Pioneers, Professionals, Returnees, Penelopes and Portnoy's Mothers." Paper presented at the Twenty-Sixth Annual Conference on Aging Women: Life Span Challenges. The Institute of Gerontology, University of Michigan and Wayne State University, 1973.

Baruch, Grace K. "Maternal Influences Upon College Women's Attitudes Toward Women and Work." *Developmental Psychology* 6 (1972):32–37.

————. "Girls Who Perceive Themselves as Competent: Some Antecedents and Correlates." *Psychology of Women Quarterly* 1 (1976):38–49.

Baxall, Martha, and Reagan, Barbara B., eds. "Women and the Workplace: The Implications of Occupational Segregation." *Signs* 1 (1976):1–317.

Bem, Sandra. "The Measurement of Psychological Androgyny." *Journal of Consulting Clinical Psychology* 42 (1974): 165–172.

Bem, Sandra, and Bem, Daryl J. "Training the Woman to Know Her Place." In Louise Kapp Howe, ed., *The Future of the Family.* New York: Simon & Schuster, 1972.

Benedek, Therese. *Psychosexual Functions in Women.* New York: Ronald Press, 1952.

Benét, Mary Kathleen. *The Secretarial Ghetto.* New York: McGraw-Hill, 1972.

Bequaert, Lucia H. *Single Women: Alone and Together.* Boston: Beacon Press, 1976.

Bernard, Jessie. "The Paradox of a Happy Marriage." In Vivian Gornick and Barbara K. Moran, eds., *Woman in Sexist Society.* New York: Basic Books, 1971.

——. "Changing Family Life Styles: One Role, Two Roles, Shared Roles." In Louise Kapp Howe, ed., *The Future of the Family.* New York: Simon and Schuster, 1972.

——. *The Future of Marriage.* New York: Bantam Books, 1973.

——. *The Future of Motherhood.* Baltimore: Penguin Books, 1975.

——. "Change and Stability in Sex-Role Norms and Behavior." *Journal of Social Issues* 32 (1976a):207–223.

——. "Where Are We Now? Some Thoughts on the Current Scene." *Psychology of Women Quarterly* 1 (1976b):21–37.

——. "Historical and Structural Barriers to Occupational Desegregation." *Signs* 1 (1976c):87–94.

Berquist, Laura. "Recycling Lives." *Ms.* 11 (1973):62ff.

Bibring, Edward. "The Mechanism of Depression." In Phyllis Greenacre, ed., *The Mechanism of Depression in Affective Disorder.* New York: International Universities Press, 1953.

Bird, Caroline. *Born Female.* Rev. ed. New York: Pocket Books, 1971.

Blake, Judith. "Coercive Pronatalism and American Population Policy." In Rose Laub Coser, ed., *The Family: Its Structures and Functions.* New York: St. Martin's Press, 1974.

Blatt, Sidney J. "Levels of Object Representation in Anaclitic and Introjective Depression." In Ruth S. Eissler, et al., eds., *The Psychoanalytic Study of the Child,* vol. 29. New Haven: Yale University Press, 1974.

Blau, Francine D., and Jusenius, Carol L. "Economists' Approaches to Sex Segregation in the Labor Market: An Appraisal." *Signs* 1 (1976):181–199.

Block, Jeanne H. "Issues, Problems, and Pitfalls in Assessing Sex Differences: A Critical Review of *The Psychology of Sex Differences.*" *Merill-Palmer Quarterly* 22 (1976):283–308.

Block, Ruth H. "American Feminine Ideals in Transition: The Rise of the Moral Mother, 1785–1815." *Feminist Studies* 4 (1978): 102–126.

Blood, Robert O., Jr., and Wolfe, Donald M. *Husbands and Wives.* New York: Free Press, 1960.

Blum, Harold P. *Female Psychology: Contemporary Psychoanalytic Views.* New York: International Universities Press, 1977.

Borque, Linda Brookover, and Back, Kurt. "Middle Years Seen Through the Life Graph." *Sociological Symposium* 3 (1969):19–30.

Boulding, Elise. "Familial Constraints on Women's Work Roles." *Signs* 1 (1976):95–117.

Boulding, Kenneth. "The Social Institutions of Occupational Segregation—Comment I." *Signs* 1 (1976):75–77.

Bourne, Patricia Gerald, and Wikler, Norma Juliet. "Commitment and the Cultural Mandate: Women in Medicine." *Social Problems* 25 (1978):430–440.

Bowlby, John. *Attachment.* New York: Basic Books, 1969.

———. *Separation.* New York: Basic Books, 1973.

Brandwein, Ruth A.; Brown, Carol A.; and Fox, Elizabeth Maury. "Women and Children Last: The Social Situation of Divorced Mothers and Their Families." *Journal of Marriage and the Family* 36 (1974):498–514.

Braverman, Harry. *Labor and Monopoly Capitalism: The Degradation of Work in the Twentieth Century.* New York: Monthly Review Press, 1974.

Brim, Orville G., Jr. "Theories of the Male Mid-Life Crisis." *The Counseling Psychologist* 6 (1976):2–9.

Broderick, Carlfred B., and Bernard, Jessie, eds. *The Individual, Sex, and Society.* Baltimore: Johns Hopkins Press, 1969.

Bromley, D. B. *The Psychology of Human Aging.* 2d ed. Harmondsworth, England: Penguin Books, 1976.

Broverman, Inge, et al. "Sex-Role Stereotypes: A Current Appraisal." *Journal of Social Issues* 28 (1972):59–78.

Brown, Carol A., et al. "Divorce: Chance of A New Lifetime." *Journal of Social Issues* 32 (1976):119–133.

Bruce, John Allen. "The Role of Mothers in the Social Placement of Daughters: Marriage or Work?" *Journal of Marriage and the Family* 36 (1974):492–497.

Burton, Cyndy, and Wintriss, Ann, eds. "Women in Midlife Crisis Conference." *Human Ecology Forum* 7 (1976):1–17.

Cagan, Elizabeth. "The Selling of the Women's Movement." *Social Policy* 9 (1978):4–12.

Caine, Lynn. *Widow.* New York: Bantam Books, 1973.

Cameron, Norman. *Personality Development and Psychopathology: A Dynamic Approach.* Boston: Houghton Mifflin, 1963.

Cardozo, Arlene Rossen. *Woman at Home.* Garden City, N.Y.: Doubleday & Co., 1976.

Carlson, Rae. "Understanding Women: Implications for Personality Theory and Research." *Journal of Social Issues* 28 (1972):17–32.

Cavan, Ruth Shonle, ed. *Marriage and Family in the Modern World.* 3d ed. New York: Thomas Y. Crowell, 1969.

Chafe, William H. *The American Woman: Her Changing Social, Economic, and Political Roles, 1920–1970.* New York: Oxford University Press, 1974.

Chafetz, Janet Saltzman. *Masculine/Feminine or Human?* Itasca, Ill.: F. E. Peacock, 1974.

Chesler, Phyllis. *Women and Madness.* New York: Doubleday, 1972.

———. *About Men.* New York: Simon and Schuster, 1978.

Chesler, Phyllis, and Goodman, Emily Jane. *Women, Money and Power.* New York: Bantam Books, 1976.

Chesser, Eustace. *Love Without Fear.* New York: Roy Publishers, 1947.

Chew, Peter. *The Inner World of the Middle-Aged Man.* Boston: Houghton Mifflin, 1977.

Chilman, Catherine S. "Some Psychosocial Aspects of Female Sexuality." *Family Coordinator* 23 (1974):123–131.

Chodorow, Nancy. "Being and Doing: A Cross-Cultural Examination of the Socialization of Males and Females." In Vivian Gornick and Barbara K. Moran, eds., *Woman in Sexist Society.* New York: Basic Books, 1971.

———. "Oedipal Asymmetries and Heterosexual Knots." *Social Problems* 23 (1976):454–468.

————. *The Reproduction of Mothering.* Berkeley: University of California Press, 1978.

Christensen, Harold, and Gregg, Christina. "Changing Sex Norms in America and Scandinavia." In Arlene Skolnick and Jerome Skolnick, eds., *Intimacy, Family, and Society.* Boston: Little, Brown, 1974.

Clavan, Sylvia. "Changing Female Sexual Behavior and Future Family Structure." *Pacific Sociological Review* 15 (1973):295–300.

Cole, David; King, Kraig; and Newcomb, Andrew. "Grade Expectations as a Function of Sex, Academic Discipline, and Sex of Instructor." *Psychology of Women Quarterly* 1 (1977):380–385.

Collins, Randall. "A Conflict Theory of Sexual Stratification." *Social Problems* 19 (1971):3–21.

Condry, John, and Dyer, Sharon. "Fear of Success: Attribution of Cause to the Victim." *Journal of Social Issues* 32 (1976):63–83.

Cook, Alice H. *The Working Mother.* Ithaca: New York State School of Industrial and Labor Relations, Cornell University, 1975.

Coser, Rose Laub, ed. *The Family: Its Structures and Functions.* 2d ed. New York: St. Martin's Press, 1974.

Cott, Nancy F. *Bonds of Womanhood.* New Haven: Yale University Press, 1977.

Cowan, Gloria. "Therapist Judgments of Clients' Sex-Role Problems." *Psychology of Women Quarterly* 1 (1976):115–124.

Cuber, John F., and Harroff, Peggy B. "The More Total View: Relationships Among Men and Women of the Upper Middle Class." *Marriage and Family Living* 25 (1963):140–145.

Cummings, Laurie Davidson. "Value Stretch in Definitions of Career Among College Women: Horatia Alger as Feminist Model." *Social Problems* 25 (1977):65–74.

Curlee, Joan. "Alcoholism and the Empty Nest." *Bulletin of the Menninger Clinic* 33 (1969):165–171.

Curtin, Katie. *Women in China.* New York: Pathfinder Press, 1975.

Dahlström, Edmund, ed. *The Changing Roles of Men and Women.* Boston: Beacon Press, 1971.

Daniels, Arlene Kaplan; Joslyn, Kersten; and Ruzek, Sheryl. "The Place of Volunteerism in the Lives of Women: Analysis of Four Types of Volunteer Experience." Final report, National Institute of Mental Health, Grant # MH 26294–01, 1975.

Darley, Susan. "Big-Time Careers for the Little Woman: A Dual-Role Dilemma." *Journal of Social Issues* 32 (1976):85–98.

Davidson, Sara. *Loose Change*. Garden City, N.Y.: Doubleday & Co., 1977.

Davitz, Joel, and Davitz, Lois. *Making It From 40 to 50*. New York: Random House, 1976.

Dean, Stanley R. "Geriatric Sexuality: Normal, Needed and Neglected." *Geriatrics* 29 (1974):134–137.

de Beauvoir, Simone. *The Second Sex*. New York: Bantam Books, 1961.

Decter, Midge. *The New Chastity and Other Arguments Against Women's Liberation*. New York: Coward, McCann & Geoghegan, 1972.

De Mott, Benjamin. "After the Sexual Revolution." *Atlantic* 238 (1976):71–93.

Densen-Gerber, Judianne. *Walk in My Shoes*. New York: Saturday Review Press, 1976.

Denzin, Norman K. *Childhood Socialization*. San Francisco: Jossey-Bass, 1977.

De Rosis, Helen A., and Pellegrino, Victoria Y. *The Book of Hope: How Women Can Overcome Depression*. New York: Bantam Books, 1977.

Deutsch, Helene. *The Psychology of Women*, vols. 1 & 2. New York: Bantam Books, 1973.

Deutscher, Irwin. "The Quality of Postparental Life: Definitions of the Situation." *Journal of Marriage and the Family* 26 (1964): 52–59.

————. "Socialization for Postparental Life." In Ruth Shonle Cavan, ed., *Marriage and Family in the Modern World*. New York: Thomas Y. Crowell, 1969a.

————. "From Parental to Postparental Life: Exploring Shifting Expectations." *Sociological Symposium* 3 (1969b):47–60.

Deykin, Eva Y., et al. "The Empty Nest: Psychosocial Aspects of Conflict Between Depressed Women and Their Grown Children." *American Journal of Psychiatry* 122 (1966):1422–1426.

Dinnerstein, Dorothy. *The Mermaid and The Minotaur.* New York: Harper & Row, 1976.

Dixon, Ruth B. "Measuring Equality Between the Sexes." *Journal of Social Issues* 32 (1976): 19–32.

Douglas, Ann. *The Feminization of American Culture.* New York: Alfred Knopf, 1977.

Douglas, Jack D. *Investigative Social Research.* Beverly Hills: Sage Publications, 1976.

Douvan, Elizabeth. "The Role of Models in Women's Professional Development." *Psychology of Women Quarterly* 1 (1976):5–20.

du Plessix Gray, Francine. *Lovers and Tyrants.* New York: Pocket Books, 1977.

Easton, Barbara Leslie. "Industrialization and Femininity: A Case Study of Nineteenth Century New England." *Social Problems* 23 (1976):389–401.

Elder, Glen H., Jr., and Rockwell, Richard. "Marital Timing on Women's Life Patterns." *Journal of Family History* 1 (1976): 34–53.

Engels, Frederick. *The Origin of the Family, Private Property, and the State.* New York: International Publishers, 1942.

Epstein, Cynthia F. *Woman's Place.* Berkeley: University of California Press, 1971.

––––––. "Law Partners and Marital Partners." *Human Relations* 24 (1971):549–564.

Epstein, Cynthia F., and Goode, William J., eds. *The Other Half: Roads to Women's Equality.* Englewood Cliffs, N.J.: Prentice-Hall, 1971.

Epstein, Joseph. *Divorced in America.* New York: Penguin Books, 1975.

Ericksen, Julia A. "An Analysis of the Journey to Work for Women." *Social Problems* 24 (1977):428–435.

Erikson, Erik H. *Childhood and Society.* New York: W. W. Norton, 1950.

———. "Inner and Outer Space: Reflections on Womanhood." In Robert Jay Lifton, ed., *The Woman in America.* Boston: Beacon Press, 1967.

———. *Identity: Youth and Crisis.* New York: W. W. Norton, 1968.

Essman, Clifford S. "Sibling Relations as Socialization for Parenthood." *The Family Coordinator* 26 (1977):259–262.

Estep, Rhoda E.; Burt, Martha R.; and Milligan, Herman J. "The Socialization of Sexual Identity." *Journal of Marriage and the Family* 39 (1977):99–112.

Etaugh, Claire, and Hadley, Terry. "Causal Attributions of Male and Female Performance by Young Children." *Psychology of Women Quarterly* 2 (1977):16–23.

Falbo, Toni. "Relationships Between Sex, Sex Role, and Social Influence." *Psychology of Women Quarterly* 2 (1977):62–72.

Farber, Leslie H. "He Said, She Said." *Review of Existential Psychology and Psychiatry* 11 (1972):116–129.

Farber, Seymour M., and Wilson, Roger H. L., eds. *The Potential of Women.* New York: McGraw-Hill, 1963.

Farrell, Warren. *The Liberated Man.* New York: Bantam Books, 1975.

Feely, Ellen, and Pyne, Helen. "The Menopause: Facts and Misconceptions." *Nursing Forum* 14 (1975):74–86.

Feeney, Helen M. "The Range and Benefits of Volunteer Service." In Rosalind K. Loring and Herbert A. Otto, eds., *New Life Options: The Working Woman's Resource Book.* New York: McGraw-Hill, 1976.

Feigen-Fasteau, Mark. *The Male Machine.* New York: McGraw-Hill, 1974.

Feldstein, Ivor. *Sex in Later Life.* Middlesex, England: Penguin Books, 1973.

Felson, Marcus, and Knoke, David. "Social Status and the Married Woman." *Journal of Marriage and the Family* 36 (1974):516–521.

Ferree, Myra Marx. "The Confused American Housewife." *Psychology Today* 10 (1976a):76 ff.

———. "Working-Class Jobs: Housework and Paid Work as Sources of Satisfaction." *Social Problems* 23 (1976b):431–441.

Filene, Peter Gabriel. *Him/Her/Self: Sex Roles in Modern America.* New York: Mentor Books, 1975.

Firestone, Shulamith. *The Dialectic of Sex: The Case for Feminist Revolution.* New York: Bantam Books, 1971.

Fisher, Seymour. *Understanding the Female Orgasm.* New York: Bantam Books, 1973.

Fishman, Pamela M. "Interaction: The Work Women Do." *Social Problems* 25 (1978):397–406.

Flax, Jane. "The Conflict Between Nurturance and Autonomy in Mother-Daughter Relationships and Within Feminism." *Feminist Studies* 4 (1978):171–189.

Flexner, Eleanor. *Century of Struggle: The Woman's Rights Movement in the United States.* New York: Atheneum, 1968.

Flint, Marcha. "The Menopause: Reward or Punishment?" *Psychosomatics* 16 (1975):161–163.

Foote, Audrey C. "The Kids Who Won't Leave Home." *Atlantic* 241 (1978):118–122.

Fox, Greer Litton. " 'Nice Girl': Social Control of Women Through a Value Construct." *Signs* 2 (1977):805–817.

Fraiberg, Selma. *Every Child's Birthright: In Defense of Mothering.* New York: Basic Books, 1977.

Frankfort, Ellen. *Vaginal Politics.* New York: Bantam Books, 1973.

Freeman, Jo. "The Social Construction of the Second Sex." In Arlene Skolnick and Jerome Skolnick, eds., *Intimacy, Family, and Society.* Boston: Little, Brown, 1974.

———, ed. *Women: A Feminist Perspective.* Palo Alto, Calif.: Mayfield Publishing, 1975.

French, Marilyn. *The Women's Room.* New York: Summit Books, 1977.

Friday, Nancy. *My Mother/My Self.* New York: Delacorte Press, 1977.

Friedan, Betty. *The Feminine Mystique.* New York: W. W. Norton, 1963.

Frieze, Irene Hanson, and Ramsey, Sheila J. "Nonverbal Maintenance of Traditional Sex Roles." *Journal of Social Issues* 32 (1976):133–141.

Fromm, Erich. *Escape from Freedom.* New York: Avon Books, 1941.

Fuchs, Estelle. *The Second Season: Life, Love and Sex—Women in the Middle Years.* Garden City, N.Y.: Anchor Press/Doubleday, 1977.

Fullerton, Howard N., Jr., and Byrne, James J. "Length of Working Life for Men and Women, 1970." Special Labor Force Report #187. U.S. Department of Labor, Bureau of Labor Statistics. Washington, D.C.: U.S. Government Printing Office, 1976.

Gagnon, John H., and Simon, William. *Sexual Conduct: The Social Sources of Human Sexuality.* Chicago: Aldine Publishing, 1973.

Gagnon, John H., and Henderson, Bruce. "The Psychology of Sexual Development." In Arlene Skolnick and Jerome Skolnick, eds., *Family in Transition.* 2d ed. Boston: Little, Brown, 1977.

Galenson, Eleanor. "Scientific Proceedings—Panel Reports." *Journal of the American Psychoanalytic Association* 24 (1976):141–160.

Gannon, Martin J., and Hendrickson, D. Hunt. "Career Orientation and Job Satisfaction Among Working Wives." *Journal of Applied Psychology* 57 (1973):339–340.

Gardiner, Judith Kegan. "A Wake for Mother: The Maternal Deathbed in Women's Fiction." *Feminist Studies* 4 (1978):146–165.

Garland, Howard. "Sometimes Nothing Succeeds Like Success: Reactions to Success and Failure in Sex-Linked Occupations." *Psychology of Women Quarterly* 2 (1977):50–61.

Garland, T. Neal. "The Better Half? The Male in the Dual Profession Family." In Constantina Safilios-Rothschild, ed., *Toward a Sociology of Women,* Lexington, Mass.: Xerox College Publishing, 1972.

Garskof, Michelle Hoffnung, ed. *Roles Women Play: Readings Toward Women's Liberation.* Belmont, Calif.: Wadsworth Publishing, 1971.

Garson, Barbara. "Women's Work." *Working Papers for a New Society* 1 (1973):5–16.

———. *All the Livelong Day*. New York: Penguin Books, 1977.

Gaylin, Willard, ed. *The Meaning of Despair*. New York: Jason Aronson, 1968.

Gilder, George F. *Sexual Suicide*. New York: Quadrangle Books, 1973.

Gillespie, Dair. "Who Has the Power? The Marital Struggle." In Hans P. Dreitzel, ed., *Family, Marriage, and the Struggle of the Sexes*. New York: Macmillan, 1972.

Gittelson, Natalie. *Dominus: A Woman Looks at Men's Lives*. New York: Farrar, Straus, Giroux, 1978.

Glaser, Barney G., and Strauss, Anselm L. *The Discovery of Grounded Theory: Strategies for Qualitative Research*. Chicago: Aldine Publishing, 1967.

Glenn, Evelyn Nakano, and Feldberg, Roslyn L. "Degraded and Deskilled: the Proletarianization of Clerical Work." *Social Problems* 25 (1977):52–64.

Glenn, Norval D. "Psychological Well-Being in the Post Parental Stage: Some Evidence from National Surveys." *Journal of Marriage and the Family* 37 (1975):105–110.

Glenn, Norval D., and Weaver, Charles N. "The Marital Happiness of Remarried Divorced Persons." *Journal of Marriage and the Family* 39 (1977):331–337.

Glick, Paul C. "Updating the Life Cycle of the Family." *Journal of Marriage and the Family* 39 (1977):5–13.

Gold, Doris B. "Women and Voluntarism." In Vivian Gornick and Barbara K. Moran, eds., *Woman in Sexist Society*. New York: Basic Books, 1971.

Goode, William J. *Women in Divorce*. New York: Free Press, 1956.

Gordon, Chad, and Johnson, Gayle, eds. *Readings in Human Sexuality: Contemporary Perspectives*. New York: Harper & Row, 1976.

Gordon, Francine E., and Strober, Myra H., eds. *Bringing Women into Management*. New York: McGraw-Hill, 1975.

Gordon, Michael, ed. *The American Family in Social-Historical Perspective*. New York: St. Martin's Press, 1973.

Gordon, Michael, and Shankweiler, Penelope. "Different Equals Less: Female Sexuality in Recent Marriage Manuals." In Arlene Skolnick and Jerome Skolnick, eds., *Intimacy, Family and Society.* Boston: Little, Brown, 1974.

Gornick, Vivian, and Moran, Barbara K., eds. *Woman in Sexist Society: Studies in Power and Powerlessness.* New York: Basic Books, 1971.

Gould, Lois. *Final Analysis.* New York: Avon Books, 1974.

Gould, Roger L. "The Phases of Adult Life: A Study in Developmental Psychology." *American Journal of Psychiatry* 129 (1972): 33–43.

———. *Transformations: Growth and Change in Adult Life.* New York: Simon and Schuster, 1978.

Gove, Walter R., and Tudor, Jeannette F. "Adult Sex Roles and Mental Illness." In Joan Huber, ed., *Changing Women in a Changing Society.* Chicago: University of Chicago Press, 1973.

Greene, Bernard L.; Lustig, Noel; and Lee, Ronald L. "Clinical Observations of Sex as a Reverberation of the Total Relationship." *Journal of Sex and Marital Therapy* 2 (1976):284–288.

Greer, Germaine. *The Female Eunuch.* New York: McGraw-Hill, 1971.

Grønseth, Erik. "The Breadwinner Trap." In Louise Kapp Howe, ed., *The Future of the Family.* New York: Simon & Schuster, 1972.

Gross, Irma H., ed. *Potentialities of Women in the Middle Years.* East Lansing: Michigan State University Press, 1956.

Grossman, Allyson Sherman. "Women in the Labor Force: The Early Years." *Monthly Labor Review* 98 (1975):3–9.

———. "Children of Working Mothers, March 1976." Special Labor Force Report #205. United States Department of Labor, Bureau of Labor Statistics. Washington, D.C.: U.S. Government Printing Office, 1976.

———. "The Labor Force Patterns of Divorced and Separated Women." *Monthly Labor Review* 100 (1977):48–53.

Group for the Advancement of Psychiatry. *The Educated Woman: Prospects and Problems.* Vol. 9, report # 92. New York: Mental Health Materials Center, 1976.

Hamburg, Beatrix A. "Coping in Early Adolescence: The Special Challenges of the Junior High School Period." In Silvano Arieti, ed., *American Handbook of Psychiatry.* 2d ed., vol. 1. New York: Basic Books, 1974.

Hammer, Signe. *Daughters and Mothers: Mothers and Daughters.* New York: Signet Books, 1975a.

———, ed. *Women: Body and Culture.* New York: Harper & Row, 1975b.

Hansson, Robert O.; Chernovetz, Mary E.; and Jones, Warren H. "Maternal Employment and Androgyny." *Psychology of Women Quarterly* 2 (1977):76–78.

Harbeson, Gladys E. *Choice and Challenge for the American Woman.* Rev. ed. Cambridge, Mass.: Schenkman Publishing, 1971.

Harkins, Elizabeth B. "Effects of Empty Nest Transition on Self-Report of Psychological and Physical Well-Being." *Journal of Marriage and the Family* 40 (1978):546–556.

Harragan, Betty Lehan. *Games Mother Never Taught You.* New York: Warner Books, 1977.

Harris, Janet. *The Prime of Ms. America: The American Woman at 40.* New York: G. P. Putnam's, 1975.

Harrison, Barbara Grizzuti. *Unlearning the Lie: Sexism in School.* New York: William Morrow, 1974.

———. " 'Write the Truth,' My Son Said. 'Write About Me.' " *Ms.* 6 (1978):14–18.

Hartmann, Heidi. "Capitalism, Patriarchy, and Job Segregation by Sex." *Signs* 1 (1976): 137–169.

———. "Comment on Marnie W. Mueller's 'The Economic Determinants of Volunteer Work by Women.' " *Signs* 1 (1976):-773–776.

Havighurst, Robert J. "Changing Roles of Women in the Middle Years." In Irma H. Gross, ed., *Potentialities of Women in the*

Middle Years. East Lansing: Michigan State University Press, 1956.

Heckman, Norma A.; Bryson, Rebecca; and Bryson, Jeff B. "Problems of Professional Couples: A Content Analysis." *Journal of Marriage and the Family* 39 (1977):323–330.

Heer, David M. "Dominance and the Working Wife." *Social Forces* 36 (1958):341–347.

Heilbrun, Alfred B., Jr. "Identification with the Father and Sex-Role Development of the Daughter." *The Family Coordinator* 25 (1976):411–416.

Helson, Ravenna. "Women Mathematicians and the Creative Personality." *Journal of Consulting and Clinical Psychology* 36 (1971):210–220.

Hennig, Margaret, and Jardim, Anne. *The Managerial Woman.* Garden City, N.Y.: Anchor Press/Doubleday, 1977.

Henry, Jules. "Forty-Year-Old Jitters in Married Urban Women." In Carolyn Perucci and Dena B. Targ, eds., *Marriage and the Family.* New York: David McKay, 1974.

Hepler, Harold R., ed. "The Sociology of the Middle Years." *Sociological Symposium* 3 (1969):1–158.

Herman, Jeanne, and Gyllstrom, Karen K. "Working Men and Women: Inter- and Intra-Role Conflict." *Psychology of Women Quarterly* 1 (1977):319–333.

Hite, Shere. *The Hite Report.* New York: Dell Publishing, 1976.

Hobbs, Daniel F., Jr., and Cole, Sue Peck. "Transition to Parenthood: A Decade Replication." *Journal of Marriage and the Family* 38 (1976):723–731.

Hochschild, Arlie Russell, ed. "The American Woman." *Transaction* 8 (1970):1–112.

———. *The Unexpected Community.* Englewood Cliffs, N.J.: Prentice-Hall, 1973.

———. "A Review of Sex Role Research." *American Journal of Sociology* 78 (1973):1011–1029.

Hoffman, Lois Wladis. "Effects of the Employment of Mothers on Parental Power Relations and the Division of Household Tasks." *Marriage and Family Living* 22 (1960):27–35.

————. "Early Childhood Experiences and Women's Achievement Motives." *Journal of Social Issues* 28 (1972):129–155.

Hoffman, Lois Wladis, and Nye, F. Ivan. *Working Mothers.* San Francisco: Jossey-Bass, 1974.

Holmstrom, Lynda L. *The Two Career Family.* Cambridge, Mass.: Schenkman Publishing, 1972.

Holter, Harriet. "Sex Roles and Social Change." *Acta Sociologica* 14 (1971):2–12.

Horner, Matina S. "Toward an Understanding of Achievement-Related Conflicts in Women." *Journal of Social Issues* 28 (1972): 157–175.

Horney, Karen. *Feminine Psychology.* London: Routledge & Kegan Paul, 1967.

————. "The Flight from Womanhood." In Jean Baker Miller, ed., *Psychoanalysis and Women.* New York: Penguin Books, 1973.

————. "The Problem of Feminine Masochism." In Jean Baker Miller, ed., *Psychoanalysis and Women.* New York: Penguin Books, 1973.

Howe, Louise Kapp, ed. *The Future of the Family.* New York: Simon & Schuster, 1972.

Huber, Joan. "Ambiguities in Identity Transformation: From Sugar and Spice to Professor." *Notre Dame Journal of Education* 2 (1972):338–347.

————, ed. *Changing Women in a Changing Society.* Chicago: University of Chicago Press, 1973.

Hunt, Janet G., and Hunt, Larry L. "Dilemmas and Contradictions of Status: The Case of the Dual-Career Family." *Social Problems* 24 (1977a):407–416.

————. "Race, Daughters and Father-Loss: Does Absence Make the Girl Grow Stronger?" *Social Problems* 25 (1977b):90–102.

Hunt, Morton. *Sexual Behavior in the 1970's.* Chicago: Playboy Press, 1974.

Hunter, Jean E. "Images of Woman." *Journal of Social Issues* 32 (1976):7–17.

Hyde, Janet S.; Rosenberg, B. G.; and Behrman, Jo Ann. "Tomboyism." *Psychology of Women Quarterly* 2 (1977):73–75.

Jacobson, Shirley, and Klerman, Gerald L. "Interpersonal Dynamics of Hospitalized Depressed Patients' Home Visits." *Journal of Marriage and the Family* 28 (1966):94–102.

Jacoby, Susan. "What Do I Do With The Next Twenty Years?" *The New York Times Magazine* (1973):10ff.

Jacques, Elliott. *Work, Creativity and Social Justice.* New York: International Universities Press, 1970.

Jaffe, A. J. "The Middle Years: Neither Too Young Nor Too Old." *Industrial Gerontology,* special issue (1971):1–90.

Janeway, Elizabeth. *Man's World, Women's Place.* New York: Delta Books, 1971.

———. "On the Power of the Weak." *Signs* 1 (1975):103–109.

Joffe, Carole E. "Child Care: Destroying the Family or Strengthening It?" In Louise Kapp Howe, ed., *The Future of the Family.* New York: Simon & Schuster, 1972.

———. *Friendly Intruders: Childcare Professionals and Family Life.* Berkeley: University of California Press, 1977.

Johnson, Miriam, et al. "Expressiveness Reevaluated." *School Review* 83 (1975):617–644.

Kagan, Jerome. "The Parental Love Trap." *Psychology Today* 12 (1978):54–61, 91.

Kagan, Jerome, and Coles, Robert, eds. *Twelve to Sixteen: Early Adolescence.* New York: W. W. Norton, 1972.

Kahne, Hilda. "Economic Perspectives on the Roles of Women in the American Economy." *Journal of Economic Literature* 13 (1975):1249–1292.

Kanter, Rosabeth Moss. "The Impact of Hierarchical Structure on the Work Behavior of Women and Men." *Social Problems* 23 (1976):415–430.

———. *Men and Women of the Corporation.* New York: Basic Books, 1977.

Kantor, David, and Lehr, William. *Inside the Family.* San Francisco: Jossey-Bass, 1975.

Keller, Suzanne. "The Future Role of Women." *Annals of the American Academy of Political and Social Science* 408 (1973):1–12.

Kelly, Joan B., and Wallerstein, Judith S. "The Effects of Parental Divorce: Experiences of the Child in Early Latency." *American Journal of Orthopsychiatry* 46 (1976):20–32.

Kernberg, Otto F. *Borderline Conditions and Pathological Narcissism.* New York: Jason Aronson, 1957.

———. "Mature Love: Prerequisites and Characteristics." *Journal of American Psychoanalytic Association* 22 (1974):743–768.

———. *Object Relations Theory and Clinical Psychoanalysis.* New York: Jason Aronson, 1976.

Kieren, Dianne; Henton, June; and Marotz, Ramona. *Hers and His: A Problem Solving Approach to Marriage.* Hinsdale, Ill.: Dryden Press, 1975.

Kingston, Maxine Hong. *The Woman Warrior.* New York: Vintage Books, 1977.

Kinsey, Alfred, et al. *Sexual Behavior in the Human Female.* Philadelphia: W. B. Saunders, 1953.

Klein, Deborah Pisetzner. "Women in the Labor Force: The Middle Years." *Monthly Labor Review* 98 (1975):10–16.

Knudsin, Ruth B., ed. *Women and Success: The Anatomy of Achievement.* New York: William Morrow, 1974.

Koedt, Anne. "The Myth of Vaginal Orgasm." In Deborah Babcox and Madeline Belkin, eds., *Liberation Now.* New York: Dell Publishing, 1971.

Koedt, Anne; Levine, Ellen; and Rapone, Anita, eds. *Radical Feminism.* New York: Quadrangle Books, 1973.

Kohlberg, Lawrence. "A Cognitive Developmental Analysis of Sex-Role Concepts." In Arlene Skolnick and Jerome Skolnick, eds., *Intimacy, Family, and Society.* Boston: Little, Brown, 1974.

Komarovsky, Mirra. "Cultural Contradictions and Sex Roles: The Masculine Case." *American Journal of Sociology* 78 (1973):873–884.

———. *Dilemmas of Masculinity.* New York: W. W. Norton, 1976.

Kraditor, Aileen S., ed. *Up From the Pedestal.* Chicago: Quadrangle Books, 1968.

Kunzle, David. "Dress Reform as Antifeminism: A Response to Helene E. Roberts' 'The Exquisite Slave: The Role of Clothes in the Making of the Victorian Woman.' " *Signs* 2 (1977): 570–579.

Kuten, Jay. "Anger, Sexuality, and the Growth of the Ego." *Journal of Sex and Marital Therapy* 2 (1976):289–296.

Lacy, Dan. "Men's Words; Women's Roles." *Saturday Review* (1975):25ff.

Lakoff, Robin. *Language and Woman's Place.* New York: Harper Colophon, 1975.

Lamb, Michael E., and Lamb, Jamie E. "The Nature and Importance of the Father-Infant Relationship." *The Family Coordinator* 25 (1976):379–385.

Lantz, Herman; Schultz, Martin; and O'Hara, Mary. "The Changing American Family from Preindustrial to the Industrial Period: A Final Report." *American Sociological Review* 42 (1977):406–421.

Lapidus, Gail Warshofsky. "Occupational Segregation and Public Policy: A Comparative Analysis of American and Soviet Patterns." *Signs* 1 (1976):119–136.

―――. "The Female Industrial Labor Force: Dilemmas, Reassessments and Options in Current Policy Debates." Conference on Problems of Industrial Labor in the U.S.S.R. The Kennan Institute for Advanced Russian Studies, Washington, D.C., September 27–29, 1977.

―――. *Women in Soviet Society.* Berkely: University of California Press, 1978.

LaRussa, Georgina Williams. "Portia's Decision: Women's Motives for Studying Law and Their Later Career Satisfaction as Attorneys." *Psychology of Women Quarterly* 1 (1977):350–364.

Lasch, Christopher. "Divorce and the Decline of the Family." In Christopher Lasch, *The World of Nations.* New York: Vintage Books, 1974.

―――. *Haven in a Heartless World: The Family Besieged.* New York: Basic Books, 1977.

Laslett, Barbara. "The Family as a Public and Private Institution: An Historical Perspective." In Arlene Skolnick and Jerome Skolnick, eds., *Intimacy, Family, and Society.* Boston: Little, Brown, 1974.

Laslett, Barbara, and Rapoport, Rhona. "Collaborative Interviewing and Interactive Research." *Journal of Marriage and the Family* 37 (1975): 968–977.

Lasoff, Anne. "Writing in the Real World." In Sara Ruddick and Pamela Daniels, eds., *Working It Out.* New York: Pantheon, 1977.

Laws, Judith Long. "Work Aspirations of Women: False Leads and New Starts." *Signs* 1 (1976):33–49.

Laws, Judith Long, and Schwartz, Pepper, eds. *Sexual Scripts: The Social Construction of Female Sexuality.* New York: Dryden Press, 1977.

Lazarre, Jane. *The Mother Knot.* New York: Dell Publishing, 1976.

———. " 'I am the mother of eight, a housewife, a feminist—and happy': Jane Broderick's Story." *Ms.* 5 (1977):51–55, 82–84.

Leavitt, Harold J. "The Social Institutions of Occupational Segregation—Comment II." *Signs* 1 (1976):78–80.

Lederer, Wolfgang. *The Fear of Women.* New York: Harcourt Brace Jovanovich, 1968.

Lee, Gary R. "Marriage and Morale in Later Life." *Journal of Marriage and the Family* 40 (1978):131–139.

Lenz, Elinor. "Women Working—Opportunities Both New and Traditional." In Rosalind K. Loring and Herbert A. Otto, eds., *New Life Options: The Working Woman's Resource Book.* New York: McGraw-Hill, 1976.

Lenzer, Gertrud. "On Masochism: A Contribution to the History of a Phantasy and Its Theory." *Signs* 1 (1975):277–324.

Lessing, Doris. *A Proper Marriage.* London: Panther Books, 1966.

Lever, Janet. "Sex Differences in the Games Children Play." *Social Problems* 23 (1976):478–487.

———. "Sex Differences in the Complexity of Children's Play." *American Sociological Review* 43 (1978):471–483.

Levine, James A. *Who Will Raise The Children?* Philadelphia: J. P. Lippincott, 1976.

Levinger, George. "A Social Psychological Perspective on Marital Dissolution." *Journal of Social Issues* 32 (1976):21–47.

Levinson, Daniel J. "Growing up with the Dream." *Psychology Today* 11 (1978):20–31, 89.

Levinson, Daniel J., et al. "Periods in the Adult Development of Men: Ages 18 to 45." *The Counseling Psychologist* 6 (1976): 21–25.

———. *The Seasons of a Man's Life.* New York: Alfred A. Knopf, 1978.

Lidz, Theodore. "The Family: The Developmental Setting." In Silvano Arieti, ed., *American Handbook of Psychiatry.* 2d ed. New York: Basic Books, 1974.

———. *The Person: His and Her Development Throughout the Life Cycle.* Rev. ed. New York: Basic Books, 1976.

Lifton, Robert Jay, ed. *The Woman in America.* Boston: Beacon Press, 1967.

Lipman-Blumen, Jean. "How Ideology Shapes Women's Lives." *Scientific American* 226 (1972):34–42.

Lipman-Blumen, Jean, and Leavitt, Harold J. "Vicarious and Direct Achievement Patterns in Adulthood." *The Counseling Psychologist* 6 (1976):26–32.

Livson, Florine. "Evolution of Self: Patterns of Personality Development in Middle-Aged Women." Ph.D. dissertation. The Wright Institute, Berkeley, California, 1974.

Lobodzinska, Barbara. "Married Women's Gainful Employment and Housework in Contemporary Poland." *Journal of Marriage and the Family* 39 (1977):405–415.

Loevinger, Jane, and Wessler, Robert. *Measuring Ego Development.* San Francisco: Jossey-Bass, 1970.

Lofland, Lyn H., ed. *Toward a Sociology of Death and Dying.* Beverly Hills: Sage Publications, 1975.

Lopata, Helena Znaniecki. *Occupation: Housewife.* New York: Oxford University Press, 1971.

Lopate, Carol. "Pay for Housework?" *Social Policy* 5 (1974):27–32.

Loring, Rosalind K. "Next Steps Up: Women as Peers and Managers." In Rosalind K. Loring and Herbert A. Otto, eds., *New Life*

Options: The Working Woman's Resource Book. New York: McGraw-Hill, 1976.

Loring, Rosalind K., and Otto, Herbert A., eds. *New Life Options: The Working Woman's Resource Book.* New York: McGraw-Hill, 1976.

Lowenthal, Marjorie Fiske. "Psychosocial Variations Across the Adult Life Course: Frontiers for Research and Policy." *Gerontologist* 15 (1975):6–12.

Lowenthal, Marjorie Fiske; Thurnher, Majda; and Chiriboga, David. *Four Stages of Life—A Comparative Study of Women and Men Facing Transitions.* San Francisco: Jossey-Bass, 1975.

Lowenthal, Marjorie Fiske, and Weiss, Lawrence. "Intimacy and Crises in Adulthood." *The Counseling Psychologist* 6 (1976): 10–15.

Lozoff, Marjorie M. "Fathers and Autonomy in Women." *Annals of the New York Academy of Sciences* 208 (1973):91–97.

Lundberg, Ferdinand, and Farnham, Maryina F. *Modern Woman, The Lost Sex.* New York: Harper & Row, 1947.

Lurie, Elinore E. "Sex and Stage Differences in Perception of Marital and Family Relationships." *Journal of Marriage and the Family* 36 (1974):260–269.

Lydon, Susan. "The Politics of Orgasm." In Robin Morgan, ed., *Sisterhood is Powerful.* New York: Vintage Books, 1970.

Lynn, David B. "Fathers and Sex-Role Development." *The Family Coordinator* 25 (1976):403–409.

Maas, Henry S., and Kuypers, Joseph A. *From Thirty to Seventy—A Forty-Year Longitudinal Study of Adult Life Styles and Personality.* San Francisco: Jossey-Bass, 1975.

Maccoby, Eleanor E. "Women's Intellect." In Seymour M. Farber and Roger H. L. Wilson, eds., *The Potential of Woman.* New York: McGraw-Hill, 1963.

———. "Sex Differences in Intellectual Functioning." In Judith M. Bardwick, ed., *Readings on the Psychology of Women.* New York: Harper & Row, 1972.

Maccoby, Eleanor E., and Jacklin, Carol N. *The Psychology of Sex Differences.* Stanford, Calif.: Stanford University Press, 1974.

Mahler, Margaret S.; Pine, Fred; and Bergman, Anni. *The Psychological Birth of the Human Infant.* New York: Basic Books, 1975.

Mainardi, Pat. "The Politics of Housework." In Robin Morgan, ed., *Sisterhood is Powerful.* New York: Vintage Books, 1970.

Mannes, Marya. "The Problems of Creative Women." In Seymour M. Farber and Roger H. L. Wilson, eds., *The Potential of Woman.* New York: McGraw-Hill, 1963.

Marmor, Judd. "Changing Patterns of Femininity: Psychoanalytic Implications." In Jean Baker Miller, ed., *Psychoanalysis and Women.* New York: Penguin Books, 1973.

Mason, Karen Oppenheim. "Social Institutions of Occupational Segregation—Comment III." *Signs* 1 (1976):81–83.

Masterson, James F. *Psychotherapy of the Borderline Adult.* New York: Bruner/Mazel, 1976.

Mayer, Thomas F. "Middle Age and Occupational Processes: An Empirical Essay." *Sociological Symposium* 3 (1969):89–106.

Mead, Margaret. "Needed: Full Partnership for Women." *Saturday Review* (1975): 26–27.

Mead, Margaret, and Metraux, Rhoda. *A Way of Seeing.* New York: William Morrow, 1974.

Medley, Morris L. "Marital Adjustment in the Post-Retirement Years." *The Family Coordinator* 26 (1977):5–11.

Meile, Richard L. "Age and Sex Differentials in Psychiatric Treatment." *Sociological Symposium* 3 (1969):107–114.

Meltzer, Leslie Marilyn. "The Aging Female: A Study of Attitudes Toward Aging and Self-Concept Held by Pre-Menopausal, Menopausal and Post-Menopausal Women." Ph.D. dissertation. Department of Psychology, University of Michigan, Ann Arbor, University Microfilms, #74–18706.

Meyer, Agnes E. "The Middle-Aged Woman in Contemporary Society." In Irma H. Gross, ed., *Potentialities of Women in the Middle Years.* East Lansing: Michigan State University Press, 1956.

Milford, Nancy. *Zelda.* New York: Harper & Row, 1970.

Miller, Brent C. "A Multivariate Developmental Model of Marital Satisfaction." *Journal of Marriage and the Family* 38 (1976): 643–657.

Miller, Jean Baker, ed. *Psychoanalysis and Women.* New York: Penguin Books, 1973.

———. *Toward a New Psychology of Women.* Boston: Beacon Press, 1976.

Miller, S. M. "On Men: The Making of a Confused Middle-Class Husband." In Arlene Skolnick and Jerome Skolnick, eds., *Intimacy, Family, and Society.* Boston: Little, Brown, 1974.

Millett, Kate. *Sexual Politics.* Garden City, N.Y.: Doubleday & Co., 1970.

Millman, Marcia. "Observations on Sex Role Research." *Journal of Marriage and the Family* 33 (1971): 772-776.

——— . *Such a Pretty Face: Being Fat in America.* New York: W.W. Norton, 1980.

Millman, Marcia, and Kanter, Rosabeth Moss, eds. *Another Voice.* Garden City, N.Y.: Anchor Books, 1975.

Mitchell, Juliet. *Woman's Estate.* New York: Vintage Books, 1973.

———. *Psychoanalysis and Feminism.* New York: Vintage Books, 1975.

Morgan, Robin, ed. *Sisterhood is Powerful.* New York: Vintage Books, 1970.

Mortimer, Jeylan; Hall, Richard; and Hill, Reubin. "Husbands' Occupational Attributes as Constraints on Wives' Employment." Paper presented at the Seventy-First Annual Meeting of the American Sociological Association. New York, N.Y., August 30–September 3, 1976.

Mozley, Paul D. "Woman's Capacity for Orgasm After Menopause." *Medical Aspects of Human Sexuality* 9 (1975):104–105, 109–110.

Mueller, Charles W., and Campbell, Blair G. "Female Occupational Achievements and Marital Status: A Research Note." *Journal of Marriage and the Family* 39 (1977):587–593.

Mueller, Marnie W. "Economic Determinants of Volunteer Work by Women." *Signs* 1 (1975):325–338.

McBride, Angela Barron. *The Growth and Development of Mothers.* New York: Harper & Row, 1973.

———. *A Married Feminist.* New York: Harper & Row, 1976.

McEaddy, Beverly Johnson. "Women in the Labor Force: The Later Years." *Monthly Labor Review* 98 (1975):7–24.

———. "Women Who Head Families: A Socioeconomic Analysis." Special Labor Force Report #190. United States Department of Labor, Bureau of Labor Statistics. Washington, D.C.: U.S. Government Printing Office, 1976.

Naffziger, Claudeen Clive, and Naffziger, Ken. "Development of Sex Role Stereotypes." *The Family Coordinator* 23 (1974):251–260.

National Institute of Industrial Gerontology. *Employment of the Middle-Aged Worker.* New York: National Council on the Aging, 1969.

Neugarten, Bernice L. "The Awareness of Middle Age." In Bernice L. Neugarten, ed., *Middle Age and Aging.* Chicago: University of Chicago Press, 1968a.

———. "Adult Personality: Toward a Psychology of the Life Cycle." In Bernice L. Neugarten, ed., *Middle Age and Aging.* Chicago: University of Chicago Press, 1968b.

———, ed. *Middle Age and Aging.* Chicago: University of Chicago Press, 1968c.

———. "Personality Change in Late Life: A Developmental Perspective." In C. Eisdorfer and M. P. Lawton, eds., *The Psychology of Adult Development and Aging.* Washington, D.C.: American Psychological Association, 1973.

———. "The Roles We Play." In American Medical Association, ed., *The Quality of Life: The Middle Years.* Acton, Mass.: Publishing Sciences Group, 1974.

———. "Adaptation and the Life Cycle." *The Counseling Psychologist* 6 (1976):16–20.

Neugarten, Bernice L., et al. "Women's Attitudes Toward the Menopause." In Bernice L. Neugarten, ed., *Middle Age and Aging.* Chicago: University of Chicago Press, 1968.

Neugarten, Bernice L., and Datan, Nancy. "The Middle Years." In Silvano Arieti, ed., *American Handbook of Psychiatry.* 2d ed. New York: Basic Books, 1974.

Niera, Veronica F., and Gutek, Barbara A. "Women and Work: A Bibliography of Psychological Research." *Catalog of Selected Documents in Psychology* 6 (1976):50.

Nilson, Linda Burzotta. "The Social Standing of a Married Woman." *Social Problems* 23 (1976):581–592.

Norton, Arthur J., and Glick, Paul C. "Marital Instability: Past, Present and Future." *Journal of Social Issues* 32 (1976): 5–20.

Nye, F. Ivan, "Emerging and Declining Family Roles." *Journal of Marriage and the Family* 36 (1974):238–245.

Nye, F. Ivan, and Hoffman, Lois W. *The Employed Mother in America.* Chicago: Rand McNally, 1963.

Oakley, Ann. *Sex, Gender and Society.* New York: Harper Colophon, 1972.

———. *Housewife.* London: Allen Lane, 1974a.

———. *The Sociology of Housework.* New York: Pantheon Books, 1974b.

O'Neill, William L., ed. *Women at Work.* Chicago: Quadrangle Books, 1972.

Oppenheimer, Valerie Kincaid. "The Sociology of Women's Economic Role in the Family." *American Sociological Review* 42 (1977):387–405.

Orden, Susan R., and Bradburn, Norman M. "Working Wives and Marriage Happiness." *American Journal of Sociology* 74 (1974): 392–407.

Otto, Herbert A., and Otto, Roberta. "The Juggling Act: Home and Career." In Rosalind K. Loring and Herbert A. Otto, eds., *New Life Options: The Working Woman's Resource Book.* New York: McGraw-Hill, 1976.

Papanek, Hanna. "Men, Women, and Work: Reflections on the Two-Person Career." *American Journal of Sociology* 78 (1973): 852–872.

Parsons, Jacquelynne E., et al. "Cognitive-Developmental Factors in Emerging Differences in Achievement-Related Expectancies." *Journal of Social Issues* 32 (1976):47–61.

Payne, Barbara, and Whittington, Frank. "Older Women: An Examination of Popular Stereotypes and Research Evidence." *Social Problems* 23 (1976):489–504.

Pearlin, Leonard I., and Johnson, Joyce S. "Marital Status, Life Strains and Depression." *American Sociological Review* 42 (1977):704–715.

Perucci, Carolyn, and Targ, Dena B., eds. *Marriage and the Family: A Critical Analysis and Proposals for Change.* New York: David McKay, 1974.

Pfeiffer, Eric; Verwoerdt, Adriann; and Davis, Glenn C. "Sexual Behavior in Middle Life." *American Journal of Psychiatry* 128 (1972):1262–1267.

Phelps, Linda. "Female Sexual Alienation." In Jo Freeman, ed., *Women: A Feminist Perspective.* Palo Alto, Calif.: Mayfield Publishing Co., 1975.

Pleck, Joseph H. "The Male Sex Role: Definitions, Problems, and Sources of Change." *Journal of Social Issues* 32 (1976):155–164.
———. "The Work-Family Role System." *Social Problems* 24 (1977):417–427.

Pleck, Joseph H., and Sawyer, Jack, eds. *Men and Masculinity.* Englewood Cliffs, N.J.: Prentice-Hall, 1974.

Pleck, Joseph H., and Brannon, Robert, eds. "Male Roles and the Male Experience." *Journal of Social Issues* 34 (1978):1–195.

Pocs, Ollie, and Godow, Annette G. "Can Students View Parents as Sexual Beings?" *The Family Coordinator* 26 (1977):31–36.

Poloma, Margaret M. "Role Conflict and the Married Professional Woman." In Constantina Safilios-Rothschild, ed., *Toward A Sociology of Women.* Lexington, Mass.: Xerox College Publishing, 1972.

Poloma, Margaret M., and Garland, T. Neal. "Jobs or Careers? The Case of the Professionally Employed Married Woman." In Andrée Michel, ed., *Family Issues of Employed Women.* Leiden, The Netherlands: E. J. Brill, 1971.

Powell, Barbara. "The Empty Nest, Employment, and Psychiatric Symptoms in College-Educated Women." *Psychology of Women Quarterly* 2 (1977):35–43.

Rabb, Theodore K., and Rotberg, Robert I., eds. *The Family in History: Interdisciplinary Essays.* New York: Harper Torchbooks, 1973.

Ramey, Estelle R. "Boredom: The Most Prevalent American Disease." *Harper's Magazine* 249 (1974):12–22.

Rapoport, Rhona, and Rapoport, Robert. *Dual-Career Families.* Middlesex, England: Penguin Books, 1971.

———. *Dual Career Families Reexamined.* New York: Harper Colophon, 1976.

Raushenbush, Esther. "Unfinished Business: Continuing Education for Women." *Educational Record* 42 (1961):261–269.

———. "Second Chance: New Education for Women." *Harper's Magazine* 225 (1962):147–152.

Rebecca, Meda; Hefner, Robert; and Oleshansky, Barbara. "A Model of Sex-Role Transcendence." *Journal of Social Issues* 32 (1976):197–206.

Reed, James. *From Private Vice to Public Virtue.* New York: Basic Books, 1978.

Reitz, Rosetta. *Menopause.* Radnor, Pa: Chilton Book Company, 1977.

Rey, Lucy D.; Noell, James J.; and Woelfel, Joseph. "Sex and the Aspiration Formation Process." Paper presented at the Seventy-First Annual Meeting of the American Sociological Association. New York, N.Y., August 30–September 3, 1976.

Rich, Adrienne. *Of Woman Born: Motherhood as Experience and Institution.* New York: W. W. Norton, 1976.

Rico-Velasco, Jesus, and Mynko, Lizbeth. "Suicide and Marital Status: A Changing Relationship?" *Journal of Marriage and the Family* 35 (1973):239–244.

Ridley, Carl A. "Exploring the Impact of Work Satisfaction and Involvement on Marital Interaction When Both Partners Are Employed." *Journal of Marriage and the Family* 35 (1973):229–237.

Roberts, Helene. "The Exquisite Slave: The Role of Clothes in the Making of the Victorian Woman." *Signs* 2 (1977):554–569.

Roberts, Joan I., ed. *Beyond Intellectual Sexism: A New Woman, A New Reality.* New York: David McKay, 1976.

Roby, Pamela. *Child Care: Who Cares?* New York: Basic Books, 1973.

Roiphe, Anne Richardson. "Occupation: Mother." In Louise Kapp Howe, ed., *The Future of the Family.* New York: Simon & Schuster, 1972.

Rollins, Boyd C., and Cannon, Kenneth. "Marital Satisfaction Over the Family Life Cycle: A Re-evaluation." *Journal of Marriage and the Family* 36 (1974):271–282.

Roper, Brent S., and Labeff, Emily. "Sex Roles and Feminism Revisited: An Intergenerational Attitude Comparison." *Journal of Marriage and the Family* 39 (1977):113–119.

Rosaldo, Michelle Zimbalist, and Lamphere, Louise, eds. *Woman, Culture and Society.* Stanford, Calif.: Stanford University Press, 1974.

Rosen, Bernard C., and Aneshensel, Carol S. "The Chameleon Syndrome: A Social Psychological Dimension of the Female Sex Role." *Journal of Marriage and the Family* 38 (1976):605–617.

Rosenberg, Florence R., and Simmons, Roberta G. "Sex Differences in the Self-Concept in Adolescence." *Sex Roles* 1 (1975):147–159.

Rosenfeld, Rachel A. "Women's Intergenerational Occupational Mobility." *American Sociological Review* 43 (1978):36–46.

Rosow, Irving. *Social Integration of the Aged.* New York: Free Press, 1967.

――. *Adult Socialization.* Berkeley: University of California Press, 1974.

Rossi, Alice S. "Equality Between the Sexes: An Immodest Proposal." In Robert Jay Lifton, ed. *The Woman in America.* Boston: Beacon Press, 1967.

――. "Transition to Parenthood." *Journal of Marriage and the Family* 30 (1968):361–376.

――. "A Biosocial Perspective on Parenting." *Daedalus* 106 (1977):1–31.

Rossi, Peter H., et al. "Measuring Household Social Standing." *Social Science Research* 3 (1974):169–190.

Roszak, Betty, and Roszak, Theodore, eds. *Masculine/Feminine.* New York: Harper Colophon, 1969

Rothman, Sheila M. *Women's Proper Place.* New York: Basic Books, 1978.

Rowbotham, Sheila. *Woman's Consciousness, Man's World.* Middlesex, England: Penguin Books, 1973.

――. *Hidden from History.* London: Pluto Press, 1974.

Rubin, Lillian B. *Busing and Backlash: White Against White in an Urban School District.* Berkeley: University of California Press, 1972.

――. *Worlds of Pain: Life in the Working-Class Family.* New York: Basic Books, 1976a.

――, ed. "Feminist Perspectives: The Sociological Challenge." *Social Problems* 23 (1976b):369–523.

――. "A Review Essay: Rosabeth Moss Kanter's *Men and Women of the Corporation* and Margaret Hennig and Anne Jardim's *The Managerial Woman.*" *Contemporary Sociology* 7 (1978):259–263.

Ruble, Diane N.; Frieze, Irene H.; and Parsons, Jacquelynne E., eds. "Sex Roles: Persistence and Change." *Journal of Social Issues* 32 (1976):1–223.

Ruble, Diane N., and Higgins, E. Tory. "Effects of Group Sex Composition on Self-Presentation and Sex-Typing." *Journal of Social Issues* 32 (1976):125–132.

Ruddick, Sara, and Daniels, Pamela, eds. *Working It Out.* New York: Pantheon Books, 1977.

Ruitenbeek, Hendrik U., ed. *Sexuality and Identity.* New York: Delta Books, 1970.

Russo, Nancy Felipe. "The Motherhood Mandate." *Journal of Social Issues* 32 (1976):143–153.

Ryan, William. *Blaming the Victim.* New York: Pantheon Books, 1971.

Saario, Terry N.; Jacklin, Carol N.; and Tittle, Carol K. "Sex Role Stereotyping in the Public Schools." *Harvard Educational Review* 43 (1973):386–416.

Sadock, Benjamin J.; Kaplan, Harold I.; and Freedman, Alfred M., eds. *The Sexual Experience.* Baltimore: Williams & Wilkins, 1976.

Safilios-Rothschild, Constantina. "Family Sociology or Wives' Family Sociology? A Cross-Cultural Examination of Decision-Making." *Journal of Marriage and the Family* 31 (1969):290–301.

———. "The Study of Family Power Structure: A Review 1960–1969." *Journal of Marriage and the Family* 32 (1970a):539–552.

———. "The Influence of the Wife's Degree of Work Commitment on Some Aspects of Family Organization and Dynamics." *Journal of Marriage and the Family* 32 (1970b):681–691.

———. "Answer to Stephen J. Bahr's 'Comment on the Study of Family Power Structure: A Review 1960–1969.'" *Journal of Marriage and the Family* 34 (1972):245–246.

———, ed. *Toward A Sociology of Women.* Lexington, Mass.: Xerox College Publishing, 1972.

———. "Dual Linkages Between the Occupational System and Family System: A Macrosociological Analysis." *Signs* 1 (1976): 51–60.

Sales, Esther (with the assistance of Rosalyn B. Katz). "Women's Adult Development." In Irene Frieze, et al., eds., *Women and Sex Roles: A Social Psychological Perspective.* New York: W. W. Norton, 1977.

Sattel, Jack W. "The Inexpressive Male: Tragedy or Sexual Politics?" *Social Problems* 23 (1976):469–478.

Scanzoni, John H. *Sexual Bargaining: Power Politics in the American Marriage.* Englewood Cliffs, N.J.: Prentice-Hall, 1972.

———. *Sex Roles, Life Styles and Childbearing: Changing Patterns in Marriage and the Family.* New York: Free Press, 1975.

Schafer, Roy. "Problems in Freud's Psychology of Women." *Journal of the American Psychoanalytic Association* 22 (1974):459–485.

Schatzman, Leonard, and Strauss, Anselm. *Field Research: Strategies for a Natural Sociology.* Englewood Cliffs, N.J.: Prentice-Hall, 1973.

Schnitzer, Phoebe Kazdin. "The Motive to Avoid Success: Exploring the Nature of the Fear." *Psychology of Women Quarterly* 1 (1977):273–282.

Schultz, Terri. *Bittersweet.* New York: Penguin Books, 1976.

Seiden, Anne M. "Overview: Research on the Psychology of Women. I. Gender Differences and Sexual and Reproductive Life." *The American Journal of Psychiatry* 133 (1976):995–1007.

———. "Overview: Research on the Psychology of Women. II. Women in Families, Work and Psychotherapy." *The American Journal of Psychiatry* 133 (1976):1111–1123.

Seifer, Nancy. *Absent from the Majority: Working Class Women in America.* New York: National Project on Ethnic America, 1973.

———. *Nobody Speaks for Me.* New York: Simon & Schuster, 1976.

Segal, Bernard E. "Suicide and Middle Age." *Sociological Symposium* 3 (1969):131–140.

Sennett, Richard. *Families Against the City.* Cambridge, Mass.: Harvard University Press, 1970.

Sennett, Richard, and Cobb, Jonathan. *The Hidden Injuries of Class.* New York: Vintage Books, 1973.

Shainess, Natalie. "Toward a New Feminine Psychology." *Notre Dame Journal of Education* 2 (1972):293–299.

———. "Sexual Problems of Women." *Journal of Sex and Marital Therapy* 1 (1974):110–123.

———. "The Effect of Changing Cultural Patterns Upon Women."

In Silvano Arieti, ed., *American Handbook of Psychiatry.* 2d ed. New York: Basic Books, 1974.

Shanas, Ethel, ed. *Aging in Contemporary Society.* Beverly Hills: Sage Publications, 1970.

Sheehy, Gail. *Passages: Predictable Crises of Adult Life.* New York: E. P. Dutton, 1976.

Sherfy, Mary Jane. *The Nature and Evolution of Female Sexuality.* New York: Vintage Books, 1973.

Sherman, Julia A. *On the Psychology of Women.* Springfield, Ill.: Charles C. Thomas, 1971.

———. "Social Values, Femininity, and the Development of Competence." *Journal of Social Issues* 32 (1976a):181–195.

———. "Comment on Gertrud Lenzer's 'On Masochism.'" *Signs* 1 (1976b):1007–1009.

Shorter, Edward. *The Making of the Modern Family.* New York: Basic Books, 1975.

Simmons, Roberta G.; Rosenberg, Florence; and Rosenberg, Morris. "Disturbance in the Self-Image at Adolescence." *American Sociological Review* 38 (1973):553–568.

Simmons, Roberta G., and Rosenberg, Florence. "Sex, Sex Roles, and Self-Image." *Journal of Youth and Adolescence* 4 (1975): 229–258.

Singer, June. *Androgyny: Toward a New Theory of Sexuality.* Garden City, N.Y.: Anchor/Doubleday, 1976.

Skolnick, Arlene S., and Skolnick, Jerome H., eds. *Intimacy, Family, and Society.* Boston: Little, Brown, 1974.

———, eds. *Family in Transition.* 2d ed. Boston: Little, Brown, 1977.

Slater, Philip E. *The Pursuit of Loneliness.* Boston: Beacon Press, 1970.

———. "Sexual Adequacy in America." In Chad Gordon and Gayle Johnson, eds., *Readings in Human Sexuality: Contemporary Perspectives.* New York: Harper & Row, 1976.

Smith, Betty. *Tomorrow Will Be Better.* New York: Harper & Row, 1971.

Smith, Marilyn. "Mom Goes to Law School." *Ms.* 6 (1977):16–18.

Smith-Rosenberg, Carroll. "The Female World of Love and Ritual: Relations Between Women in Nineteenth-Century America." *Signs* 1 (1975):1–29.

Sokolowska, Magdalena. "Some Reflections on the Different Attitudes of Men and Women Towards Work." *International Labour Review* 92 (1965):35–50.

Somerville, Rose M. "The Future of Family Relationships in the Middle and Older Years: Clues in Fiction." *The Family Coordinator* 21 (1972):487–498.

Sontag, Susan. "The Double Standard of Aging." *Saturday Review* (1972):29–38.

Spangler, Eve; Gordon, Marsha A.; and Pipkin, Ronald M. "Token Women: An Empirical Test of Kanter's Hypothesis." *American Journal of Sociology* 84 (1978):160–170.

Spanier, Graham B. "Romanticism and Marital Adjustment." *Journal of Marriage and the Family* 34 (1972):481–487.

Spence, Donald, and Lonner, Thomas. "The Empty Nest: A Transition Within Motherhood." *The Family Coordinator* 20 (1971): 369–375.

Spiegel, John. *Transactions: The Interplay Between Individual, Family, and Society.* New York: Science House, 1971.

Sprey, Jetse. "Family Power Structure: A Critical Comment." *Journal of Marriage and the Family* 34 (1972):235–238.

Stacey, Judith; Breines, Wini; and Cerullo, Margaret. "Alice Rossi's Sociobiology and Anti-Feminist Backlash." *Berkeley Journal of Sociology* 22 (1978):167–177.

Stafford, Rebecca; Backman, Elaine; and Dibona, Pamela. "The Division of Labor Among Cohabiting and Married Couples." *Journal of Marriage and the Family* 39 (1977):43–57.

Stewart, Abigail J., and Winter, David G. "The Nature and Causes of Female Suppression." *Signs* 2 (1977):531–553.

Stinnett, Nick, et al. "Older Persons' Perception of Their Marriages." *Journal of Marriage and the Family* 34 (1972):665–670.

Stone, Lawrence. *Family, Sex and Marriage.* New York: Harper & Row, 1977.

Storr, Catherine. "Freud and the Concept of Parental Guilt." In

Arlene Skolnick and Jerome Skolnick, eds., *Intimacy, Family, and Society.* Boston: Little, Brown, 1974.

Strouse, Jean, ed. *Women and Analysis.* New York: Dell Publishing, 1975.

Sutherland, Sharon L. "The Unambitious Female: Women's Low Professional Aspirations." *Signs* 3 (1978):774–794.

Tangri, Sandra S. "Determinants of Occupational Role Innovation Among College Women." *Journal of Social Issues* 28 (1972): 177–199.

———. "Social Institutions of Occupational Segregation—Comment IV." *Signs* 1 (1976):84–86.

Tanner, Leslie B., ed. *Voices from Women's Liberation.* New York: Signet Books, 1970.

Thompson, Clara M. *On Women.* New York: New American Library, 1971.

Tittle, Carol Kehr, and Denker, Eleanor Rubin. "Re-entry Women: A Selective Review of the Educational Process, Career Choice, and Interest Measurement." *Review of Education Research* 47 (1977):531–584.

Tresemer, David. "Do Women Fear Success?" *Signs* 1 (1976): 863–874.

Trigg, Linda J., and Perlman, Daniel. "Social Influences on Women's Pursuit of a Nontraditional Career." *Psychology of Women Quarterly* 1 (1976):138–150.

Troll, Lillian E. "The Family of Later Life: A Decade Review." *Journal of Marriage and the Family* 33 (1971):263–282.

Turk, James L., and Bell, Norman W. "Measuring Power in Families." *Journal of Marriage and the Family* 34 (1972): 215–223.

Ullman, Liv. *Changing.* New York: Bantam Books, 1978.

United States Bureau of the Census. *1970 Subject Reports: Marital Status.* PC (2)–4C. Washington, D.C.: U.S. Government Printing Office, 1975.

————. "Number, Timing, and Duration of Marriages and Divorces in the United States: June 1975." *Current Population Reports,* Series P-20, #297. Washington, D.C.: U.S. Government Printing Office, 1976a.

————. *Statistical Abstract of the United States: 1976.* 97th ed. Washington, D.C.: U.S. Government Printing Office, 1976b.

————. *Social Indicators, 1976.* Washington, D.C.: U.S. Government Printing Office, 1977.

United States Commission on Civil Rights. Staff Report. *Women and Poverty.* Washington, D.C.: U.S. Government Printing Office, 1974.

United States Department of Labor. *Dual Careers: A Longitudinal Study of Labor Market Experience of Women.* Vols. 1, 2, 3, 4. Manpower Research Monograph #21. Washington, D.C.: U.S. Government Printing Office, 1970–1976.

————. Bureau of Labor Statistics. "Going Back to School at 35." Special Labor Force Report #159. Washington, D.C.: U.S. Government Printing Office, 1973.

————. "Job Satisfaction: Is There a Trend?" Manpower Research Monograph #30. Washington, D.C.: U.S. Government Printing Office, 1974.

————. Women's Bureau. *1975 Handbook on Women Workers.* Washington, D.C.: U.S. Government Printing Office, 1975.

————. Bureau of Labor Statistics. "Marital and Family Characteristics of the Labor Force, March 1975." Special Labor Force Report #183. Washington, D.C.: U.S. Government Printing Office, 1975.

————. Bureau of Labor Statistics. "Families and the Rise of Working Wives: An Overview." Special Labor Force Report #189. Washington, D.C.: U.S. Government Printing Office, 1976.

————. Bureau of Labor Statistics. *U.S. Working Women: A Databook.* Washington, D.C.: U.S. Government Printing Office, 1977a.

————. Employment and Training Administration. *Women and Work.* R & D Monograph #46. Washington, D.C.: U.S. Government Printing Office, 1977b.

United States Public Health Service. *Vital Statistics of the United States, Vol. III, Marriage and Divorce.* Washington, D.C.: U.S. Government Printing Office, 1975.

Vaillant, George E. *Adaptation to Life.* Boston: Little, Brown, 1977.

Van de Velde, Th. H. *Ideal Marriage: Its Physiology and Technique.* New York: Random House, 1930.

Veroff, Joseph, and Feld, Sheila. *Marriage and Work in America.* New York: Van Nostrand Reinhold, 1970.

Vicinus, Martha, ed. *Suffer and Be Still: Women in the Victorian Age.* Bloomington: University of Indiana Press, 1973.

———. *A Widening Sphere: Changing Roles of Victorian Women.* Bloomington: University of Indiana Press, 1977.

Waite, Linda J. "Working Wives: 1940–1960." *American Sociological Review* 41 (1976):65–80.

Wales, Jeffrey B. "Sexuality in Middle and Old Age: A Critical Review of the Literature." *Case Western Reserve Journal of Sociology* 6 (1974):82–105.

Walker, Kathryn E. "Time Spent in Household Work by Homemakers." *Family Economic Review* (1969):5–6.

———. "Time Spent by Husbands in Household Work." *Family Economic Review* (1970):8–11.

Wallace, Michele. *Black Macho and the Myth of the Superwoman.* New York: Dial Press, 1978.

Wallerstein, Judith S., and Kelly, Joan B. "The Effects of Parental Divorce: The Adolescent Experience." In Anthony Koupernik, ed., *The Child in His Family . . . Children at a Psychiatric Risk.* New York: John Wiley, 1974.

———. "The Effects of Parental Divorce: Experiences of the Preschool Child." *Journal of the American Academy of Child Psychiatry* 14 (1975):600–616.

———. "The Effects of Parental Divorce: Experiences of the Child in Later Latency." *American Journal of Orthopsychiatry* 46 (1976):257–290.

Walstedt, Joyce Jennings. "The Altruistic Other Orientation: An

Exploration of Female Powerlessness." *Psychology of Women Quarterly* 2 (1977):162–176.

Watson, J. Allen, and Kovett, Vira R. "Influences on the Life Satisfaction of Older Fathers." *The Family Coordinator* 25 (1976): 482–488.

Weiss, Jane A.; Ramirez, Francisco O.; and Tracy, Terry. "Female Participation in the Occupational System: A Comparative Institutional Analysis." *Social Problems* 23 (1976):593–608.

Weiss, Nancy Pottishman. "The Mother-Child Dyad Revisited: Perceptions of Mothers and Children in Twentieth Century Child-Rearing Manuals." *Journal of Social Issues* 34 (1978): 29–45.

Weiss, Robert S. *Marital Separation.* New York: Basic Books, 1975.

———. "The Emotional Impact of Marital Separation." *Journal of Social Issues* 32 (1976):135–145.

Weissman, Myrna M., et al. "The Educated Housewife: Mild Depression and the Search for Work." *American Journal of Orthopsychiatry* 43 (1973):565–573.

Weissman, Myrna M., and Paykel, Eugene S. *The Depressed Woman: A Study of Social Relationships.* Chicago: University of Chicago Press, 1974.

Weisstein, Naomi. "Kinder, Kuche, Kirche: Psychology Constructs the Female." In Robin Morgan, ed., *Sisterhood is Powerful.* New York: Vintage Books, 1970.

Weitzman, Lenore J., et al. "Sex-Role Socialization in Picture Books for Preschool Children." *American Journal of Sociology* 77 (1972):1125–1150.

Wells, Theodora. "Handling Sexism at Work: Nondefensive Communication." In Rosalind K. Loring and Herbert A. Otto, eds., *New Life Options: The Working Woman's Resource Book.* New York: McGraw-Hill, 1976.

Westoff, Charles F. "Trends in Contraceptive Practice: 1965–1973." *Family Planning Perspectives* 8 (1976):54–57.

Westoff, Charles F., and Jones, Elise F. "Contraception and Sterilization in the United States, 1965–1975." *Family Planning Perspectives* 9 (1977):153–157.

Westoff, Leslie Aldridge. *The Second Time Around: Remarriage in America.* New York: Penguin Books, 1978.

Whitely, Marilyn Peddicord, and Poulsen, Susan B. "Assertiveness and Sexual Satisfaction in Employed Professional Women." *Journal of Marriage and the Family* 37 (1975):573–581.

Williams, Juanita H. *Psychology of Women—Behavior in a Biosocial Context.* New York: W. W. Norton, 1977.

Williamson, Nancy E. "Sex Preferences, Sex Control, and the Status of Women." *Signs* 1 (1976):847–862.

Wirtenberg, T. Jeana, and Nakamura, Charles Y. "Education: Barrier or Boon to Changing Occupational Roles of Women?" *Journal of Social Issues* 32 (1976):165–179.

Wiseman, Jacqueline P., ed. *The Social Psychology of Sex.* New York: Harper & Row, 1976.

Woolf, Virginia. *A Room of One's Own.* Frogmore, St. Albans: Triad/Panther Books, 1977.

Wortis, Helen, and Rabinowitz, Clara, eds. *The Women's Movement: Social and Psychological Perspectives.* New York: John Wiley, 1972.

Wortis, Rochelle Paul. "The Acceptance of the Concept of the Maternal Role by Behavioral Scientists: Its Effects On Women." In Arlene Skolnick and Jerome Skolnick, eds., *Intimacy, Family, and Society.* Boston: Little, Brown, 1974.

Yates, Martha. *Coping: A Survival Manual for Women Alone.* Englewood Cliffs, N.J.: Prentice-Hall, 1976.

Young, Michael, and Willmott, Peter. *The Symmetrical Family.* New York: Penguin Books, 1975.

Zaretsky, Eli. *Capitalism, the Family and Personal Life:.* New York: Harper Colophon, 1976.

Zellman, Gail L. "The Role of Structural Factors in Limiting Women's Institutional Participation." *Journal of Social Issues* 32 (1976):33–46.

Index

marriage *(cont'd)*
  see also divorce; remarriage
masochism, 78–79
mental health:
  effect of employment, 230 n.11
  standards for women and men,
    248–49 n.4
middle-class families:
  educational expectations, 48
middle-class women:
  age of marriage, 226 n.4
  children's departure, 19
  definition, 215
  educational background, 169–73
  in labor force, 166–71, 175–78
midlife transition, 7–8, 12, 24,
    178–208
midlife women:
  decisions about future, 123–54
  expectations, 18
  statistics, 10–11
mixed messages to girls, 45–51
mother:
  as powerful, 69–71
  unwed, 245 n.37
motherhood, 233 n.40
  cultural myths, 243 n.20
  as destiny, 24, 110, 115, 11′, 121
  failure, sense of, 20–23
  ideal, 24–25, 26–27, 28
  loss of role, 13–40, 228 n.3, 231
    n.25
  responsibility, 29–30
"mystery" of a woman, 43
"mythic woman," 236 n.7
myths:
  dangerous mother, 68–71
  empty nest, 13–40, 228 n.3, 229
    n.9, 231 n.25
  madonna-mother, 24–25, 26–27, 28
  about motherhood, 243 n.10
  vaginal orgasm, 86

naïveté, sexual, 75–77, 85
natural mother, 26
  see also madonna-mother myth
never-married women:
  statistics, 8, 226 n.8

"nice girl" expectation, 44, 53,
    236–37 n.10

opposition to returning to school, 4,
    179–80, 195
orgasm, 74, 76, 78, 80–81, 242–43
    n.17, 245 n.36
  faked, 88–93
  female:
    male responsibility, 77, 242 n.13
    increased potential after child-birth,
      81–82, 243 n.18
  multiple, 87
  vaginal, 86
overweight, 54, 197–98, 239 n.25,
    259 n.24

paid work, 2, 104–22, 160–70
  as economic necessity, 24–25,
    164–67
  transition from volunteer work,
    160–65
  see also career; salary; women in
    labor force
parental expectations, 45–51
passivity, 78–79, 151, 154, 203, 204
pay, 161, 163, 164, 176, 199–200,
    250 n.15, 257 n.14
performance, sexual, 87, 88, 91
personality differences, male and
    female, 238–39 n.22
physical appearance as self-definition,
    54
pleasure, 148
  sexual, 77–79, 93–95, 243 n.17,
    245 n.37
"politics of housework," 259 n.19
  see also domestic tasks: apportioning
population, female, 227 n.23
postparental marital contentment, 228
    n.3, 229 n.6
power:
  in American society, 106
  fear of, 67–71
  on the job, 162–63
  in marriage, 98–102, 152–54, 183,
    203
  of mother, 69–71